A New Life with Opportunities and Challenges

*The settlement experiences
of South Sudanese-Australians*

Dr William Abur

ISBN 978-0-6486541-8-6
© Dr William Abur, 2019

Published by Africa World Books Pty. Ltd.
(www.africaworldbooks.com)

All rights reserved. No part of this publication may be reproduced, stored in a retrieval system, or transmitted, in any form, or by any means, electronic, mechanical, photocopying, recording or otherwise, without the prior permission of the publishers.

This book is sold subject to the conditions that it shall not, by way of trade or otherwise, be lent, re-sold, hired out or otherwise circulated without the publisher's prior consent in any form of binding or cover other than in which it is published and without a similar condition including the condition being imposed on the subsequent purchaser.

Design and typesetting: Africa World Books

ABOUT THE AUTHOR

Dr William Abur, PhD

Migration and resettlement is a process that involved an individual or a family moving to another country to seek for a better life and opportunities. This can be a new beginning in life for families and individuals as they are more likely to get opportunities such as better education, employment and peace of mind from uncertainty. At the same time, there are some new challenges to be faced by families and individuals while they are settling in their new country. These new challenges include language, cultural shock, integrating into new systems and laws, prejudices and discrimination of "being refugee" and being different in appearance from mainstream community. Migration and settlement of refugees can be challenging and is a journey that required support and tolerance in order for settlers to find the ways forward to overcome challenging issues.

This book provides an insight into some of the critical challenges that were encountered by the South Sudanese-Australians during their settlement journey in Australia. The settlement issues presented in this book are confined not only to the South Sudanese-Australians but apply to other communities with refugee backgrounds who may have had similar experiences to South Sudanese-Australians. Therefore, this book is very valuable to those who are working with South Sudanese-Australians, both young people and families as well as other refugees.

I have covered some critical settlement issues such as lack of employment, benefits of participating in employment and sport, racism and discrimination, issues regarding young people and families.

Table of Contents

PREFACE The background of the Author and motivation
for the research   13

CHAPTER 1 MIGRATION AND SETTLEMENT
OF SOUTH SUDANESE-AUSTRALIANS   16
1 Aim and significant contribution of the book   22
2 Settlement issues for South Sudanese-Australians   24
3 Mental Health and Trauma   25
4 Social and Cultural Changes   26
5 Raising Family: A challenges facing
   South Sudanese -Australian parents   28
6 Opportunities in Australia for
   South Sudanese-Australians   29

CHAPTER 2 SOCIAL AND POLITICAL BACKGROUND
OF SOUTH SUDANESE PEOPLE   31
1 The history of South Sudan and its people   31
2 People and society of South Sudan   35
3 Family values and cultural practice   37
4 Political history and conflicts   39
5 History of Civil war in South Sudan and its impact   41
6 South Sudanese community in Australia   43
7 Age and sex of South Sudanese in Australia   45
8 Ancestry of South Sudanese in Australia   46
9 Language of South Sudanese in Australia   46
10 Religion of South Sudanese in Australia   46
11 Education, employment, and income
   of South Sudanese in Australia   48
12 Occupation in workforce   48
13 Incomes of South Sudanese in Australia   48
14 Social and Settlement issues of
   the South Sudanese community in Australia   50

CHAPTER 3   THE MARGINALISATION OF REFUGEES: SETTLEMENT
            EXPERIENCE OF SOUTH SUDANESE-AUSTRALIANS   53
            1 Settlement of Refugees: a challenging process   55
            2 Policy and Practice: refugee settlement in Australia 59
            3 The South Sudanese in Australia:
               Cultural Challenges   62
            4 Post-trauma and wellbeing for
               South Sudanese refugees   65
            5 Mental Health and General Wellbeing for
               South Sudanese Refugees   69
            6 Family Functioning and Social Problems   74
            7 Financial hardship   76
            8 Settlement experiences   81
            9 Learning English   89
            10 Family dynamics and social change   91
            11 Gender role and difficulties   92
            12 Challenging issues with young people   94
            13 Integration and lack of integration   97
            14 The need for advocacy services on behalf of
               South Sudanese-Australians.   102
            15 Community role and support for
               vulnerable families and young people   107

CHAPTER 4   RACISM IS STILL A WAR IN OUR MODERN TIME   112
            1 Racism is a national hazard in face
               of multicultural society.   118
            2 Subtle racism and discrimination   122
            3 Institutional racism in school.   128
            4 Discrimination and racism in employment.   131
            5 Relationship between police
               and youth of African backgrounds.   135

CHAPTER 5 EMPLOYMENT AND UNEMPLOYMENT FOR REFUGEES 138
1 Impacts of unemployment 141
2 Benefits of employment for a refugee community 142
3 Participation in employment 143
4 Economic capital and financial benefits
   of employment 147
5 Psychological capital 150
6 Social capital 154
7 Cultural capital: learning experiences
   from employment 159
8 Unemployment, social and psychological impacts 166
9 Discrimination and racism in employment 176

CHAPTER 6 PARTICIPATION OF SOUTH SUDANESE-AUSTRALIANS
           IN SPORT 182
1 Benefits of Sport for the Refugee Community 185
2 Gaps in Sport for Refugees and their Community 187
3 Sport for Social Change. 190
4 Problems of Sport for Refugee Community 192
5 Gender Division in Sport Sociology 195
6 Physical capital 198
7 Psychological capital 201
8 Cultural capital 205
9 Social capital 209
10 Economic capital 213
11 Gaps in sport for the refugee community 215
12 Sport as a settlement strategy for refugees 217
13 Problematic aspects of sports participation 221
14 Racism and discrimination in Sport 224
15 Concluding remark 228

References 236

Acknowledgements

Although I remain the sole author of this book, it is in my interest to acknowledge several individuals who have provided some support during the journey of research and writing. Some made their contributions throughout my research passage in different ways, including encouragement from both elders and young people, and some with simple academic advice and correction. I take great pleasure in acknowledging all the individuals and thanking them for their encouragement, support, and guidance during my busy years of working on my research. I'm very thankful to all my South Sudanese-participants for their contributions in sharing their settlement knowledge and experiences with me during my research. I thank each and every person who participated in the in-depth interview. You can now enjoy reading the data in this book.

Dedication

I dedicated this book to my family, my wife Elizabeth Nyandeng Abuoi and children for their understanding and persevering with me while I spent hours working on the research which has resulted in this book. You challenged me and motivated me at the same time. I'm very proud of you all.

To my lovely uncle, General Francis Marial Abur who saw something in me and convinced my father and my siblings that I have to go with you to the bush (SPLA's liberated area) and join school. Over the years you have truly motivated me and guided me well. I'm very proud of you, uncle.

PREFACE

The Background of the Author and Motivation to do the Research

Since we migrated and resettled in Australia as refugees, Dr William Abur, PhD, Australia has provided my family and myself with different opportunities which I would otherwise not have dreamt of if we were in Africa. One such opportunity (and privilege) is education. This was a new beginning with new opportunities and challenges. I was able to complete my PhD on the migration and settlement of refugees using as a case study of the South Sudanese community in Melbourne. This book is a review of data collected from participants who are members of the South Sudanese community in Melbourne. The book also provided a voice to the South Sudanese community on the critical settlement challenges they have witnessed during their settlement.

I am a South Sudanese migrant from a refugee background and I have conducted research, as an insider, into my own community and culture. I wanted to document and tell the stories of both marginalisation and new opportunities for my people as they encountered the many challenges – including constant racial vilification in the media and workplaces.

I am also a qualified social worker with extensive experience in the field of refugee settlement. I am a lecturer in social work at Deakin University, teaching critical social work theories and practices such as oppressive and anti-oppressive theories, system theory, strengths-based theory, human rights and social justice. As such, I bring a wealth of both personal and professional experiences to bear on this book. This has made me very aware that employment and sports participation are the most meaningful areas of refugee settlement and key areas for my research.

My personal experience includes leaving South Sudan during

great upheaval and violent conflict and spending ten years in a refugee camp in Kakuma, Kenya before pursuing resettlement to a third country – Australia. I met my wife in Kakuma refugee camp and our eldest son was born there. When I was in the camp, I did not know whether my family and I would to end up in Australia or the United States, as many of my friends and peers did. I have now spent over ten years in Australia, raising a family of six children, while studying and working. I am now a citizen of Australia, yet I am constantly aware of my refugee background and I am deeply involved in humanitarian issues facing refugees at a both professional and personal level.

My professional experience as a Social Worker in Australia is built on my experiences acquired from the refugee camp where I worked as a Counsellor with the Jesuit Refugee Services (JRS). My qualifications in Social Work and community development have allowed me the privilege of working with refugee communities in Melbourne and responding to the complex settlement needs of families and individuals. Based on my professional experience and my first-hand understanding of settlement challenges, the idea for this study emerged. It was to explore and develop strategies in the field of refugee settlement based on a systematic and critical exploration of the social issues facing refugee families and individuals, particularly young people.

In my working life as a Social Worker, the families and individuals with whom I work have regularly raised the issue of unemployment and the resulting financial difficulties. They also raised the issue of feeling a lack of connection to the broader community and a lack of knowledge about opportunities for young people to engage in recreational and leisure activities. These were some of the key factors that motivated me to conduct research on sport and employment as important factors in the settlement of refugees. As a Social Worker, I noted that many youths from the South Sudanese community in Melbourne were engaged in basketball, something which has brought them a great deal of personal satisfaction, hope and success.

I also chose to include employment in my research so as to better understand the economic conditions of families in the South Sudanese community and explore the settlement processes of families with different work histories. As a Social Worker and community member, I noted that employment challenges were commonly discussed among South Sudanese Australians. Many were looking for work but were either unsuccessful or felt that they were locked into undesirable, low-skilled, low-paid and precarious positions.

My research work explores the ways in which participation in employment and sport can assist refugees to accumulate capital – economic, social, cultural, psychological and physical capital – and use it to enhance their ability to navigate the settlement process. This knowledge can inform future policy, programs and practice pertaining to these two areas of settlement so as to improve the quality of life of South Sudanese Australians and their families.

Among many factors that help people establish themselves in a new country is engagement with host communities via areas such as employment, education and leisure activities such as organised sport and non-professional, community-organised sport. Without strategic thinking and engagement, the settlement will remain challenging for both refugees and host communities due to the social issues that arise for people settling in a new cultural context. The processes of gaining employment can be particularly fraught and a lack of employment can have a serious impact on both individuals and families, making basics such as appropriate housing difficult to access. On the other hand, participation in sport can contribute greatly to positive settlement experiences and further access to networks and integration into the broader community. Sport can also create structure for unemployed people and help in developing a range of skills that may be useful in obtaining employment. The challenges of being, or having been, a refugee and settling in a new cultural and geographic context can be difficult to comprehend for those in the broader community who have not experienced it. Many South Sudanese have experienced extreme levels of conflict, displacement, racism and discrimination prior to coming to Australia. It is important that South Sudanese-Australians are able to freely voice these experiences without fear of recrimination and that these experiences are made widely known. This book provides an opportunity for the South Sudanese to relate their settlement experiences, focusing especifically on areas of employment and sports participation in Melbourne. These experiences and my analysis of them make an important contribution to theoretical knowledge and an understanding of refugee settlement and to the broader context of social and public policies on the settlement of refugees.

CHAPTER 1

Migration and Settlement of South Sudanese-Australians

Migration and settlement of people from refugee backgrounds is very complex and difficult when both the culture and language of the host country is very different and they have very little knowledge of them. Settlement challenges can be marginalising, and heart-breaking, for the vulnerable families and individuals who survived a long, despicable civil war and then find themselves struggling with settlement challenges in Australia. During these difficulties, many families went through separation and divorce, some young people ended up in prison with criminal records, recorded against them. Also, divorced and separated families go through emotional grieving as it is traumatic and shocking to some of the families and individuals.

The ability to read and write English is a common problem for migrants and refugees from non-English speaking countries. For example, when walking at Footscray Shopping Centre in Melbourne I saw many people from African countries, including my own, in need of support services and someone who could help them to understand official letters which had been sent direct to their home address, and who could make phone calls on their behalf to find out what the letters meant and what needed to be done.

As a Social Worker working with young people and families, I decided to write this book to explain the difficulties facing refugees settling in Melbourne. This book captures most of the experiences of the South Sudanese people settling in Australia. The material

A NEW LIFE WITH OPPORTUNITIES AND CHALLENGES

came from a PhD in which participants from the South Sudanese community living in Melbourne were interviewed about their settlement journey in Australia. Settlement experiences of migrants into Australia are very different and complex, and can often be overwhelming. I know this from personal experience. Working together as a family was vital Also, divorced and separated families go through emotional grieving as it is traumatic and shocking to some of the families and individuals.

It was a not 'a piece of cake' – or 'a cup of tea'!

As a South Sudanese who lived for ten years in Kenya as a refugee in Kakuma refugee camp, I know much about life in a refugee camp and about some of the behaviour of local Kenyans directed at the refugees living in their country. I have seen the sorrows caused by critical social problems effecting refugee families and individuals both overseas and here in Australia as I worked with refugee families and individuals from different nationalities and continents. I have witnessed some of the despicable discrimination and abuse done to some of my colleagues in a refugee camp by Kenyan citizens including government official like police officers. I have also witnessed racism and discrimination in Australia directed to people from refugee backgrounds.

Children with black skin walking to school and having done nothing wrong were racially abused on the street by two adult Caucasian men – just one example of racism and how some people choose to treat other people in their community instead of with a welcoming spirit with support.

when I was in Africa, we always had jokes about the settlement challenges that faced refugee families and individuals from African backgrounds resettling in western countries like the United States of America, Canada and Australia. When I came to Australia, I came to realise that some, if not all of these stories told in the refugee camp in Kenya about these challenges were true.

In 2002, many of my friends and contemporaries who had grown up with me in the refugee camp in Kenya and displacement camps in South Sudan were resettled in United States of America. They were called 'The Lost Boys of Sudan' by the American settlement worker who interviewed them at Kakuma for resettlement in the United Stated of America. She discovered that many of the boys had no recollection of where their parents were during the interview periods. Some did not even know whether their parents were alive or dead. This would have been true because there were no avenues of communication at that time to remote villages in South Sudan where many parents of lost boys may have been residing.

By then, I had no idea where I was going to be, however, I knew a bit about Australia in my studies and that was about the kangaroo which carried its baby in its pouch. A few years later, some of my close friends and relatives had the opportunity to resettle in Australia for a better life and opportunities. As insecurity continued in the refugee camp where I was living, I was later convinced by friends and relatives not to ignore this resettlement opportunity since the situation in the camp and in South Sudan was hopeless.

Being able to speak English overseas was a great help. I have been volunteering by assisting people struggling with re-settlement problems. This ranges from small tasks such as interpreting letters and making phone calls to more major ones such as accompanying individuals or families to courts and hospitals and interpreting. I was also in the process of re-settlement myself and was committed to studies in Community Services from which I subsequently graduated with a Bachelor of Social Work, Master of International Community Development and Diploma of Community Welfare Work and many other professional development trainings.

The experience of South Sudanese-Australians is mixed. Some have obtained a high level of education and opportunities which they would have not achieved in refugee camps or in South Sudan. However, migration and settlements can involve challenges such as the need to learn a new language, negotiate different cultural and societal values and address emotional trauma (Bunde-Birouste 2012). The settlement experiences of South Sudanese community members in Australia can be viewed as being particularly challenging due to the critical social issues of young people which mainstream media label as "gangs" in Melbourne (Baker-Lewton, et al 2017, Marjoribanks, et al 2010). For instance, in 2007, the South Sudanese community in Melbourne was criticised by the former Immigration Minister, Kevin Andrews, over what he termed a "failure" to integrate or assimilate into the Australian way of life. Refugee groups "don't seem to be settling and adjusting into the Australian way of life as quickly as we would hope," he argued (Henry-Waring 2008, p. 3; Marlowe 2010, p. 2).

> I have no control over my children, I wanted to take them back to Africa. I don't want them to die in the jail.
>
> A South Sudanese mother who her two girls and boys became addicted to alcohol and other drugs.

This mother had lost control of her own children due to the pressures of re-settlement, inter-generational conflict, lack of positive relationships and the negative influence among youths faced with freedom of choice. The aim of this book is to identify these settlement challenges facing the South Sudanese community when they arrive in Australia as refugees. It provides some information on the social issues based on the community's experiences in areas of unemployment, housing, racism and discrimination, parenting in new cultural surroundings and relationships in welfare states.

The South Sudanese community migrated to Australia in large numbers between 2003 and 2006 in which many families and individuals were granted a humanitarian visas through resettlement programmes. Some refugee families often arrive in Australia with high expectations of rebuilding their lives within a short time. Unforeseen challenges are often underestimated. Rebuilding a life that has suffered traumas and has been deprived by conflict is not easy without considering other barriers arising through being newly-arrived in a country with its own bureaucratic systems. Understanding refugees' social conditions, historical, cultural, economic and political backgrounds, including difficulties encountered during the settlement period, is fundamentally important at many levels. This includes reshaping settlement policy. Settlement and refugee experiences have been debated numerous times in Australia and in other many parts of the world. Assimilating refugee groups in host communities is not simple. African refugees and migrants who have resettled in countries with higher incomes (such as Australia faced challenges including family breakdown, parenting, unemployment, racism and discrimination issues (Renzaho 2011). Among the pressing challenges that refugees and migrant settlers face is a struggle and need to adjust to the new culture and to integrate in mainstream services. This happens because the practices and values that are being reflected in their new environment are sometimes inconsistent with the African communities' values and traditional ways of engaging in and with community groups.

In 2019, I wrote the article titled *South Sudanese Community in Australia and their Social Problems*. The aim of my writing was to explain some of the critical issues affecting the South Sudanese community members settling in Australia. Many people from the South Sudanese community in Australia arrived as refugees for resettlement in Australia after living for some years in refugee camps. Resettlement in a new country is a dream for many refugees worldwide, including people from South Sudan who left their country because of war. Leaving a country during war can be traumatic, since people leave in very challenging circumstances and travel to neighbouring countries with experiences different from their own experiences and knowledge. In addition, refugees are often not able to return to their home countries, because the causes of their departure continue to apply in their country of origin. It is important to highlight the global situation and crisis of refugees seeking asylum due to constant forcible displacement. This article discusses some social issues and challenges facing South Sudanese-Australia while integrating. The challenges and struggles of refugees are multi-faceted and include dealing with difficult decisions such as abandoning their homes and jettisoning their belongings. These issues significantly affect their lives because their social networks and economic livelihoods have been disrupted by displacement and forced migration and they are often exposed to danger and uncertain journeys. Large numbers of South Sudanese families who are currently living in Australia came from refugee camps such as the Kakuma refugee camp in Kenya, camps in Uganda, Ethiopia and urban cities in Egypt. These camps are characterised by shortages of food, inadequate medical services, and lack of sanitation.

Aim and Significant Contribution of the Book

The book makes both theoretical and empirical contributions in the migration and settlement journey of the South Sudanese-Australians. Refugees from South Sudan came to Australia to re-establish themselves while recovering from a long civil war in which many lost their property and moved to refugee camps where some stayed for a long time. Some refugee camps include Kakuma camp in Kenya, and camps in Uganda, Ethiopia, and Egypt (Ager 1999; Ajak et al. 2015; Marlowe 2011a). The South Sudanese community is one of the newly-emerging refugee communities in Australia and is a fast-growing community among African community groups in Australia, particularly in Melbourne. They have arrived through the humanitarian process and settled in different states and suburbs. Their settlement has been challenging, as many issues were debated in public media as well as social media because social change and lack of support and social connection with mainstream community groups have made it more difficult to move quickly beyond settlement challenges (Abur 2012; Ajak et al. 2015).

The findings suggest that people from refugee backgrounds are highly vulnerable to social isolation, unemployment and racism and discrimination. The settlement difficulties of refugees include the need to learn new languages, negotiating differing cultural and societal values, and addressing emotional trauma (Bunde-Birouste et al. 2012). The existing support and provision of settlement services are no longer sufficient to address such problems facing refugees in Melbourne. A society with little or no engagement in employment or sport through its young people often encounters serious social issues such as social isolation, family breakdown, mental health problems, criminal activities or substance abuse (Blustein 2008; Cullen 1999).

Employment and unemployment are issues for which many refugees have not been prepared while living in refugee camps, although they are aware they are in a process of transition to one of the UNHCR's durable solutions, known as resettlement. When refugees are resettled, employment becomes a central aim for refugees. Finding a job is a main step towards a meaningful settlement outcome (Mamer 2010), as becoming socially connected is also viewed as crucially important to as a settlement outcome.

The research question for this study is derived from the earlier aim and objectives of: How do employment and sport participation affect the settlement process of the South Sudanese community in Melbourne, Australia? The aim of this study is to explore the role of employment and sport participation in the refugee settlement process, through a case study of the South Sudanese community in Melbourne, Australia. The following were the overarching objectives of study.

Explore South Sudanese community members' settlement experiences and engagement in employment and sport.

Examine the benefits members of the South Sudanese community derive from employment and participation in sport.

Develop policy recommendations on how employment and sport participation can better assist this community to navigate their settlement challenges.

Significant contributions

This book makes a significant contribution to knowledge about refugee settlement. There has been no research in Australia to date that has systematically compared the roles played by employment and sport participation in the settlement process for refugee communities and, in particular, South Sudanese refugees. At the same time, there are countless cases where those refugees have had extreme difficulty in adjusting to life in a new country, and where lack of community participation has been a part of these difficulties. The book discusses the ways in which participation in employment and sport can assist refugees to accumulate capital – particularly social, economic, cultural, psychological, and physical capital – and use it to enhance the settlement process.

Settlement issues for South Sudanese-Australians

Settlement issues of people from refugee backgrounds can be complexed and required ongoing assistances and support from the host community, government, and non-government agencies to address different settlement challenges. Sometimes families and individuals can make their ways to achieve better or successful settlement. However, the question of successful settlement is still debatable and what this means for refugees. There are various understandings of what it means to be "well settled" in a new country. These include feeling safe from racism and discrimination, obtaining secure and well-paid employment, buying a home, children feeling well supported at school and in the community, and playing sport with the host community, all without experiencing aggressive or abusive language. Sometimes, settlement can be a two-way process of mutual understanding of cultural expectations, with the host community working in partnership with refugees. South Sudanese community/African have recently encountered racial vilification in media by some politicians because of trouble caused by young people who were making poor choices. Some families are/were not able to control their teenage young people who choose to integrate in the mainstream society in wrong way, by choosing to follow or hang around criminal who happened to train them with criminal activities. Some parents are to be blamed by failing to keep young people or family in control. One of the problems is a high of separations and divorces due to social security reasons and social change which I will discuss in point four below.

Mental Health and Trauma

Mental health issues or trauma are existing any society, but very common with people who comes from conflict affected areas and other difficulties such as displacement and migration to a place where culture and lifestyle is different to their own. Unfortunately, mental health or trauma is not often discussed by the South Sudanese or African families because of traditional beliefs and taboos associated with mental health. When discussing mental health or trauma issues with people from South Sudan, their responding can be very different compared to the western societies. The cultural beliefs and taboos associating with mental health perspective sometimes can make more difficult for professional to offer counselling services to families and individuals that may benefit from professional counselling. Sometimes we have qualified social workers and counsellors who are willing to assist families and individuals within the South Sudanese community to address some challenging issues related to mental health before it is too late, but people are not open enough to seek for support for some reasons. For example, people tend to decline services because it is not part of their belief system.

Mental health issues and other social problems are clearly holding some families and individuals back from progressing and overcoming settlement difficulties. Mental health and post-traumatic stress disorder (PTSD) are impacting and ruining lives of young families and individuals. This is not about diagnosing or labelling people or families, but about acknowledging trauma as one of the settlement challenges when people from refugee backgrounds settle in a new country after experiencing some appalling situations, including whilst in refugee camps. Their experiences in conflict areas and later in refugee camps influence their ability to resettle. There is ample evidence from the literature which suggests those with a refugee background have experienced some form of abuse, rape, oppression, or have witnessed extermination, killing, looting, and destruction of personal wealth; they have been in slavery, forced to live in exile and in shocking conditions in refugee camps (Abur, 2018 and Abur & Spaaj, 2016). These experiences evidently affect many refugees, including those from the South Sudan, who may have been forced to live in refugee camps for many years. They bring these difficult experiences with them when engaging in resettlement programs (Abur 2018, Abur, 2012).

Social and Cultural Changes

Moving to the new environment and new culture comes with some social and cultural changes. South Sudanese-Australians are juggling with cultural and social changes in family level. There is a high level of confusion between living in new culture with some freedoms and traditional- conservative culture in South Sudan. One of the problems is that some men and women are losing their traditional responsibilities of raising family or children in right way. People are struggling with social change as a result of living in the western culture. However, culture and social change are not static; it depends with individuals and families how they want to manage their social and cultural changes.

We know that changes can happen anytime and anywhere. Many changes occur between one generation and the next, but changes often needed carful and cautious handing, because things can easily go wrong. This is a real problem with some of the South Sudanese-Australians. Social and cultural changes have been mishandled as we sees crisis with young people who are involved in criminal activities such as stealing in shopping centres, carjacking, drugs and alcohol consumptions which often resulted into violence behaviours.

Culture refers to a way of doing things within a particular country or in ethnic community groups, which include shared beliefs, values, and norms of governing. The changes in human ways of life and movement have far-reaching effects. Large numbers of people in today's society, do live in cities and towns rather than rural villages. For refugees, culture and social change are a huge part of their experience. For example, being a refugee and resettling in an unfamiliar environment carries many complex experiences including loss, life, and cultural change. One must work hard to understand the culture of a host country and entitlement system which required certain levels of education fully understand. The adjustment to a new culture and new environment is a challenging process that each refugee is likely to go through regardless of where he or she comes from. Often, refugees tend to be marginalised in their new societies and in many cases treated as aliens, which causes further suffering and feelings of alienation, struggling to accept a lower status than that which they held previously (Abur, 2018). The experiences of refugees in the settlement process often involve unforeseen issues such as meeting new groups of people and challenging social norms. Upon arrival, the socially constructed norms and values of place turn refugees' lives upside down (Abur, 2018). Therefore, culture and social change impact on refugees who have moved to resettle in a new environment and society, which is different from their own experiences and social norms of their upbringing, (Abur, 2017, Abur 2012). There is also a general expectation that refugees will adjust quickly to the expectations of the host society, which (erroneously) assumes that acculturation and integration are straightforward, if not seamless, processes.

Raising Family: a challenges facing South Sudanese-Australian parents

Raising a family in a new culture to one's own is a challenge for South Sudanese and many African migrant families with very little knowledge of western parenting (Abur, 2018, Abur, 2017). Children and teenagers tend to adapt new culture quickly, but their parents still hold on to their own cultures and parenting styles based on where they grow up. As children and teenagers find their ways to adapt or integrate in new culture, they are more likely to struggle with identity issues, lack of mentoring and guiding to right paths. This is a case with many young people and their families from South Sudanese community in Australia. There is often tension between parents and teenagers conflicting over the two cultures. Sometimes, parents are left with speechless with their teenagers are caught in criminal activities. Sometimes it can be too late to fix the problem in sophisticated legal systems.

Unfortunately, some parents do have hands in the failure of their young people because they were not able to address their relationship problems. I'm afraid to say this fact, but it has to be raised as I'm aware of many families and individuals who let down their young people for some selfish-reasons. Some men and women who ended their relationships choose to be young again by attending night parties and neglected their young children and teenagers' needs. This is one of the reasons why many teenagers become rebellious against their parents.

Some parents within South Sudanese or African community groups failed to understand that child rearing is very complex in western societies compared to African society where a child is raised by the whole village. I'm proudly here to say I was raised by the whole village during my time in South Sudan. My parents had no many difficulties like the current issues we are facing with young people. For instance, drugs and alcohol is available everywhere and can easily accessed by young people. Often, there is considerable debate within the South Sudanese community among different generations about where they really belong. Some people consider themselves more Australian by adapting to Australian ways of life and have criticised South Sudanese ways.

The differences in cultural values between Australian and South Sudanese societies have been the main issue causing anxiety among parents. Some South Sudanese parents in Australia are greatly concerned about their young people having contact with those outside their own culture and resist any kind of relationship that a young person can form in their own community (Abur 2018). Some young people may choose not to attend school, and not listen or respect parents' opinions because they think that their parents or adults don't understand them and their needs. This brings critical challenges for parents in terms of responsibilities within the family Many parents feel their responsibilities and respect are undermined by local authorities to discipline and management their children according their tradition culture. Thus, parenting children in a new culture has been one of the challenging tasks for South Sudanese families. Refugees from the South Sudan (and Africa in general) who have resettled in Australia face new challenges in raising families, particularly managing and raising their children in a new culture, which is contrary to their original culture (Abur, 2018).

Opportunities in Australia for South Sudanese-Australians

There are opportunities and challenges in Australia, depending on how families and individuals' level of approach and engagement with mainstream community groups Australia is regarded as a lucky country for different generation of migrants who settled successful and raised their young generations. South Sudanese families can also work hard by focusing on positive aspects on things they can achieve. Parents must really accept the challenge of social change and work together for the benefit of their children. People must seek help from different mentors to mentor them in order to reach to the next level. Grown up adults must not waste their times discussing politics in community and neglected their families and young people. Both young people and adults or parents must the challenge as an opportunity to work harder by concentrating in either school or employment rather than engaging in negative behaviours or wasting their time in parties.

Social issues or settlement issues can only be addressed well when there is goodwill to engage individuals and families in activities that connect them with mainstream services, which go beyond existing settlement services. People do need to engage in some useful activities depending on their ages. For examples, participation in employment and sport assists refugees to enhance different forms of capital. For instance, employment has a crucial role in assisting them to improve connections with their new society and, of course, earn income for their families. Employment is helpful for refugees, not only for financial gain, but also for identity, learning, and connection. Sport is one of many potentially powerful strategies to engage young people in pro-social activities, alongside employment for those who are work-ready. Sport fosters social connections for young people from refugee backgrounds, even if they themselves may not be refugees. Its power lies in bringing together people from different backgrounds. Sport can link them to resources and give them a sense of belonging. Sport not only generates health benefits through direct participation in physical activity, but through that participation, a platform for communication and social interaction. Participation in sport is thus powerful in motivating and inspiring individuals and their community to socially interact. Participation in both sport and employment provide social, cultural, economic, psychological, and physical capital.

CHAPTER 2

Social and Political Background of South Sudanese People

This chapter provided an overview of social and political background of South Sudan, its people and culture, the civil war, and the composition of the refugee community in Australia. Particular attention is given to the conflicts that displaced many South Sudanese, and the trauma that South Sudanese refugees subsequently suffered as a result of long civil war and difficulties in refugee camps. The chapter also discussed the settlement process in Australia, and a demographic analysis of Australia's South Sudanese community as they were resettled in different states of Australia.

The history of South Sudan and its people

South Sudan is a newest nation in Africa and has a challenging and protracted history of struggle to gain independent status. The region was known as Southern Sudan during its colonisation. The Republic of South Sudan was declared an independent nation in July 2011, a result of the Comprehensive Peace Agreement (CPA) signed between the government of Sudan and the guerrilla movement in Southern Sudan, known as the Sudan People's Liberation Movement/Army (SPLM/A) (Deng 2005b). The CPA was signed in 2005 to end hostilities between the people of South Sudan and the government in Khartoum, predominantly led by those with Arab backgrounds (Kevlihan 2013). The CPA was established for a six-year interim period, during which time a number of provisions were to be implemented to assess the possibility of a unified Sudan, and to ensure that peace prevailed in the country. The CPA also provided an opportunity for the people from South Sudan to hold a referendum to determine if they wanted Sudan to remain as one country or to choose separation at the end of the interim period. The result of this referendum led to secession from Sudan. Historically, South Sudan has a long history of conflict, which has led to ongoing internal violence within community groups. The region was first colonised by Great Britain from 1882 and later granted independence in 1956, when Arabs took over the nation's governance with no special provision for the indigenous peoples of the south. As a consequence of the lack of services for these people, the first civil war broke out in 1955. This is referred to as the Anya-Nya I War (Deng 2005a). It ended with the Addis Ababa Peace Agreement in 1972, which promised self-government to people from the southern region, with little interference from the Khartoum Government in the north. However, this agreement was dishonoured by the Khartoum Government and people of South Sudan in 1983 formed the Anya-Nya II Movement against the government (Kevlihan 2013). The people of Southern Sudan fought for years to have a state independent of the Khartoum regime, and while they made the occasional gain, the end result was political chaos and enormous economic hardship. In short, a long history of conflict has shaped the identity of South Sudan, with the underlying cause being the imposition of Arab and Islamic culture from Northern Sudan (Daly 2004; Ryan 2014). It is important to remember that the history of the Republic of South Sudan is very different from Northern Sudan in a number of ways, especially regarding the development – and frequent neglect – of country, culture, and identity (Deng 2005b).

On 9 July 2011, the Republic of South Sudan was born, and its people waved an emphatic goodbye to Khartoum. The transitional period had taken six-and-a-half years after the CPA was signed. Unfortunately, there was no development or structure of the system put in placement during the six years and half transitional period. This later on leads to many serious internal conflict among people of South Sudan. President

Kiir's leadership was criticised by the same politicians who were holding ministerial positions including vice President Dr Riek Machar who was seeking support from public to overthrow President Kiir. Sadly, most of these politicians who criticised President Kiir are the main people who involved in very high level of corruption. They looted public money during six years interim periods and after independence while they were in government together with President Kiir.

Geographically, South Sudan is a landlocked country located in central-east Africa, which is part of Eastern Africa according to the United Nations sub-regional divisions. The River Nile flows north through the country and constitutes a major geographic feature, supporting agriculture and large numbers of wild animals. South Sudan is rich in terms of natural resources, including oil, gold, and wildlife, but the long civil war has restricted development. The Republic of South Sudan borders a number of countries: Sudan to the north, Ethiopia to the east, Uganda and Kenya to the southeast, the Democratic Republic of the Congo to the southwest, and the Central African Republic to the west. It has an area of 619,745 square kilometres comprised of 28 states, according to the governing system. The original ten states (and their administrative centres) for administrative services were Central Equatoria (Juba town), Western Equatoria (Yambio), Eastern Equatoria (Torit), Jonglei (Bor), Unity (Bentiu), Upper Nile (Malakal), Lakes (Rumbek), Warrap (Kuacjok), Western Bahr el Ghazal (Wau), and Northern Bahr el Ghazal (Aweil) (Lejukole 2008). The following map shows the geographical location of these states.

In 2015, under the leadership of President Salva Kiir Mayardit, South Sudan was divided into 28 states with the aim of bringing services closer to people in rural areas. The 28-states-policy was supported by a majority of citizens but opposed by the opposition leader and some rebel groups. In 2017, President also added more states to make 32 states. However, there is still demands of more in the Republic of South Sudan. The following is the list of 32 states created by President Kiir Mayardit's government.

A NEW LIFE WITH OPPORTUNITIES AND CHALLENGES

S/No	State	Capital	Counties
The Greater Upper Nile Region (13 States)			
1	Jonglei	Bor	Bor, Twic East and Duk
2	Fangak state	Ayod	Ayod, and Fangak
3	Bieh State	Waat	Uror and Nyirol
4	Akobo State	Akobo	Akobo County
5	Maiwut State	Maiwut	Longchuk, Koma, and Maiwut
6	Latjor State	Nasir	Ulang and Nasir
7	Boma State	Pibor	Pochalla, and Pibor
8	Central Upper Nile State	Malakal	Akoka, Pigi, Baliet and Panyikang
9	Northern Upper Nile State	Renk	Renk, Maban and Melut
10	Fashoda State	Kodok	Kodok and Manyo
11	Ruweng State	Panriang	Panriang and Abiemnhom
12	Southern Liech State	Leer	Mayendit, Leer and Panyijiar
13	Northern Liech State	Bentiu	Mayom, Koch, Rubkona and Guit
The Greater Bahr el ghazal Region (10 States)			
14	Gogrial State	Kuacjok	Gogrial West and Gogrial East
15	Twic State	Mayen-Abun	Twic County
16	Tonj State	Tonj	Tonj North, Tonj East and Tonj South
17	Gok State	Cueibet	Cueibet County
18	Western Lake State	Rumbek	Rumbek North, Rumbek East, Rumbek Center and Wulu
19	Eastern Lake State	Yirol	Yirol East, Yirol West and Awerial
20	Aweil East State	Wanjok	Aweil East county

21	Lol State	Raja	Raja, Aweil North and Aweil West
22	Aweil State	Aweil	Aweil South and Aweil Centre
23	Wau State	Wau	Jur River and Bagari
The Greater Equatoria Region (9 States)			
24	Jubek State	Juba	Juba County (Bari, Lokoya, Nyangwara communities)
25	Terekeka State	Terekeka	Terekeka, Jemeiza, Gwor, Tali and Tigor
26	Yei River State	Yei	Yei, Lainya, Morobo and Kajo Keji
27	Tambura State	Tambura	Tambura and Nagero
28	Gbudwe State	Yambio	Yambio, Ezo, and Anzara
29	Amadi State	Mundri	Mvolo, Mundri West and Mundri East
30	Maridi State	Maridi	Lopa, Torit, Ikotos and Magwi
31	Imatong State	Torit	Lopa, Torit, Ikotos and Magwi
32	Kapoeta State	Kapoeta	Kapoeta North, Kapoeta East, Kapoeta South and Budi

People and society of South Sudan

People from South Sudan do come from diverse backgrounds in terms of language, cultural practice, and lifestyle, but all originated from two main groups or tribes, the Nilotic and non-Nilotic groups. The largest tribal groups in South Sudan come from Nilotic and they are: Dinka, Nuer, Kakwa, Bari, Azande, Shilluk, Kuku, Murle, Mandari, Didinga, Ndogo, Bviri, Lndi, Anuak, Bongo, Lango, Dungotana, and

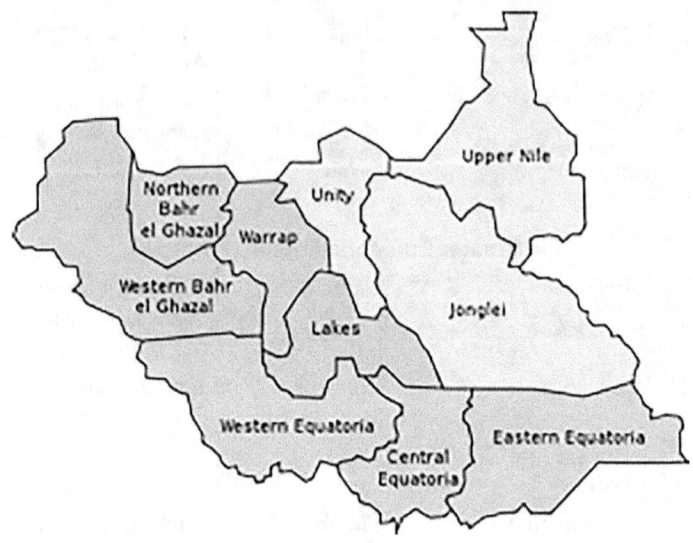

Figure 2:1: Map of South Sudan and its old states.
Source: Republic of South Sudan website (http://www.goss.org).
(Note: there are different versions of maps of South Sudan due to the divisions of states within South Sudan.)

Acholi (Lejukole 2008; Makol 2012). The religions practiced by these community groups are predominantly Christian and Animist creeds. The national languages are Arabic-Juba and English. These are the common languages used in social settings, commercial transactions, and other official communication in the country (Mamer 2010). Most South Sudanese believe their original background was from the Nilotic group, meaning the group that was created and lived alongside the River Nile, or were the first group that entered the land of South Sudan before the 10th century CE. Many often talk about their Nilotic values and ways of responding to their visitors. They are very proud of their hospitable spirit and cultural values. This Nilotic group includes the Dinka, Nuer, and Shilluk tribes. The second group is the non-Nilotic group, which includes the Azande or Zande people who entered South Sudan in the 16th century. They comprise the third largest group in South Sudan (Makol 2012; Ryan 2014).

Social and Political Background of South Sudanese People

The social lives and politics of the South Sudanese have been heavily influenced by the civil war, which undermined the social fabric of their communities in relation to their communal and traditional histories. There is a high level of poverty in villages, which lack education and traditional farming practices. However, the people are proud of being South Sudanese regardless of difficulties due to lack of services and infrastructure. Many communities still live in tribal groups as a way of supporting and caring for each other. Each tribe has a distinct area of land for which they are responsible, as the issue of land is about power in relation to cultural tradition. Each tribe is led by a chief, who is responsible for maintaining law-and-order throughout the community (Deng, FM 2011). The politics and social settings of each tribe are similar in many ways, but differ in terms of marriage practices and cattle keeping. Some tribes heavily invest their time in herding and keeping cattle as a form of wealth. When they marry, they use cattle to pay a dowry to the family of the bride as a form of appreciation for raising their daughter in a respectful and responsible manner. This practice is common in Dinka and Nuer as well as other tribes.

Traditional culture and values are an important part of South Sudanese life. Major life events are commonly celebrated by tribes, and include births, adulthood, marriage, ageing, and the death of a chief or leader as a mark of his or her work in the community. The ceremony for the death of a chief or leader often continues for seven days, and many domestic animals may be sacrificed as community gifts (Deng 2011; Makol 2012).

Family values and cultural practice

The family unit is an important part of South Sudanese culture and has been integrated into all tribes as part of community life. Most South Sudanese families hold strongly to the notion of extended family (as distinct from the nuclear family). Such traditional values and customs dictate the notions of family. Therefore, a South Sudanese family commonly consists of grandparents, mothers, fathers, children, uncles, aunts, cousins, nephews and nieces (Dei Wal 2004; Ethnic Council of Shepparton and District Inc. 2013).

There are roles and responsibilities for each family member. Children have roles to play in the family in supporting their parents to bring up younger siblings, or to undertake some domestic duties, such as looking after cattle, goats, and sheep. Aunts and uncles have separate roles in bringing up children in the family. Girls are often attached to their aunts who are expected to teach them to be respectful and responsible for members of the community and to be good mothers for their own family in due course. Uncles are responsible for teaching boys, including how to protect family and property. Regarding health and welfare issues, every family is responsible for caring for family members and their welfare. Each adult is expected to contribute to the sharing of responsibilities and other tasks (Juuk 2013).

The child-naming process is very important to all tribes, and can express the circumstances of birth, describe a historical event, or the character of the child. A name can also be given to honour a patriarch of the clan or family member who served as a leader. For some tribes who pay a dowry to marry, a child can be given the name of their best cow or bull. The child can be given any number of names and may add or change names at pivotal points in his/her life. It is also common that the child is named after a midwife, who is then responsible for helping with the child's education (Dei Wal 2004; Duany & Duany 2005).

Traditionally, men are the head of family and responsible for providing food and protection. The traditional role of the father is to keep the family together and to distribute wealth to family members. Family members go to the father or consult him when they need something. When he dies, his wealth and responsibilities are usually passed to the oldest son. Uncles and aunts support the oldest son during transition and teach or encourage him to learn to be the responsible man in the family. Women are responsible for domestic duties, such as caring for children, the sick, and the elderly at home, although many of these responsibilities have been taken over by centralised services delivered in large towns and cities.

However, armed conflicts have placed the burden of these social services on women because many men joined the fight for independence and lost their lives. Many women remain the sole carers for their children, including among those families who resettled in Australia (Abur 2012; Dei Wal 2004; Juuk 2013). It is important to acknowledge that the social and cultural values of South Sudanese families in Australia (and other western countries, for that matter) have changed due to the influence of more cosmopolitan cultures and lifestyles acquired on the way to resettlement. For instance, in Australia, gender roles are more flexible, and these local values and practices have generated serious debate in the South Sudanese community. The western style of dressing and partying has also challenged gender norms and traditional expectations in both men and women. The greater sense of freedom in Australia has also caused intergenerational and gender conflicts within families and communities (Ethnic Council of Shepparton and District Inc. 2013; Juuk 2013).

Political history and conflicts

From 1930 to 1953, the Anglo-Egyptian Condominium governed northern and southern Sudan separately because of contentious issues in religion and traditional practices, but the southern region was under-resourced despite its natural resources such as oil and gold (Atem 2011b; Deng, FM 2011; Kebbede 1997; Lejukole 2008). The civil war began a year before independence in 1955 and continued until the Addis Ababa Agreement of 1972 granted regional autonomy to the South (Daly 2004; Deng 2011). Sudan gained its independence from the Anglo-Egyptian Condominium on 1 January 1956. The northern area of Sudan was, and remains, predominantly Muslim, while the southern region (today, the Republic of South Sudan) was, and remains, mostly dominated by Christians and animists.

A NEW LIFE WITH OPPORTUNITIES AND CHALLENGES

According to FM Deng (2011), the great challenge of preserving Christianity in the Sudan, especially in the southern part of the country, was closely linked to the civil war between Sudan's North (Muslim) and South (predominantly Christian). This war has raged intermittently since 1955, making it possibly the longest civil conflict in the world. Ethnographically, Sudan has never been one broad community: it consists of two parts – south and north – which differ in ethno-linguistic composition and religious affiliation. Religious tensions, particularly to do with the spread of Islam, together with land and ethnic divisions have been the main contributory factors to civil war (Ajak et al. 2015, Mamer 2010). In recent years, the Sudanese Civil War has been well documented. The civil war was kept internal until 1983 when many groups from South Sudan took up arms to liberate themselves from what they believed was an oppressive regime of the Khartoum Islamic Government (Ajak et al. 2015).

Thus, the international community knew little about the civil conflict, community, and particularly how badly the Khartoum regime was oppressing people in the south, including denying people basic human services and development opportunities. People were forced to practice Islam against their will in order to obtain services and minor posts in government. The roots of this war lie in longstanding ethnic and religious hostility, fuelled by the discovery of oil in the southern provinces (Ajak et al. 2015; Kebbede 1997). Many people lost their lives, properties were destroyed, and millions became homeless and displaced as a consequence of this conflict (Coker 2004; Duany & Duany 2005).

The referendum of January 2011 was a key part of the CPA and allowed people from Southern Sudan to vote overwhelmingly for secession, resulting in South Sudan becoming independent (Ajak et al. 2015; Brosché 2008). Although South Sudan remains independent, the secession has its own problems as tension on contentious issues continues, including the demarcation of the north-south border and the status of the oil-rich Abyei region, which has always been claimed by both countries (Deng, 2005b). Lengthy peace talks have failed on many occasions to find solutions to some key issues despite both nations depending heavily on oil revenues. South Sudan has three-quarters of the oil, but important infrastructure including pipelines, refineries and a Red Sea port are still in the north. Khartoum lost significant revenue from oil when South Sudan became independent (Ajak et al. 2015; Deng 2005b).

Many elements involved in Sudan's political and civil crises. The problems of cultural, political, and religious alienation of the south from the north are an outcome of more recent Sudanese government policies as well as a legacy of British/Egyptian colonial rule (Mitchell 1989). The distribution of political power and social and economic advantage became crucial to the maintenance of government in Sudan, as it maintained colonial rule (Ajak et al. 2015; Deng 2005b). Those rulers who followed continued the colonial practice of ruling by division. The Sudanese government has a poor human rights reputation and is currently under international sanction for killing vulnerable citizens from the south and from Darfur in the west. Nevertheless, the fact that some of the root causes of Sudan's civil wars were due to former British colonial administration, which left South Sudan impoverished at the end of its rule in 1956, should not be forgotten (Mitchell 1989).

History of Civil war in South Sudan and its impact

The civil war is generally viewed as a conflict between the Arab Muslim north and black animist or Christian south over oil money, political power, and religious issues (Ajak et al. 2015; Deng 2005a; Makol 2012). The civil war has affected people of South Sudan in many ways, including displacement, torturing and witnessing the killing of relatives – often innocent children and women – in South Sudan. This war also made many things worse in the region, such as shortages of food and medical services. From 1988 to 1998, lives were lost because of famine due to food shortages in the region (Khawaja et al. 2008). Widespread destruction of property and violations of human rights also occurred. A significant number of people were displaced from the region and an estimated 390,000 South Sudanese refugees are still living in camps in Egypt, Chad, Uganda, Kenya, and Ethiopia (Abur 2012). The consequences of civil war have extended from generation to generation in South Sudan. Land and properties were stolen and some who took refuge in neighbouring countries later resettled in western countries, including Australia (Abur 2012). The United Nations estimated 2 million deaths and 4 million displaced people (Atem 2011b; Deng 2005b). Urban refugees also reside in Cairo, Kampala, Nairobi, and Addis Ababa (Abur 2012). Some Sudanese Australians returned to their ancestral homeland when the conflict officially ended in 2005.

For those who were resettled in the West, the process often began in refugee camps with help from the UNHCR and Australia's Offshore Humanitarian Program (OHP). The conditions in refugee camps were often unbearable, as the UNHCR could only provide basic services (Abur 2012). On arriving in Australia, these refugees faced considerable challenges in adapting to a new life, new social system, and new culture, and needed time to adapt to a new location, language, and cultural framework. Their abilities and skills were often eroded by their experiences in refugee camps and conflict, and their self-esteem and confidence were shaken by settlement difficulties. On the other hand, many refugees were psychologically resilient, and spent considerable time supporting their 'fellow travellers' (Atem 2011a).

However, there are many barriers and limitations South Sudanese community members face in providing assistance to vulnerable young people and families who are continuing to face settlement challenges. They tend to live in different suburbs, yet they see themselves as one community and celebrate common social activities together, such as birthday parties, marriages, and funerals (Abur 2012).

South Sudanese community in Australia

South Sudanese people began arriving in Australia in 1997 and a second wave occurred since 2007 through offshore humanitarian programs. The early group established a community to support newly arrived families and individuals. One of the aims in forming a community was to assist individuals and family members who were still in refugee camps. People who register with the UNHCR as refugees are often granted visas to be resettled. South Sudanese people who arrived in Australia were resettled in different states of Australia.

The South Sudanese in Australia have been one of the fastest growing communities and one of the more disadvantaged groups regarding settlement needs – in particular, with regard to employ-

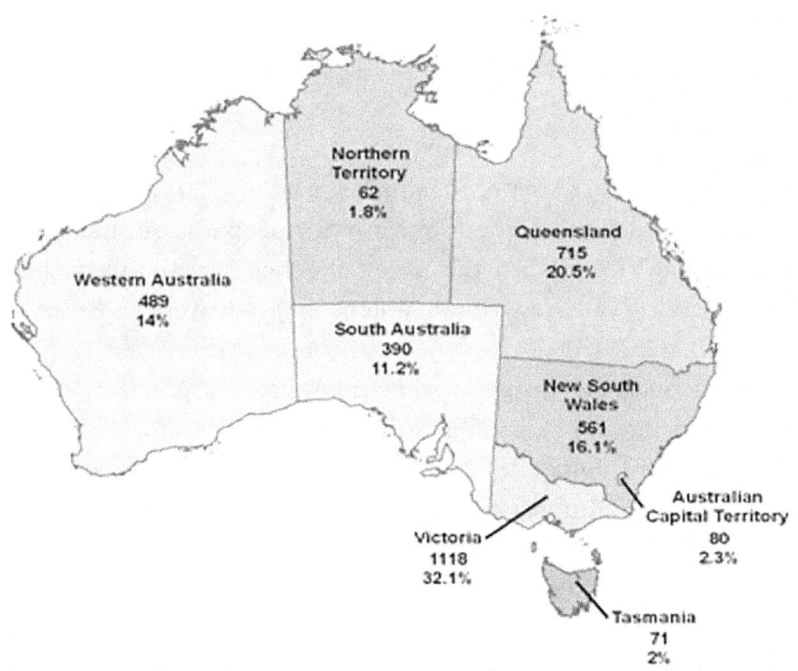

Figure 2:2: South Sudan-born people in Australia.
Source: Department of Immigration and Citizenship (2013)

A NEW LIFE WITH OPPORTUNITIES AND CHALLENGES

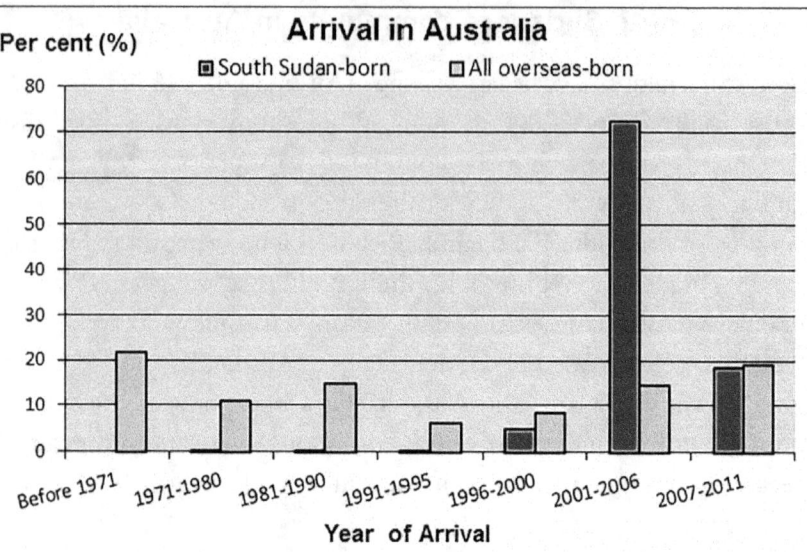

Figure 2:3: Arrival periods of South Sudan-born people in Australia.
Source: Department of Immigration and Citizenship (2013)

ment and housing (Abur & Spaaij 2016, Marlowe 2011a). The 2011 Census recorded 3487 South Sudan-born people in Australia, and showed that Victoria had the largest number (1118), followed by Queensland (715), New South Wales (561) and Western Australia (489) (DIAC, 2013).

South Sudanese people arrived in Australia at different times, including before 1971 according to the 2011 Census, as shown in Figure 6.6. The largest number of families and individuals arrived between 2001 and 2006. Among the total South Sudan-born in Australia at the time of the 2011 Census, 72.4% arrived between 2001 and 2006, and 18.4% arrived between 2007 and 2011. Compared to the 62% of total overseas-born population who arrived before 2001, only 5.6 % of South Sudan-born people living in Australia arrived before that time.

Social and Political Background of South Sudanese People

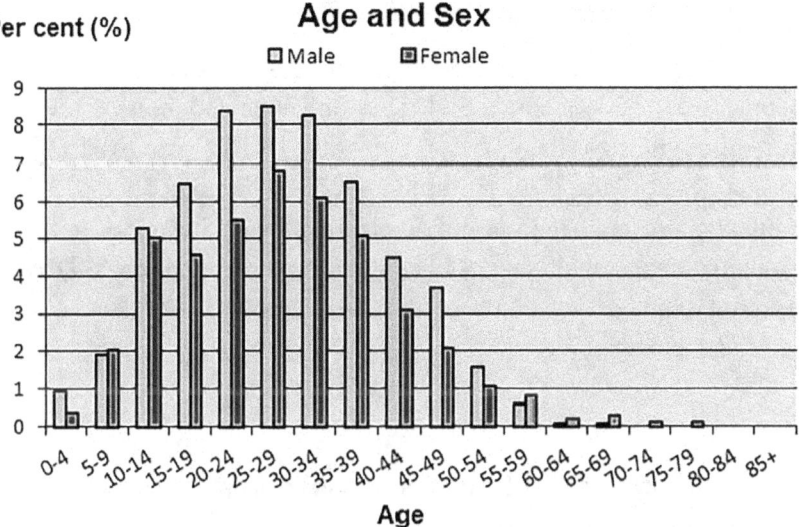

Figure 2:4 : Age and sex of South Sudanese in Australia.
Source: Department of Immigration and Citizenship (2013)

Age and sex of South Sudanese in Australia

The median age of South Sudan-born arrivals in 2011 was 27 years, compared with 45 years for all overseas-born arrivals, and 37 years for the total Australian population. The age distribution showed 15.5% were aged 0–14 years, 24.9% 15–24 years, 48.9% 25–44 years, 10.1% 45–64 years, and 0.6% were 65 years and over. There were 1979 males (56.7%) and 1509 females (43.3%) among those born in South Sudan who now live in Australia. The sex ratio was 131.1:100 males to females (see DIAC 2013).

Ancestry of South Sudanese in Australia

In the 2011 Census, the top ancestry responses for South Sudan-born people were 55.0% South Sudanese, Sudanese (15.4%), African – not otherwise described (7.7%) and other African groups (16.2%). In that census, Australians reported about 300 different ancestries by ethnicity. A total of 4825 responses claimed South Sudanese ancestry. However, there are difficulties in confirming these numbers, as DIAC was not then set up to distinguish between South Sudanese and Sudanese-born people.

Language of South Sudanese in Australia

The main languages spoken at home by South Sudan-born people in Australia were Dinka (1811), Arabic (656) and Nuer (259). Of the 3388 South Sudan-born people who spoke a language other than English at home, 80.5% spoke English very well or well, and 16.4% spoke English not well or not at all.

Religion of South Sudanese in Australia

At the time of the 2011 Census, the major religious affiliations amongst South Sudan-born were Catholic (1488), Anglican (1222) and Presbyterian and Reformed (238). The percentage for South Sudan-born who stated, "No Religion" (0.6%) was lower than in the total Australian population (22.3%), and a further 1.7% did not state a religion.

Social and Political Background of South Sudanese People

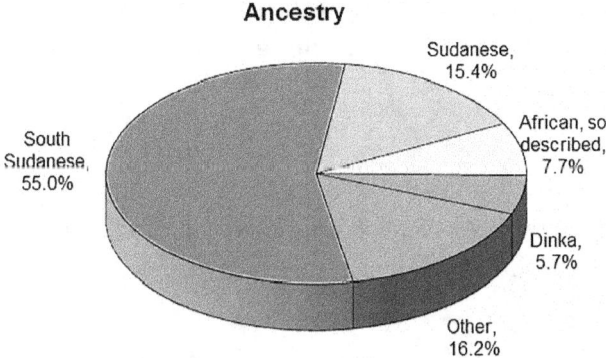

Figure 2:5: Ancestry of South Sudanese in Australia
Source: Department of Immigration and Citizenship (2013)

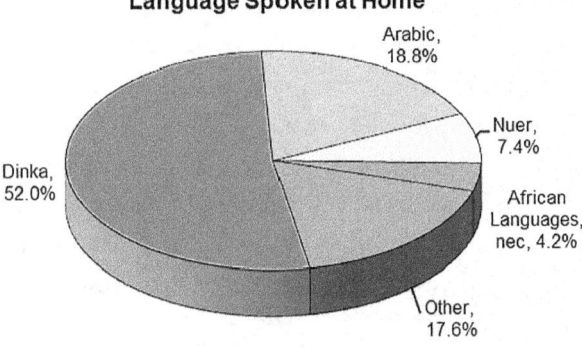

Figure 2:6: Language spoken at home by South Sudanese in Australia
Source: Department of Immigration and Citizenship (2013)

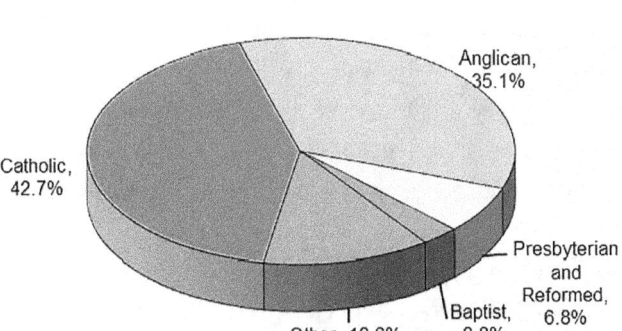

Figure 2:7: Religious beliefs of South Sudanese in Australia
Source: Department of Immigration and Citizenship (2013)

Education, employment and income of South Sudanese in Australia

The 2011 Census showed that 43.2% of South Sudan-born people aged 15 years and over had some form of higher, non-school qualifications compared to 55.9% of the general Australian population. Of that percentage, 34.4% were still attending an educational institution. The corresponding rate for the total Australian population was 8.6%.

Occupation in workforce

In the 2011 Census, the participation rate in the labour force was 50.7% among South Sudan-born people aged 15 years and over. The unemployment rate was 28.6%. Corresponding rates in the total Australian population were 65% and 5.6%, respectively. In other words, the unemployment rate among South Sudanese in Australia was more than four times that of the general Australian population. Of the 1028 South Sudan-born people who were employed, 18.8% were employed in a skilled, managerial, and professional or trade occupation. The corresponding rate in the total Australian population was 48.4%.

Incomes of South Sudanese in Australia

The median income at the time of the 2011 Census recorded the individual weekly income for South Sudan-born people in Australia, aged 15 years and over as $272, compared with $538 for all overseas-born respondents, and $597 for all Australian-born. The total Australian population had a median individual weekly income of $577.

Before their arrival in Australia, people from the South Sudanese community had different experiences, including being victims of civil war, staying in refugee camps, or living in transit in neighbouring countries such as Kenya (Atem 2011a; Juuk 2013). As a result of such

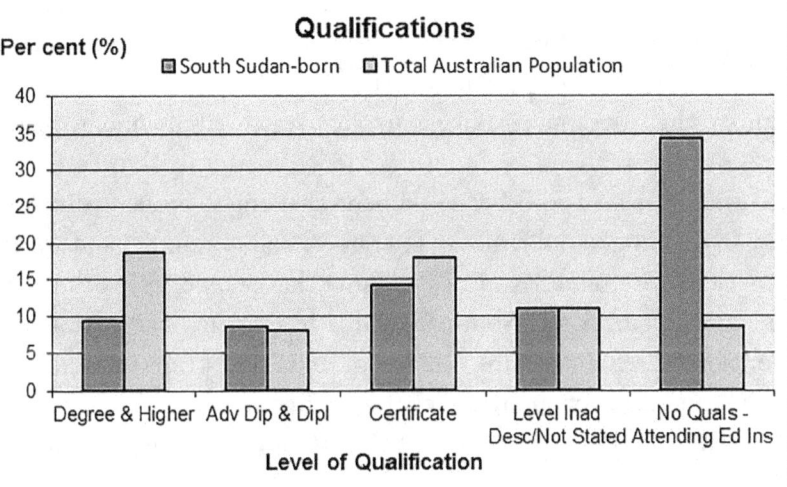

Figure 2:8: Level of educational qualifications of South Sudanese in Australia
Source: Department of Immigration and Citizenship (2013)

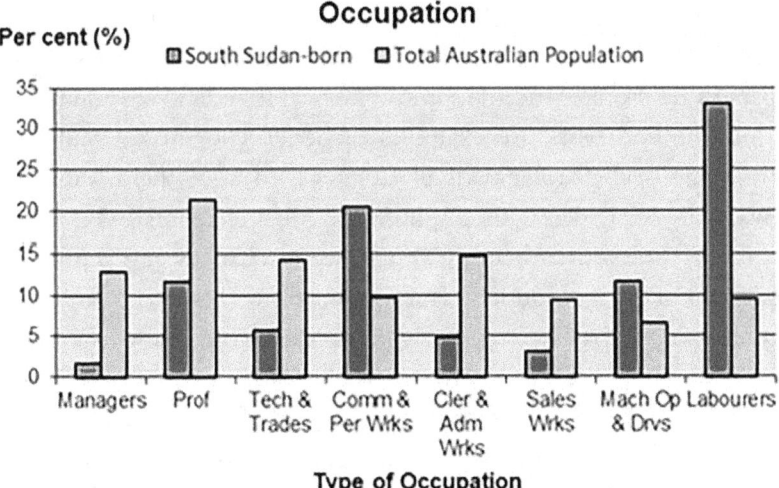

Figure 2:9: Occupation in workforce of South Sudanese in Australia
Source: Department of Immigration and Citizenship (2013)

challenging journeys, many have missed development opportunities, including education. People are aware of the importance of education in their lives and the lives of their children, but conflict and transition denied them the rights to education (Juuk 2013). Similar challenges face refugees in the area of employment. Many have arrived with no or little experience in the workforce (Abur 2012). This, added to other settlement challenges, presents difficulties in gaining employment. Therefore, solid training and work experience are often required to ensure that people are work ready. In some instances, the South Sudanese immigrants had performed work in the refugee camps, including driving UN cars, undertaking restaurant work for men, while women frequently sold tea or food in small shops in the camps (see Ethnic Council of Shepparton and District Inc. 2013).

Social and Settlement issues of the South Sudanese community in Australia

Settlement of the South Sudanese people in Australia brings many social changes, ranging across community and family levels. Some changes are problematic and some beneficial to individuals and family. Education and work are examples of benefits for South Sudanese, while one of the problematic challenges is to understand Australian law. Many struggles with disputes and disagreements, which lead to family breakdown because of the social changes and misunderstandings of the law. South Sudanese come from a system of family and customary law that does not apply in Australia. Thus, many individuals struggle to hold their family together. These family issues are exposed upon arrival because of different values, beliefs, and processes; they are largely unaware of the laws and regulations governing family life (Abur 2012, Milos 2011).

Given the social and family issues, it is cleared that South Sudanese community groups need assistance to be better educated about family law and its procedures (Juuk 2013; Milos 2011). The community need to be informed about the role and function of the law and law enforcement agencies. It also needs to be informed about individual rights when dealing with the legal system (Juuk 2013; Milos 2011). South Sudanese customary law is highly developed and has been established throughout centuries of usage, so cultural and practical differences provide a stark contrast between the two legal systems (Milos 2011). When it comes to family problems or civil matters, South Sudanese refugees have trouble understanding legal issues. A lack of school-based education and poor provision of general information about Australia prior to arrival, and difficulties surrounding language, cause difficulties for many South Sudanese during their settlement period, particularly in Australia (Abur 2012, Juuk 2013).

The South Sudanese community supports its members through advocacy, connecting families and individuals, organising cultural activities and celebrations, as well as assisting families and individuals who are in crisis (e.g. mourning and funerals). The perception of community in South Sudan is linked to a sense of responsibility and respect, especially to their own ethnic group. Community leaders have been working hard to assist families and individuals to settle by observing the legal issues in Australia more carefully. The community leader's role in helping families has been viewed as vital in the research context, but nothing has been offered to assist community leaders to continue this important work.

Keeping the community stable is of the highest importance for community leaders, who are still expected to hear disputes in the community and apply fair and just outcomes for all. There is a lot of pressure on community leaders and elders to keep peace and stability in the community. However, this vital role of the community leaders is not recognised in the Australian legal system (Milos 2011, p. 13).

This chapter two has provided a brief history of post-colonial South Sudan in both political and social contexts, as well as the settlement and composition of the South Sudanese community in Australia.

A NEW LIFE WITH OPPORTUNITIES AND CHALLENGES

It has explained the settlement and social problems faced by the South Sudanese refugee community whose members have endured a long civil war. Some are recovering from trauma, which sometimes makes things difficult for individuals and families to organise themselves and move on with their lives. The demographic data in this chapter has provided an overview of the South Sudanese community in Australia, which can assist readers to not only understand the origins, customs, and cultural traditions of the South Sudanese, but also to appreciate the challenges they face in adjusting to a new life in a foreign country.

CHAPTER 3

The Marginalisation of refugees: Settlement experience of South Sudanese-Australians

I have focused on settlement difficulties and backgrounds of the South Sudanese-Australians from academic perspective in the above chapters. This chapter presented the findings or the voice of community members who were interviewed during my PhD research in the area of migration and settlement of the South Sudanese community in Australia. During the interviews, participants discussed common themes that they considered important to their families, themselves and to their South Sudanese community. They were also able to share some of their personal experiences of settlement in Australia. Therefore, I have presented the selected texts from the interviews as primary voices of participants according to their personal experiences and their reflection about community's experience as general.

The forced migration of people from South Sudan to Australia started in the 1990s due to an extended civil war between North Sudan and Southern Sudan. As a result of that war, over 30,000 plus Sudanese arrived in Australia and many of them have since obtained their Australian citizenship (Abur, 2018, Abur & Spaaji 2016). The largest number of humanitarian entrants from Sudan arrived between 2000 and 2006, often after spending several years in refugee camps. Many South Sudanese-Australians were resettled to Australia after spending years in refugee camps. The concept of refugee protection emerged during World War II, resulting in the Convention on

Refugees and subsequently the establishment of the UNHCR (Abur & Spaaij, 2016; McDonald et al. 2008; UNHCR 2015). Refugees are people who have fled their homeland often as a result of political instability, repression, and violent conflict. They leave in order to escape oppressive discrimination, or severe physical and mental harm (Abur & Spaaij, 2016, Mamer 2010). Such sudden departures generally mean that refugees do not have the time or opportunity to pack their belongings or to farewell loved ones (Abur 2012; Mamer 2010, Marlowe 2011a). Often, they leave secretly for fear of persecution, without knowing if they will ever be able to return. Typically, refugees are then exposed to uncertain and dangerous journeys (Mamer 2010).

'Refugee resettlement' is a term used to describe the relocation of refugees from a country of asylum to a third country for permanent integration, with the aim of addressing the needs of refugees through integration in that third country. While the resettlement process is complex, it is widely viewed as a durable solution for refugee problems (see Marlowe, Harris & Lyons 2014; Refugee Council of Australia 2010; Tipping 2011). Refugees are assessed and accepted for resettlement when they meet the criteria set out by the UN Convention (Colic-Peisker & Tilbury 2007; Fozdar & Hartley 2012; McDonald et al. 2008). The challenges that refugees experienced are significant and multi-faceted (Abur 2012; Fozdar & Hartley 2013) Large numbers of refugees, who are waiting to be assessed and resettled currently live in refugee and displacement camps worldwide, such as the Kakuma refugee camp in Kenya, from where many South Sudanese have lived before migrating to Australia, as well as camps in Uganda, Ethiopia, and Egypt. These camps are characterised by shortages of food, inadequate medical services, and lack of sanitation (Ager 1999; Ajak et al. 2015; Marlowe 2011a).

In addition to these physical deprivations and hardships, many refugees experience highly traumatising events prior to their arrival in the camps, such as witnessing executions, the death of loved ones, different forms of abuse, rape, and oppression as well as looting and widespread destruction. These experiences can have profound emotional and psychological impacts on families and individuals and it has been widely recognised that as a result many refugees suffer from varying degrees of Post-Traumatic Stress Disorder (PTSD) (Abur & Spaaij, 2016, Ajak et al. 2015, Marlowe 2011a, Tipping 2011). The complexity of the pre-settlement experiences of refugees and the impact of these experiences of individuals and families put pressure on countries receiving refugees to ensure that they can be adequately supported at both a policy and service level (Ajak et al. 2015; Marlowe 2011a). Countries providing resettlement programs do so voluntarily as part of the global sharing of responsibility to protect refugees and provide a durable solution to those who cannot return to their countries of origin (UNHCR 2015). The receiving country is expected to provide refugees with support services and access to resources that facilitate successful integration into the host society (Hurstfield et al. 2004; UNHCR 2015; Bloch 2000, 2008; Korac 2003; Peisker & Tilbury 2003). These issues discussed in the literature review are very critical and important issues for the South Sudanese community in Australia and in the context of this study. Families and individuals are struggling with resettlement and settlement issues, and may need some support services in order to overcome settlement issues.

Settlement of Refugees: a challenging process

While resettlement issues for refugees in general have been discussed above, this section discusses *settlement* issues for refugees that are of particular significance to the South Sudanese community in Australia. 'Refugee settlement' is a term used when refugees arrive in Australia and require a range of support services to establish themselves and become independent in a new cultural and social context (see Abur & Spaaij 2016, DIAC 2013). Settlement is a complex process that requires support from the host community, government, and non-government agencies to address different challenges (Abur 2012, Abur & Spaaij 2016 Lejukole 2008).

Refugees have sometimes been perceived as a burden on receiving countries. This notion of a burden has been central to both policy and research debates about displacement and protection (Zetter 2015, p. 17). Such political and community concerns are indicative of the global challenge of refugee resettlement amidst a trend of decreasing numbers of refugees being able to return voluntarily to their countries (Correa-Velez, Barnett, & Gifford 2015). The complexity of settlement is magnified by attachment to place – how refugees identify with the country that they settle in and how they create a sense of belonging (Hiruy 2009). Arguably this is very much influenced by how they are received; as burdensome or as being able to make an important contribution. Based on the 1951 Convention Relating to the Status of Refugees and Protection, the countries where refugees are resettled must act responsibly in a non-discriminatory manner by ensuring that those people have the opportunity to participate fully in society (Abur & Spaaij, 2016, UNHCR 2015).

Ideally, settlement can be seen as a two-way process of mutual understanding of cultural expectations, with the host community working in partnership with refugees. As the Refugee Council of Australia (2011) (RCA) argues:

> Settlement is not just something that a refugee must do, but there is also a need for the wider community to adapt to accommodate the refugees. A "spirit of hospitality", where refugees are made to feel welcome in a community, underpins successful refugee settlement programs.

Settlement is meant to be the final stage for refugees and migrants to integrate into Australian society and it is a time when families and individuals require support to gain social connection and to develop economic independence (Bennett & Adriel 2014; DIAC 2012). However, Lejukole (2008) has argued that settlement cannot ever be completed;

it is an ongoing process that involves the challenges of adapting to a new place and gradually connecting with the host community. At the beginning the challenges of settlement can overshadow its benefits for refugees. These challenges include lack of social capital and language to assist the integration process. Settling in a new environment and social context is a daunting task for anyone, regardless of the educational level one may or may not have obtained (Abur 2012; Abur & Spaaij 2016). The impact of integrating into a new society can cause high levels of stress and anxiety (Pisano 1995; Refugee Council of Australia 2010). Refugees often experience a high level of homesickness and isolation and this is aggravated by culture shock that further hinders their ability to begin a new life in Australia (Abur & Spaaij 2016) As well as promoting optimal levels of wellbeing required to deal with the stress and adjustments involved in resettlement, integration programs that support emotional and personal rebuilding approach can help to prevent the development of more serious mental health difficulties (Marlowe 2010, p. 6, cited in UNHCR 2002, p. 231).

The settlement of refugees has generated a vast body of research globally. Studies in this field have covered a broad array of themes critical to setting the context for this current PhD research in terms of understanding forced migration and displacement. Prominent themes of particular relevance include drivers of displacement and forced migration, legal and moral frameworks, and experiences in refugee camps and countries of resettlement (see, for example, Abur & Spaaij 2016, Colic-Peisker & Tilbury 2007; Fozdar & Hartley 2012; McDonald et al. 2008). Factors which have been identified as making a significant positive contribution to settlement include: feeling safe from racism and discrimination, obtaining secure and well-paid employment, being able to buy a home, and one's children feeling well supported at school and in the community (Abur & Spaaij 2016, Ager 1999; Fozdar & Hartley 2012, Fozdar & Hartley 2012, Refugee Council of Australia, 2010). As I have discussed the general settlement issues the general settlement challenges for refugees in Australia, I still believe that there is a great need to critique settlement policy and ways forward to address some of the bigger issues which people from refugee backgrounds still experiencing in Australia.

Issues such as unemployment, discrimination and vilification by the main Medias, health and wellbeing, social networks and family/parenting are some of the difficulties which faced the South Sudanese-Australians and other groups with refugee backgrounds in Australia. For example, poor states of mental health can contribute to barriers to refugees gaining employment, however obtaining employment can significantly improve overall-wellbeing.

When a host country provides assistance to enable newly arrived refugees to integrate into their new society, services and treatment of refugees are influenced by the politics within the country (Allerdice 2011). In Australia, refugee settlement policy-making, management, and funding are centralised at the Commonwealth level. For the past few years, discussion of refugees in Australia has increasingly focused on refugees from African countries and the recent arrival of boats seeking asylum in Australia (Abur & Spaaij 2016, Baker-Lewton, et al 2017, Marjoribanks, et al 2010). Many of these recent debates in the media have attempted to distinguish between "bad" and "good" refugees. "Bad" refugees are those who "jump the queue", meaning they arrive by boat and not through the formal UNHCR channel (Abur & Spaaij 2016; Marjoribanks, et al 2010).

The majority of South Sudanese in Australia arrived through the work of the UNHCR in refugee camps. Despite this, they are still often labelled as "undesirable" refugees in Government and media discourse because of their settlement-related challenges in Australia, which have been both exaggerated and widely misreported by the mainstream media (Abur & Spaaij 2016, Marjoribanks, et al 2010, Baker-Lewton, et al 2017). Therefore, understanding these history and challenging issues facing people from refugee backgrounds in Australia including people from the South Sudanese community is very vital in policy and practice contexts.

Policy and Practice: refugee settlement in Australia

Australia has a history of resettling refugees and people in humanitarian need, and is a signatory to the United Nations 1951 Convention relating to the Status of Refugees and to the subsequent 1967 Protocol (Cope & Kalantzis 1999, Smith 1998). The Humanitarian Resettlement Program in Australia began in 1947, with the resettlement of European Displaced Persons (DPs) who were displaced by World War II (see Australian Government, Department of Immigration and Border Protection 2013) and brought to Australia where they were accommodated under the auspices of the International Refugee Organization (IRO), the immediate precursor of the UNHCR. Since 1947, more than 800,000 refugees from a broad range of nationalities have been resettled and have rebuilt their lives in Australia (Abur & Spaaij 2016, Atem 2011; DIAC 2013; Pisano 1995; Refugee Council of Australia 2010). Between 1933 and 1939, for example, more than 7,000 Jews fleeing Nazi Germany were settled (Neuman 2006). In 1937, the Australian Jewish Welfare Society pioneered the first refugee settlement support services, with financial assistance from the Australian government. (Refugee Council of Australia 2012). However, Australia also has a history of discriminating against certain ethnicities. After Federation, the Restriction Act 1901, which became known as the White Australia Policy, limited immigration to Australia on the basis of ethnicity (Atem 2011, Refugee Council of Australia 2010).

The White Australia Policy formally ended in 1975 with the introduction of the Racial Discrimination Act. A multicultural political agenda was beginning, but it took until 1989 for the federal government to translate it into policy in the form of a National Agenda for Multicultural Australia. The aim of the policy was to achieve a harmonious society based on Australian values by recognising diversity as a positive contribution to the workforce within Australian culture (see Australian Government 2012). Since 1975 when the first Vietnamese refugees arrived in Australia by boat, many more refugees have arrived from Asia, the Middle East, and Africa. In the last decade, refugees have come from Burma, Bhutan, Afghanistan, Iraq, South Sudan, Sudan, Somalia, Congo, and Burundi (Abur & Spaaij 2016, Atem 2011, DIAC 2011, and Refugee Council of Australia 2010).

As a public policy, multiculturalism encompasses government measures designed to respond to diversity and differences. The government has identified three dimensions of its multicultural policy. The first is cultural identity, which is the right of all Australians, within carefully defined limits, to express and share their individual cultural heritage, including their language and religion. The second is social justice, the right of all Australians to equality of treatment and opportunity, and the removal of barriers of race, ethnicity, culture, religion, language, gender, or place of birth. The third dimension is economic efficiency, the need to maintain, develop, and utilise effectively the skills and talents of all Australians, regardless of background (Australian Government 2014).

With this multicultural society in mind, refugee community groups are considered to be disadvantaged, and thus deserving of special consideration under social inclusion services after a realisation that some community groups are being excluded (Calma 2008). Social inclusion has become an important policy initiative for state governments, and it often generates debate about which groups are socially excluded, and why (Calma 2008 and see Australian Government 2012). Social exclusion is viewed as a significant social cost, since it pushes new arrivals to the edge of society and prevents them from participating fully by virtue of their poverty, lack of basic competencies, limited lifelong learning opportunities, and ongoing discrimination (Abur & Spaaij 2016). Many refugees have experienced poverty in their home countries as well as the interim country prior to settlement, which in addition to war and conflict has led to poor quality or interrupted education – or in some cases the total absence of formal education. Refugees have varying degrees of written literacy in their own language, and may have very low levels of English language. If they have been living in a refugee camp prior to their arrival, they may also have no concept of how to interact with society and its institutions such as banks, hotels, etc (Abur 2012). A combination of lack of familiarity with systems that are necessary in the navigation of daily life and a lack of ability/confidence with language can result in a struggle to gain meaningful or any employment. This results in limited participation in society with little access to power and decision-making bodies and, thus, often feel powerless and unable to take control over decisions that affect their lives (Abur & Spaaij 2016, Stratigaki 2005).

Social inclusion policy, on the other hand, aims to preserve human and cultural rights, especially in relation to language retention, participation in economic production, recognition of qualifications of refugees and skilled migrants, and participation in decision-making (Calma 2008). The basic values of multiculturalism and social inclusion policy in Australia include the following principles: **Principle 1**, a commitment to celebrate and value the benefits of cultural diversity for all Australians, within the broader aims of national unity, community harmony and maintenance of our democratic values, **Principle 2**, a commitment to a just, inclusive and socially cohesive society where everyone can participate in the opportunities that Australia offers and where government services are responsive to the needs of Australians from culturally and linguistically diverse backgrounds (Australian Government 2014, p.6).

These principles highlight a mutual obligation for all citizens, whether migrants or Australian-born, to accept that everyone has the right to retain, express, and share their own cultural heritage in return for an overriding commitment to Australian norms (which include the country's laws, democratic form of governance, and adoption of English as a national language). The government's social policy and vision of a socially inclusive society effectively means that all Australians should feel valued and have the opportunity to participate fully in society. It states that all Australians must have an equal opportunity to be involved in learning by participating in education and training; to be involved in the workforce by participating in employment, in voluntary work, and in family and caring; to engage by connecting with people and using their local community's resources; and to have a voice so they can influence decisions that affect them (Abur & Spaaij 2016, Australia Government 2012).

The South Sudanese in Australia: Cultural Challenges

There is a general expectation that refugees will adjust quickly to the expectations of the host society, which (erroneously) assumes that acculturation and integration are straightforward, if not seamless, processes. However, cultural differences between the refugee community and that of the host country can mean that integration is complex. For instance, some mainstream community members were quick to blame the culture of South Sudanese or African in general due to some poor behaviours of young people who tended to act out and involves in criminal activities for some reasons. Culture has been defined as knowledge, social activities, and the interpretation of life or worldview with which individuals or groups associate, as well as an understanding of their society (Habermas et al 1985).

This study is built from study which I conducted in 2012 for my master's degree, which found that South Sudanese community was and is facing complex issues in adjusting to their new environment including cultural change (Abur 2012). Atem (2011) found that settlement of Sudanese refugees in Australia is complicated by cultural differences and by their experiences prior to arrival. Large numbers of people in today's society now live in cities and towns rather than rural villages (Giddins 1989). Some of families and individuals in the South Sudanese community to Australia with mixed experiences and lifestyles. Some had opportunity of living in cities and town, but some families and individuals were from village to refugee camps and from refugee camps to settle in urban areas in Australia which is different from their experiences in refugee camps or in the villages.

In South Sudanese culture life events such as the birth, sickness, death (mourning), marriage, and reunion are very important as they bring family, relatives, extended family, and friends together in either celebration or to support each other through difficult/sad times. *Togetherness* is essential in Dinka (the largest tribal group in Southern Sudan) culture and is one of the reasons why the Dinka people live in large groups or extended families that can reach beyond 12 families in a kinship chain close in blood relations (Juuk 2013; Makol 2012). This cultural beliefs and practices are still impacting the South Sudanese families and individuals in Australia in different ways. Some families find it hard to raise their children in Australia because cultural reasons that may be against Australian culture and lifestyles.

Renzaho & Vignjevic (2011) argued that raising a family in a culture new to one's own is a challenge for many African migrant families with very little knowledge of western parenting. Children of migrants tend to adapt quickly, but their parents still hold on to their own cultures and parenting styles. As children adapt to those systems and cultures of their new country, they are often required to interpret the new culture for their parents or other adult family members who are struggling with certain issues (Juuk 2013; Renzaho & Vignjevic 2011). These include social issues relating to child rearing, child protection, and school issues. For example, a teenager may choose not to attend school, and not listen to or respect parents' opinions because he/she is more expert in certain areas of interpreting for parents (Abur 2012; Renzaho & Vignjevic 2011). This brings critical challenges for parents in terms of responsibilities within the family (Lejukole 2008). Many parents feel their responsibilities and respect are undermined when local authorities' initiate programs to discipline and manage their children (Bye & Alvarez 2007).

Thus, parenting children in a new culture has been one of the challenging tasks for South Sudanese families (Renzaho & Vignjevic 2011). Resettling can be highly disruptive and is often a lengthy transitional process. It often involves losing structures that may have provided significant support for child protection and development, and individual and general family functioning (Juuk 2013). Often, there is considerable debate within the South Sudanese community among different generations about where they really belong. Some people consider themselves more Australian by adapting to Australian ways of life, and have criticised South Sudanese ways. The differences in cultural values between Australian and South Sudanese societies have been the main issue causing anxiety among parents. Some South Sudanese parents in Australia are greatly concerned about their young people having contact with those outside their own culture, and resist any kind of relationship that a young person can form in their own community (Abur 2012; Renzaho & Vignjevic 2011). One of the things that adults or parents fear is the difference between Australia's liberal values and South Sudan's traditional and conservative values. This frequently leads to intergenerational disagreement and conflict in the family, as well as in the community and among different generations.

The rise of intergenerational conflict among refugees and migrant families due to difference in cultural values and practices is a major social problem. Social workers and people working in the criminal justice system believe that it is a major source of family breakdown (Marlowe, Harris & Lyons 2014; Renzaho & Vignjevic 2011). Maintaining one's original culture in the family is important in many societies and carries considerable weight in terms of an argument as to why people want to keep the values of their cultural practice and family relations (Abur 2012; Atem 2011). African, and particularly Sudanese, parents are a case in point. They often want their children to maintain traditional values and roles, but this creates tensions for teenagers who have grown up in Australia, who will confidently challenge such expectations and demands from their parents (Juuk 2013). The difficulties teenagers face in accepting traditional values and cultural expectations from parents include pressure from friends, directly and indirectly, to adopt an Australian or western culture rather than continuing to value their traditional cultures. Conflict can occur within families whose members are all new migrants, as well as within families whose children have been born in Australia (Abur 2012; Juuk

2013). Clashes of this type generally arise regarding modes of dress and behaviour, differences in child-rearing practice and, in particular, a greater sense of independence amongst young people.

Post-trauma and wellbeing for South Sudanese refugees

During the resettlement and settlement process, refugees face many challenges including learning a new language, finding employment, gaining an understanding the systems and culture of the host country and dealing with discrimination (Abur & Spaaij 2016, Baker-Lewton, et al 2017). There are also stresses associated with being separated from family members and/or family reunification process in Australia, as well as profound feelings of homesickness and isolation (Abur & Spaaij 2016). These challenges can impede refugees from achieving well-being in the resettlement context (Marlowe, Harris & Lyons 2014, Lejukole 2008; Tipping 2011, Renzaho & Vignjevic 2011). The length of time needed for refugees to settle and to feel settled– is closely linked to the number of support services provided. Support with income, housing, employment, education and health care assists integration into the local community and plays an important role in enabling refugees to rebuild their lives and sense of self (Abur & Spaaij 2016, Marlowe 2010).

This body of literature demonstrates that both resettlement and settlement difficulties cause some of the mental health and wellbeing issues for families and individuals from refugee backgrounds, in addition to their conflict and displacement experiences before arriving at refugee camps. From this study's perspective, understanding post-trauma and wellbeing issues of South Sudanese community families and individuals is a very important part of this study. There is no doubt that some, if not many, South Sudanese families and individuals have experienced some trauma and other wellbeing issues due to post-settlement and settlement experiences.

There are some less tangible factors that play a vital role in the settlement process include feeling safe and secure, gradually being able to restore a sense of self-worth and dignity, regaining a sense of control over one's life, resolving guilt, and processing grief around the loss of identity and country (Refugee Council of Australia, 2010). One of the ongoing problems for refugees is post-traumatic stress disorder (PTSD), which is often not discussed openly, but it is a significant issue when it comes to resettlement. Support programs contribute to refugee individual's overall well-being and can decrease both daily and long-term stress, which is a part of PTSD (Abur 2012, Marlowe 2010, and Tipping 2011)

Settlement issues affect the well-being of individuals and families from refugee backgrounds during their settlement period, and often become overwhelming (Atem 2011; Hadgkiss et al. 2012). Generally, there are significant wellbeing and mental health issues that required some urgent preventions for refugees in order for them to overcome some settlement issues (Lejukole 2008; Mamer 2010). The wellbeing and mental health issues include post-traumatic stress disorder (PTSD). There is no intention here to either diagnose or label all refugees, but rather to acknowledge trauma as one of the settlement challenges for people from refugee backgrounds who have experienced appalling situations, including whilst in refugee camps (Marlowe 2010, 2011a). Their experiences in conflict areas and later in refugee camps influence their ability to resettle.

There is ample evidence in the literature to suggest that those with a refugee background have experienced some form of abuse, rape, oppression, or have witnessed horrific atrocities, including killings, looting, and destruction of personal wealth. Some have been in slavery, forced to live in exile and in shocking conditions in refugee camps (see Lejukole 2008; Mamer 2010; Marlowe 2010, 2011a). These experiences evidently affect many refugees, including those from the South Sudan, who may have been forced to live in refugee camps for many years. They bring these difficult experiences with them when engaging in resettlement programs (Mamer 2010).

South Sudanese refugees have been studied for years for post-trauma issues because of their background in the civil war, displacement, and their lives in refugee camps (see Lejukole 2008; Mamer 2010; Marlowe 2010, 2011a). In Australia, most people from South Sudanese community have no idea what trauma means, or how to seek help if one has encountered traumatic challenges (Abur 2012 and Lejukole 2008). In some respects, trauma presents a powerful argument that helps people claim for recognition as refugees (Marlowe 2011a). Trauma is something that has helped many refugees gain entry into refugee camps, acquire refugee status, and access services in Australia (Marlowe 2011b). However, traumatic experiences – or being labelled as having trauma issues – can limit opportunities for refugees to integrate into their host society, as well as to obtain decent employment and participate in decision-making (Westoby 2008).

Post-trauma is a condition that is not often discussed by refugees because of traditional beliefs and taboos associated with mental health (Abur 2012). When discussing trauma issues, South Sudanese people respond very differently to those raised in western societies (Marlowe 2010 and Tipping 2011). This has sometimes made it difficult to offer counselling for trauma to particular refugees such as those in the South Sudanese community. People are more likely to decline services because it is not part of their belief system (Marlowe 2010). More specifically, it is not uncommon for cultures such as the South Sudanese to decline to discuss their trauma or mental health issues. Trauma is a new concept for them. It is often viewed as a weakness to talk about mental health issues. This is a general observation in relation to common attitudes and feelings around trauma and this is confirmed by other research (Abur 2012; Marlowe 2010). Some of the strengths, resilience, and coping mechanisms that assist the South Sudanese to deal internally with trauma issues, stating that many do not want to hear about post-trauma, as it labels them in negative ways (Marlowe 2010). This does not mean that there is no trauma among at least some South Sudanese people who have resettled in western countries such as Australia, and among those still living in South Sudan because of the long civil war, they have witnessed. As part of transition and settlement confrontation, families and individuals would find themselves with fewer or no skills to deal with past and present challenges in the new environment (Abur 2012; Tipping 2011).

Having social connections enhances the well-being and health of people through daily contact and support for social issues (Bloom 2014). Personal social wellbeing involves a person's relationship with others and how that person communicates, interacts, and socialises (Bloom 2014, Mikkonen & Raphael 2010). It can also relate to how people make friends and whether they have a sense of belonging. For example, going to the movies with friends can help to ease the daily stress of social isolation (Mikkonen & Raphael 2010). Social health and wellbeing refer to the social hierarchy of people, their financial status, living conditions, social support, level of education, acceptance of race, gender, religion, and behaviours, and access to health care (Hadgkiss et al. 2012). For refugee community groups, such as the South Sudanese community in Melbourne, their social well-being can be measured by a broad range of indicators. They include the level of income of members and their families, social participation and social support networks, current and previous education, understanding social and political systems, understanding critical challenges of settlement (such as living conditions, racism and discrimination, and culture shock), and other factors such as city lifestyle (Mikkonen & Raphael 2010).

The complex roles played by these social determinants of the health and well-being of those who feel socially excluded are at an extreme level for the disadvantaged and may be experienced both directly and indirectly (Hadgkiss et al. 2012). The disadvantaged are more likely to experience social exclusion from decent employment opportunities, due to their backgrounds as refugees, having English as a second language or lacking certain skills and qualifications (Abur

& Spaaij 2016). It is very common for refugees to lack supportive relationships, suffer social isolation, and face mistrust of and by others. Racism and discrimination further increase stress and other unsettling emotions (Abur & Spaaij 2016). Stressful living conditions make it extremely hard to take up physical leisure activities or to practice healthy eating habits because most of one's energy is directed simply at coping day to day. Such conditions can cause continuing feelings of shame, insecurity, and worthlessness, which affect psychological health (Bloom 2014, Mikkonen &Raphael 2010). The social environment brings a new complexity in terms of health and wellbeing (Hadgkiss et al. 2012). For instance, lack of employment and participation in sport can cause many problems for individuals; there is no doubt that a lack of participation in social activities within the local community creates inequality, and feelings of stigma and social isolation, which can lead to serious health and wellbeing issues.

Therefore, obtaining employment-related income is perhaps the most important social determinant of good health. The level of income shapes overall living conditions affects psychological functioning and influences health-related behaviours, such as the quality of diet, the extent of physical activity, tobacco and excessive alcohol use, which are likely factors among refugee community groups in Australia. Participation in employment and sports brings especial connections to individual people who are either would have suffered social isolation in societies.

Mental Health and General Wellbeing for South Sudanese Refugees

The aftermath of conflict, displacement and migration comes with other level of difficulties. The level of mental health problems raised highly in community while was no proper support services put in place to deal with mental health issues.

> Mental health issues in community are not only affecting individuals who are mentally sick but does have cascading consequences on general society. It is happening now in community on social media issues, people are abusing each other and creating serious allegations or defamations
>
> *Participant 7, 38-year-old male, 10 years in Australia*

People who experienced conflict and lived long in a difficult situation such as refugee camps are more likely to encounter trauma and other mental health problems (Abur, 2018). More importantly, the continuation of conflict and poverty in many parts of Africa has caused historical serious mental health problems (Tempany, 2009). Both government and private agencies have overlooked the importance of addressing mental health issues in war affected communities. For instance, people living with severe mental health conditions such as schizophrenia, bipolar mood disorder and severe depression (Kakuma, at el, 2010). South Sudan is one of the countries affected by war, poverty, infectious diseases and mental health problems. The South Sudanese people who migrated and settled in Australia are also facing serious mental health issues as the aftermaths of conflict and settlement difficulties.

> In many cases, we are confused by the difficulties and many issues that make our mind not function well as we were previously. Men are abandoning their families and some women are not copping well with children. This is just iceberg of mental health and general wellbeing matters facing South Sudanese-Australians. We know that a woman driven her own children into a lake in western suburb of Melbourne. She was not normal to me
>
> *Participant 18, 30-year-old female, 15 years in Australia*

One of the ongoing problems in the South Sudanese community is post-traumatic stress disorder (PTSD), which is often not discussed openly, but it is a significant issue when it comes to general wellbeing of family and community. This area of mental health is largely ignored or neglected in the South Sudanese community. There are some support services in mainstream Australian systems that supported individuals and families that are struggling with mental health issues or general wellbeing issues. For the South Sudanese people, they are more unwilling to seek mental health support services because cultural related fear of taboo associating with mental illness (Abur 2012, Marlowe 2010, and Tipping 2011).

> Mental health issues are often not appropriately addressed in African community groups because some people refused not to discuss their mental health issues with families or friends. They also don't seek support services outside of community
> Participant 11, 28-year-old female, 8 years in Australia

Mental health problems are not often discussed by the South Sudanese people because of traditional beliefs and taboos associated with mental illness (Abur 2012). When discussing mental health issues, South Sudanese people respond very differently to those raised in western societies (Abur, 2018, Marlowe 2010). This has sometimes made it difficult to offer counselling for trauma to particular refugees such as those in the South Sudanese community. People are more likely to decline services because it is not part of their belief system (Marlowe 2010).

> There are many people in the South Sudanese community who are struggling with settlement issues and this led to many other mental health problems. Some people remained isolated because of their mental health problems (
> Participant 12, 22-year-old female, 11 years in Australia

Settlement issues affect the well-being of individuals and families from refugee backgrounds during their settlement period, and often become overwhelming (Atem 2011; Hadgkiss et al. 2012). Generally, there are significant wellbeing and mental health issues that required some urgent preventions for refugees in order for them to overcome some settlement issues (Lejukole 2008; Mamer 2010). The wellbeing and mental health issues include post-traumatic stress disorder (PTSD). There is no intention here to either diagnose or label all refugees, but rather to acknowledge trauma as one of the settlement challenges for people from refugee backgrounds who have experienced appalling situations, including whilst in refugee camps (Marlowe 2010, 2011a). Their experiences in conflict areas and later in refugee camps influence their ability to resettle.

> Settlement journey and experiences can be frustrating sometimes. One can feel lost in the jungle sometimes and not knowing where to start and what to do. There are too many problems, starting with family, children are going their own ways, wife and husband are not agreeing on small issues. if you are a man, you think of taking your bag and go back to war and leave children with their mother
> *Participant 14, 23-year-old male, 9 years in Australia*

During the resettlement and settlement process, refugees face many challenges including learning a new language, finding employment, gaining an understanding the systems and culture of the host country and dealing with discrimination (Abur & Spaaij 2016, Baker-Lewton, et al 2017). There are also stresses associated with being separated from family members and/or family reunification process in Australia, as well as profound feelings of homesickness and isolation (Abur & Spaaij 2016). These challenges can impede refugees from achieving well-being in the resettlement context (Marlowe, Harris & Lyons 2014, Lejukole 2008; Tipping 2011, Renzaho & Vignjevic 2011). The length of time needed for refugees to settle and to feel settled– is closely linked to the number of support services provided. Support with income, housing, employment, education and health care assists integration into the local community and plays an important role in enabling refugees to rebuild their lives and sense of self (Abur & Spaaij 2016, Marlowe 2010).

Settlement difficulties and experience of war and displacement often caused some of the mental health and wellbeing issues for families and individuals from refugee backgrounds, in addition to their conflict and displacement experiences before arriving at refugee camps (Abur, 2018 and Abur & Spaaji 2016). Understanding post-trauma and wellbeing issues of South Sudanese community families and individuals is a very important part in term of delivering support services and policy making. There is no doubt that some, if not many, South Sudanese families and individuals have experienced some trauma and other wellbeing issues due to post-settlement and settlement experiences. There are some less tangible factors that play a vital role in the settlement process include feeling safe and secure, gradually being able to restore a sense of self-worth and dignity, regaining a sense of control over one's life, resolving guilt, and processing grief around the loss of identity and country (Abur, 2018, Refugee Council of Australia, 2010).

Social isolation is one of the settlement difficulties for people who have no network and other support around them. Some of the members within south Sudanese community are extremely engaged in hate speech through social media. Psychological stress and despair are caused by lack of participation and connection during the settlement period. The experience of social isolation is a problem that could lead to self-isolation, stress, frustration and anger, negative thoughts about general life and purpose of living. There is always a trend of ignorance about the extent of mental problems in community and how the stigma/taboo of mental illness can be avoided.

> Social isolation is a big thing for people who stay at home without socialising outside their homes. Sometimes they become aggressive to themselves and their family members and cannot learn or see the world in a big picture [sic]
> *Participant 8, 25-year-old female, 14 years in Australia*

Family Functioning and Social Problems

Family settling in new country is not an easy journey for many South Sudanese people who migrated and settled in Australia or other parts of the world. There is often a high level of confusion for many families and individuals when confronted with social change and settlement issues. There is a strong trend towards family dysfunction because of social change and welfare dependency. Many families have experienced some pressure in maintaining relationships either between parents or between parents and their children, especially teenagers ((Renzaho, et al 2011). These relationship issues in families is a result of social and cultural change due to settlement pressures. Family breakdown and intergenerational conflict were trends raised by participants as part of their settlement challenges.

> Culture is a big thing; people are struggling with change and fear of losing your own culture and replacing it with a different culture. Change is not an easy thing for many people; there is a fear of [the] unknown attached to change. There are lots of cultural issues that still exist or [are] practised within the South Sudanese community. I think people need to ask themselves where they want to be in the next 10 or 20 years. If people want to remain in Australia, they must accept change and be ready to go through changes and beyond. Unless they want to go back to South Sudan, then that is a question in terms of accepting change and adjusting to Australia.
> *Participant 18, 30-year-old female, 15 years in Australia*

Cultural change is one of the big issues faced by the South Sudanese families in Australia during their settlement journey. Another participant echoed the preceding quote that social change and culture was affecting South Sudanese people and other African people in Australia as they were born and raised in a different environment to Australia.

Culture and social changes affect South Sudanese people and African migrants as they adapt to Australian social life. People who were born in Africa were raised in a different social environment, which is not the same as the Australian way of life/ social situations.

Participant 9, 30-year-old female, 12 years in Australia

The following is just a case example of a family of how the social change affecting the family.

A family of four children migrated to Australia and settled in Melbourne. Dad got job in Sharpton in Victoria and decided to take family to Sharpton to live there with him while working in farm. For some reasons, things did not work well for the family. Dad decided to return to Africa (South Sudan). Three boys become teenagers and two of them decided to back to Melbourne where some of their friends. For some reasons, they decided to join wrong crowd. One of the boys was arrested and jailed for a year. The other boy was charged by police, but released on bail application with conditions to report to police every day. Third boy struggle cope with pressure due to the situations where his two brothers were in. He decided not to go to school although he was only 16 years old. However, he was still living with his mother and younger sibling. None of them is working and financial pressure is amounting on the family. They were told to leave their rental house soon as possible. Mother was left devastated, crying for help, but no service that pick up her case to work with her. You are now assigned to the case, discuss the following with your colleague or supervisor about the situation of this family.

Questions for discussion
1. If dad was still in Australia, do you think boys would have been in different situation?

2. What support does this mother need?
3. Why there was no service provider that pick up the case early enough?
4. Do you think settlement difficulties played a big role in disengagement of boys and their involvement in criminal activities?
5. Why there was no support for the boys in Melbourne?

Financial hardship

As mentioned in the above case example, lack of employment and financial hardship can contribute to other settlement problems such as paying cost of renting for families and individuals who are not working (Abur;2018, Abdelkerim & Grace,2012). There is linked between mental health problems and unemployment, given the high level of financial stress that families and individuals from refugee backgrounds go through they are not employed (Abur, 2018, Abur & Spaaji, 2016). The condition of mental illness increased when there is lack of financial security in different ways. This can happen through increasing trauma and stress on individuals and families (Abur, 2018). The experience of financial difficulties for families and individuals was commonly talked about among the South Sudanese people who are not employed. Some families are struggling to pay for school equipment for their children.

> The cost of renting a house was very high and everything was tough. We later lost the house because of financial problems. We joined one [of] our family members in Melbourne and shared the accommodation which was later better, but again the house was not [big] enough for us all. Sometimes, living as a family is better than living alone in terms of housing: accommodation can be so challenging and difficult to manage financially when you are not working. Getting housing is one

of the many challenges that refugees face, especially when they have no work. They cannot afford to pay rent through Centrelink payments.

Participant 7, 38-year-old male, 10 years in Australia

Modern employment theory argues that there are significant benefits of employment for refugee communities in Australia (Abdelkerim & Grace, 2012, Abur & Spaaji, 2016) Employment has important social benefits for individuals, families, neighbourhoods, and communities. Financial benefit of employment is linked to stable family situation and mental health outcome such as decreased crime rates, reduced drug and alcohol abuse, and stable healthy families (Cullen 1999; Forstater 2006). Employment is particularly significant for refugee communities as it assists in enabling people to integrate more easily into the host community. Financial independence, opportunities to enhance skills, build social networks and contribute to society all aid in the process of establishing a sense of home in a new country and creating a positive self-identity (Cholewinski 2010; Trewin 2001). Supports from community members to newly arrived individuals and families help to reduce some of the settlement difficulties for those who have no relatives to assist them.

> Some of us have no formal or informal network and connection when came here. Everything appeared complicated to do it by your own. Parents are stressed and young people are also stressed with what is happening between schools and home. I'm aware of some people who are almost to give up on their lives because of settlement difficulties and trauma
>
> *Participant 8, 25-year-old female, 14 years in Australia.*

Successful settlement and integration come when there are enough support services to obtain advice, guidance, and active participation in education and employment, as well as in sport, particularly for young people. During this study, participants were asked to describe the settlement process from their own personal experiences and understanding. One participant highlighted the broad range of description:

> Settlement is a hard thing to measure, how to define successful settlement? Settlement and integration have been misunderstood: integration and settlement are long-term work, which cannot be achieved within a short time. People can still work, doing jobs they do not really like or enjoy. This can make them feel homesick sometimes when they feel unwelcome due to some issues. Some people struggle with settlement issues such as housing, unemployment and other [things] such as racism and discrimination. To me, there are people who are really doing well in terms of settlement and there are people that are struggling with challenges. But the thing is: how do you define successful settlement and unsettlement?
>
> *Participant 18, 30-year-old females, 15 years in Australia*

There were also differences in the settlement experience between young people and their parents in the South Sudanese community. Some parents or adults were and still struggling because they miss their networks and their old ways of life.

> Some are settling well, and some are still having difficulties in settling, especially the adults or parents who are still struggling lots with settlement challenges. Their ways of living in Africa are very different to the lifestyle here. They have no network and neighbourhood support as they used to chat freely in the village. Here, they have to think about bills and issues of children at school or work[ing] to pay bills.
>
> *Participant 17, 25-year-old female, 12 years in Australia.*

Trusting on other people to tell you how to deal with little issues can be a big shock and change for some people who, perhaps, are used to being independent. Some parents in the South Sudanese community relied on their children to tell them what to do in Australia because of problems learning English as they did not know what to do, even in reading basic information.

Finding housing for family is one of the settlement problems for newly arrived people from refugee backgrounds. Some families and individuals from the South Sudanese community encountered accommodation problems as part of their settlement experiences.

> When I came to Australia, things were really new for me and my family. We thought and said to ourselves, "This will be interesting". Indeed, things became harder and harder, particularly when we were looking for accommodation, it was so difficult because none of us were working. No-one was helping us to find a house, and we had no experience in dealing with estate agents. Later on, someone helped us to get a house, but we found it difficult because we had no money to pay rent. We tried to apply for government housing, but this was also hard to get because there were many people on the waiting list. The waiting list can go for more than five years, depending on your case/situation of your family.
> *Participant 20, 19-year-old female, 9 years in Australia*

In Australia, most people from South Sudanese community have no idea what trauma means, or how to seek help if one has encountered traumatic challenges (Abur 2012 and Lejukole 2008). In some respects, trauma presents a powerful argument that helps people claim for recognition as refugees (Marlowe 2011a). Trauma is something that has helped many refugees gain entry into refugee camps, acquire refugee status, and access services in Australia (Marlowe 2011b). However, traumatic experiences – or being labelled as having trauma issues – can limit opportunities for refugees to integrate into their host society, as well as to obtain decent employment and participate in decision-making (Westoby 2008).

More specifically, it is not uncommon for cultures such as the South

Sudanese to decline to discuss their trauma or mental health issues. Trauma is a new concept for them. It is often viewed as a weakness to talk about mental health issues. This is a general observation in relation to common attitudes and feelings around trauma and this is confirmed by other research (Abur 2012; Marlowe 2010). Some of the strengths, resilience, and coping mechanisms that assist the South Sudanese to deal internally with trauma issues, stating that many do not want to hear about post-trauma, as it labels them in negative ways (Marlowe 2010). This does not mean that there is no trauma among at least some South Sudanese people who have resettled in western countries such as Australia, and among those still living in South Sudan because of the long civil war, they have witnessed. As part of transition and settlement confrontation, families and individuals would find themselves with fewer or no skills to deal with past and present challenges in the new environment (Abur 2012; Tipping 2011).

Having social connections enhances the wellbeing and health of people through daily contact and support for social issues (Bloom 2014). Personal social wellbeing involves a person's relationship with others and how that person communicates, interacts, and socialises (Bloom 2014, Mikkonen & Raphael 2010). It can also relate to how people make friends and whether they have a sense of belonging. For example, going to the movies with friends can help to ease the daily stress of social isolation (Mikkonen & Raphael 2010). Social health and wellbeing refer to the social hierarchy of people, their financial status, living conditions, social support, level of education, acceptance of race, gender, religion, and behaviours, and access to health care (Hadgkiss et al. 2012). For refugee community groups, such as the South Sudanese community in Melbourne, their social well-being can be measured by a broad range of indicators. They include the level of income of members and their families, social participation and social support networks, current and previous education, understanding social and political systems, understanding critical challenges of settlement (such as living conditions, racism and discrimination, and culture shock), and other factors such as city lifestyle (Mikkonen & Raphael 2010).

The complex roles played by these social determinants of the health and well-being of those who feel socially excluded are at an extreme level for the disadvantaged and may be experienced both directly and indirectly (Hadgkiss et al. 2012). The disadvantaged are more likely to experience social exclusion from decent employment opportunities, due to their backgrounds as refugees, having English as a second language or lacking certain skills and qualifications (Abur & Spaaij 2016). It is very common for refugees to lack supportive relationships, suffer social isolation, and face mistrust of and by others. Racism and discrimination further increase stress and other unsettling emotions (Abur & Spaaij 2016). Stressful living conditions make it extremely hard to take up physical leisure activities or to practice healthy eating habits because most of one's energy is directed simply at coping day to day. Such conditions can cause continuing feelings of shame, insecurity, and worthlessness, which affect psychological health (Bloom 2014, Mikkonen &Raphael 2010). The social environment brings a new complexity in terms of health and wellbeing (Hadgkiss et al. 2012). For instance, lack of employment and participation in sport can cause many problems for individuals; there is no doubt that a lack of participation in social activities within the local community creates inequality, and feelings of stigma and social isolation, which can lead to serious health and wellbeing issues.

Settlement experiences

The overarching area of research for this study is the settlement experience of the South Sudanese community in Melbourne, Australia. The understanding of the settlement experience of this community comes with mixed experiences. These mixed experiences are negative and positive, for individuals and families – depending on social connections with the host society and learning experiences.

A NEW LIFE WITH OPPORTUNITIES AND CHALLENGES

Some people managed to settle better within a shorter time, and some continued to struggle to overcome settlement issues.

Successful settlement and integration comes when there are enough support services to obtain advice, guidance, and active participation in education and employment, as well as in sport, particularly for young people. During this study, participants were asked to describe the settlement process from their own personal experiences and understanding. One participant highlighted the broad range of description:

> Settlement is a hard thing to measure, how to define successful settlement? Settlement and integration have been misunderstood: integration and settlement are long-term work, which cannot be achieved within a short time. People can still work, doing jobs they do not really like or enjoy. This can make them feel homesick sometimes when they feel unwelcome due to some issues. Some people struggle with settlement issues such as housing, unemployment and other [things] such as racism and discrimination. To me, there are people who are really doing well in terms of settlement and there are people that are struggling with challenges. But the thing is: how do you define successful settlement and unsettlement?
>
> *Participant 18, 30-year-old females, 15 years in Australia*

The above explanation illustrates some of the challenges facing people from South Sudanese community in Melbourne when it comes to settlement and integration. Lack of understanding of settlement difficulties and challenges by the general population or some policy makers in relation to integration are clearly demonstrated in the above explanation.

Participants also demonstrated the difficulties faced when they were new in Australia. They described their experiences as initially routine, and as involving little more than simply eating and sleeping. However, things got better over time.

> When we came to Australia for a better life and other opportunities, our settlement experiences were very boring at first because we knew nothing about Australia. We just eat and sleep, eat and sleep. Life was a bit hard when we were new but at the end of the day because we were able to be outside in the park, play, and watch people playing sport we became active in different things, which helped us to understand our settlement better. We later managed to do [new] things, which made our lives better compared to the time we just eat and sleep, eat and sleep.
> *Participant 8, 25-year-old female, 14 years in Australia*

There were also differences in the settlement experience between young people and their parents in the South Sudanese community. Some parents or adults were and still struggling because they miss their networks and their old ways of life.

> Some are settling well and some are still having difficulties in settling, especially the adults or parents who are still struggling lots with settlement challenges. Their ways of living in Africa are very different to the lifestyle here. They have no network and neighbourhood support as they used to chat freely in the village. Here, they have to think about bills and issues of children at school or work[ing] to pay bills.
> *Participant 17, 25-year-old female, 12 years in Australia.*

Relying on other people to tell you how to deal with little issues can be a big shock and change for some people who, perhaps, are used to being independent. Some parents in the South Sudanese community relied on their children to tell them what to do in Australia because of problems learning English as they did not know what to do, even in reading basic information.

> So, for me, there is no doubt that many people in the South Sudanese community struggle with settlement issues. Not

> knowing what to do is big, if even reading basic information or letters can be big for people who cannot read and write. They also rely on other people to get information. Some parents rely on their teenagers or children to read a letter to them. This can change the whole responsibility [role] in families when teenagers seem to be the ones taking responsibility for telling parents what to do.
> *Participant 12, 22-year-old female, 11 years in Australia*

Finding housing for family is one of the settlement problems for newly arrived people from refugee backgrounds. Some families and individuals from the South Sudanese community encountered accommodation problems as part of their settlement experiences.

> When I came to Australia, things were really new for me and my family. We thought and said to ourselves, "This will be interesting". Indeed, things became harder and harder, particularly when we were looking for accommodation, it was so difficult because none of us were working. No-one was helping us to find a house, and we had no experience in dealing with estate agents. Later on, someone helped us to get a house, but we found it difficult because we had no money to pay rent. We tried to apply for government housing, but this was also hard to get because there were many people on the waiting list. The waiting list can go for more than five years, depending on your case/situation of your family.
> *Participant 20, 19-year-old female, 9 years in Australia*

Financial problem can contribute to other settlement problems such as paying cost of renting for families and individuals who are not working. The experience of financial difficulties for families and individuals was commonly talked about among participants. Among some of the South Sudanese community members this experience was one of the most challenging. According to Participant 7:

> The cost of renting a house was very high and everything was tough. We later lost the house because of financial problems. We joined one [of] our family members in Melbourne and shared the accommodation which was later better, but again the house was not [big] enough for us all. Sometimes living as a family is better than living alone in terms of housing: accommodation can be so challenging and difficult to manage financially when you are not working. Getting housing is one of the many challenges that refugees face, especially when they have no work. They cannot afford to pay rent through Centrelink payments.
> *Participant 7, 38-year-old male, 10 years in Australia*

Further, the cost of child care was also affecting parenting of young children as parents would want to put their children in childcare to allow them attend English classes or other activities that may assist them with settlement issues. In the words of some community members:

> Financial hardship was one of the many issues that we have been struggling with, I was not able to put my children in childcare because of the cost.
> *Participant 16, 28-year-old, 10 years in Australia*

Social isolation is one of the settlement difficulties for people with refugee backgrounds who have no connection with the mainstream community. Psychological stress and despair are caused by lack of participation and connection during the settlement period. The experience of social isolation is a problem that could lead to self-isolation, stress, frustration, and negative thoughts in a new country of resettlement. In the words of Participant 8:

> Social isolation is a big thing for people who stay at home without socialising outside their homes. Sometimes they become aggressive to themselves and their family members

A NEW LIFE WITH OPPORTUNITIES AND CHALLENGES

and cannot learn or see the world in a big picture [sic]
Participant 8, 25-year-old female, 14 years in Australia

A lack of internal and external supports was noted as part of the problems faced during the settlement period by participants. Many of the South Sudanese families and individuals left some of their close relatives overseas. Those who had their family members with them found it a bit easier to settle because they were able to help each other more than those without close relatives or family members.

> Settlement can be easy if you have a family, but if [you] don't have a family; settlement can be a difficult and challenging experience because you don't have enough support and interaction with people.
> *Participant 8, 25-year-old female, 14 years in Australia*

Supports from community members to newly arrived individuals and families help to reduce some of the settlement difficulties for those who have no relatives to assist them.

> People from your network in the community can help you settle better if they came here before you. They can drive you in their cars and show [you] places and what you need to do to get organised and move on.
> *Participant 8, 25-year-old female, 14 years in Australia*

> Good things, I was welcome in Australia and had a great support from the community. Everything was provided to me freely, which was great.
> *Participant 1, 24-year-old male, 8 years in Australia*

Good planning with clear goals and vision is helpful when you are in new place. Some members in the South Sudanese community who had clear vision and willing to seek some advice from the first members who have settled or have some experiences of how to deal with some settlement issues were able to settle well. Participant 15 hinted at strategies for successful settlement:

> When it comes to settlement experiences and contentment, there are people who have settled well and there are people who have not settled well. Those who have settled well are those who seek advice, educate themselves, look for employment or engage in good activities, which they benefit from. They have a high level of dreams or goals. They want to contribute to the Australian community through doing good things and to be seen by those who are not actively engaged for some reason. People who have support services or seek support from others had positive experiences in relation to their settlement outcomes.
>
> *Participant 15, 28-year-old male, 10 years in Australia*

Living in a new country often requires a person to make cautious decisions every day. Such decisions mean that one needs to ignore some activities that may be problematic both in the short term and long term. It also means that people need to seek advice from host community members who are willing to advise, as well as those with refugee backgrounds who have enough experience and understanding of issues.

> The settlement required people to be little bit wise by focusing on things that can help them to grow and ignore negative things like people who try to put them down. It is always important to focus on people who help you grow as a person and not people who put you down for their own interests. I met people who helped me to grow as a person and also people who put me down. Those who put me down were the people who don't want me to grow and I quickly understood their intent.
>
> *Participant 3, 20-year-old male, 11 years in Australia*

A NEW LIFE WITH OPPORTUNITIES AND CHALLENGES

Settling well in a new country required some sacrifices, commitments, hard work and making the right choices for future directions. These include active involvement in sport and other activities, such as education and work, to access connections and other resources. However, participants noticed the differences between young people and adults in their ability to adapt within the South Sudanese community. Young people adapted more quickly to the Australian way of life, whereas adults tended to struggle more with settlement challenges. Participant 17 gave a perceptive analysis of how settlement went on as a generational issue:

> There are generations of young people in the South Sudanese community who are settling or have settled well because they have adapted to the Australian way of living quickly and [are] moving beyond their settlement issues. Those who used the freedom and the opportunity of education to educate themselves and work for themselves are settling well. They have open minds and use their opportunities very well. For example, there are lots of opportunities and freedom for women here. Some had never had the freedom and opportunities before. To settle better, you have to be open-minded, ready to learn and to face new challenges. In the end, you will find yourself knowing much about Australian culture, systems and ways of living. You can organise your life easily and end up being satisfied with your settlement.
> *Participant 17, 25-year-old female, 12 years in Australia*

Participants acknowledged that there were improvements in community in terms of settlement difficulties compared to the time many of the community members were new in Australia or in Melbourne. Indicators of this improvement were captured in Participant 16's explanation below:

> I have seen a big improvement in terms of the community

settling in Australia. When we arrived, we were really struggling with settlement issues. We were not able to drive cars for shopping, but now many South Sudanese people are able to drive. It was really hard to see someone going shopping with three children and a push pram.

Participant 16, 28-year-old female, 10 years in Australia

Learning English

Settling in a new country and learning the language is not an easy task, regardless of cultural background and language. Some migrants and refugees from non-English speaking countries often face pressure to learn English as quickly as possible, to benefit from daily communication and reading simple information. Many were not able to communicate in English because they had no prior opportunity to learn English. For example, the English-language barrier was a bigger problem for some South Sudanese in Australia, as many of them had not had opportunity to learn English before their arrival for resettlement in Australia.

> The settlement was very difficult when I came because of the English barrier; it was hard to understand the Australian way of living, culture and English as well as understanding life and different ways of doing things. However, I find it easy now because I am able to communicate or express myself in English. The bad things for me were [that] I missed my family and relatives because they were not here with me.
>
> *Participant 4, 24-year-old male, 9 years in Australia*

In addition

> Learning English was challenging for me because I was not able to express words correctly in English. I always feel scared and not ready to talk because people will correct my English. I was not able to use correct words or was unsure about some

words. I felt scared to talk to people and felt like I was not part of this society.
>
> *Participant 1, 24-year-old male, 8 years in Australia*

Difficulties in language barrier is part of the South Sudanese experiences in Australia and cannot be underestimated. Participants stated that the language barrier made their settlement with their family members difficult when they arrived in Australia, but they have overcome this by learning English.

> Some people are having a hard time settling in because of the language barrier. It is a big thing; I remembered from my family members when we came it was difficult for some of us, but we are overcome.
>
> *Participant 12, 22-year-old female, 11 years in Australia*

Some participants noted that many South Sudanese people are multilingual and English became a third or fourth language for them, which makes it harder for them to express themselves well in English without thinking in their other languages.

> One of the challenges for settlement is learning English, [because] English is a second or third language for the South Sudanese people. Sometimes it can be so difficult to express yourself well in English and this can be frustrating, especially when there is no one to assist you. English is so hard for us, especially when you choose hard subjects: it can be so difficult for you because no support is available for you as a learner. Lots of people become frustrated with the new challenges; some choose to isolate themselves from the community or groups. This is where depression kicks in and the settlement became so difficult and challenging in many ways.
>
> *Participant 9, 30-year-old female, 12 years in Australia*

Participants were quick to challenge the general expectations of wanting them to learn English and adopt Australian ways of life as part of integration and adjustment.

> It is ridiculous with a high expectation of wanting people to learn perfect English in six years, and move on quickly to get a job and manage settlement issues or cope with difficult situations in a new culture.
> Participant 19, 27-year-old female, 11 years in Australia

Family dynamics and social change

There is often a high level of confusion for many families and individuals when confronted with social change and settlement issues. There is a strong trend towards family dysfunction because of social change and welfare dependency. Many families have experienced some pressure in maintaining relationships either between parents or between parents and their children, especially teenagers. These relationship issues in families is a result of social and cultural change due to settlement pressures. Family breakdown and intergenerational conflict were trends raised by participants as part of their settlement challenges.

> Culture is a big thing; people are struggling with change and fear of losing your own culture and replacing it with a different culture. Change is not an easy thing for many people; there is a fear of [the] unknown attached to change. There are lots of cultural issues that still exist or [are] practised within the South Sudanese community. I think people need to ask themselves where they want to be in the next 10 or 20 years. If people want to remain in Australia, they must accept change and be ready to go through changes and beyond. Unless they want to go back to South Sudan, then that is a question in terms of accepting change and adjusting to Australia.
> Participant 18, 30-year-old female, 15 years in Australia

Cultural change is one of the big issues faced by the South Sudanese families in Australia during their settlement journey. Another participant echoed the preceding quote that social change and culture was affecting South Sudanese people and other African people in Australia as they were born and raised in a different environment to Australia.

> Culture and social changes affect South Sudanese people and African migrants as they adapt to Australian social life. People who were born in Africa were raised in a different social environment, which is not the same as the Australian way of life/ social situations.
> *Participant 9, 30-year-old female, 12 years in Australia*

Gender role and difficulties

There are different and specific views about gender-related issues in the South Sudanese community. Participants believed that South Sudanese men were struggling with social change within their families because of migration and settlement in a new culture. This changed some of their roles and expectations in family. One of the female participants had offered her advice to South Sudanese men to learn some soft skills that may be useful to them in their families.

> Men need to learn soft social skills and be ready to embrace the changes. Their hard or tough skills are not working in Australia as they used to be tough on women and children. Running away to avoid family challenges is not the solution. Willingness and [readiness] to learn soft social skills is a way forward that can help men from African backgrounds.
> *Participant 17, 25-year-old female, 12 years in Australia*

The tension of gender issues was part of social change and family problems. Another female participant stated that South Sudanese women tended to have more power in Australia than their male partners. Some told their male partners that Australia was not Africa, meaning that men had no voice or authority to tell their female partners to do things they may otherwise not want to do in their house.

> Some families have experienced difficult relationships because of settlement; changes have been so dynamic and have caused some difficulties in relationships between men and women. Sometimes each side starts blaming the other, or sometimes women would tell men: "This is not Africa." Women have more freedom in Australia than in Africa. This has raised many tensions in families and men appear to be not coping with the changes. The only way for men is to escape from Australia and go back to Africa.
> *Participant 17, 25-year-old female, 12 years in Australia*

Young women in the South Sudanese community were also facing some issues of blame in their families and in the community. This blame related to gender tension because young women who grew up in Australia were working their way towards Australian values, which could be seen as going against their family's wishes and culture. Some people blame young women for abandoning relationships and choosing to be single mothers.

> Young women/women are going off-track in the community because the system (Centrelink) supports them to remain single to get more payments because she is a single mother. Many married women now take advantage of this [assistance] and kick [sic] their men/husbands away because of the Centrelink support. This help is short-term for single mothers, but in the long-term, their children will remain disadvantaged because some will miss the role of their fathers. I see that in the long-term, it is destroying the community. I have seen some young women having children with different fathers, and this is causing a bit of a problem as in traditional South Sudanese

culture [where] it is not good to have children by different fathers; it has shamed [them] and stigma [is] attached.
Participant 9, 30-year-old female, 12 years in Australia

Challenging issues with young people

Youth are the future of any society if they are well trained and brought up with good behaviours to meet the society expectations. Displaying bad behaviours is not part of the society expectation according to South Sudanese culture. Youth issues have been the centre of media scrutiny in recent years. The specific youth issues are linked to parenting responsibility and the lack of role models for young family members. Parenting is one of the challenging issues for South Sudanese families. The task of single parenting is not easy for many parents. In South Sudan, war has caused single parent issues as many men lost their lives in conflict, and some male parents were forced to separate from their families due to the conflict. Another cause is cultural change or culture shock in Australia. These issues have torn many relationships apart and left the responsibility of caring for children with one parent, most likely to be the mother. During interviews, single parenting emerged as one of the difficult issues in discussions about family matters. It is very clear that single parents in the South Sudanese community were struggling with their teenage children, who were taking different directions.

> Many young people are lacking parenting discipline; many families or young people are being parented by single parents – particularly by mothers. Many of my friends and cousins are lacking male parenting or male role models because their fathers are not here in Australia. Some lost their fathers during the war in South Sudan/Sudan
> *Participant 9, 30-year-old female, 12 years in Australia*

Youths who spend some of the time socialising in public places, such as train stations, were viewed by their parents as wasting time instead of spending their time focusing on education. Participants raised concerns about youth congregating at train stations and shopping centres as ways of killing time. Those youths who choose to do so were blamed in the community, because the community had a view that they were wasting their time. They should instead be engaged in education or helping their families at home instead of walking around aimless.

> Those youths who choose to spend their time walking in the streets, shopping centres or hanging around public transport stations will not be settled in my opinion, because there is nothing important that they are focusing on, unless they focus on things that are good for their future aspirations.
> *Participant 10, 21-year-old male, 8 years in Australia*

There were also different understandings and perceptions of issues faced by parents and young people. It appears that young people were aware of their needs and challenging issues related to them. Participants believed that some parents had no understanding of the issues affecting young people. This is just one of the gaps between South Sudanese young people and their parents.

> Young people are facing many challenges, which their parents cannot understand. These challenges can generate conflict between parents and young people who are not supported by their parents at home. The South Sudanese think that learning in Australia is similar to learning in Africa. Young people find it hard to deal with their education without support from parents or relatives and that is why some young people drop out from their schooling.
> *Participant 4, 24-year-old male, 9 years in Australia*

Parents from the South Sudanese community do have high expectations and tough parenting strategies, which can sometimes cause great tension between young people and parents. Although there were some tensions between parents and young people, some young people acknowledged that what their parents had done for them could not be easily forgotten by their generation. They also acknowledged the issues of the past as difficult issues, but felt these should not hold them back from progressing.

> We have gone through tough times and many challenging issues during our settling time, but I think if young people from our community learn from what their parents and older siblings, cousins went through, the next generation will be better. The South Sudanese community is a young community; we are still working on many things to establish ourselves better. The past will be passed, and there will be a better future, although we will not forget what our parents have gone through, but it will not hold us back as a young generation to do better in my opinion.
> *Participant 3, 20-year-old male, 11 years in Australia*

Lack of central meeting places for youth groups is one wish the community has for its young people. Participants reported that youth issues increased because there was no space for them to run their social activities and programs.

> Community centres for young people from refugee backgrounds need to be provided; young people don't have places to do their activities. We find it hard to go to mainstream youth places because of certain attitudes people display toward us. This makes settlement hard for young people whose parents are juggling no jobs and responsibility for their kids.
> *Participant 20, 19-year-old female, 9 years in Australia*

Lack of educational support at schools was reported as one of the many problems affecting young people. Some young people from the

South Sudanese community dropped out from due to challenging issues they have faced in school without sufficient support services. Participants believed that this was due to institutional racism in school and lack of support to young people and their families.

> Our children are facing huge challenges at school because there is no strong support for them and adults are facing issues of unemployment, no work for them. This makes the settlement a bit difficult for some families within some communities and African groups.
> Participant 11, 28-year-old female, 8 years in Australia

The consequences of not participating in sport and the workforce are greater for youths from the South Sudanese community due to their backgrounds. Participants believed that youths who were not engaged in sport and the workforce would always remain as victims of settlement challenges unless they made informed choices to get involved in something useful for their future.

> Refugee youths who are not engaged in the workforce and sport, many of them will be victim of settlement challenges because they have nothing productive to engage in, such as work and sport.
> Participant 17, 25-year-old female, 12 years in Australia

Integration and lack of integration

The concept of integration is something that has been discussed and promoted well by some politicians for emerging communities such as the South Sudanese community. The expectation is that newly arrived community groups are to integrate as quickly as possible into the mainstream community (Ager & Strang 2004). In recent years, there were some discussions targeting the South Sudanese community as one of the communities that have not been integrating well, due to several settlement issues discussed in this book. During interview, participants believe that some South Sudanese people are integrating well by adopting Australian ways of life. They also acknowledge the settlement challenges as hard to overcome in a short period.

> I remember when the South Sudanese community was labelled as a community that has not been integrated well in Australia. I think this is not true because we have people who are doing well in education, people who are working and people who have taken mortgages for their families. I think we are part of the Australian community. It is only a small proportion of people who are struggling or heading in the wrong direction, because of lack of support, as they are new to Australia.
> *Participant 6, 27-year-old male, 11 years in Australia*

Members of the South Sudanese community were fully aware of those who were integrating well and those who were not integrating due to settlement difficulties. All participants believed that that some individuals and families managed to settle well, but some were struggling with integration.

> There are families and individuals who are doing well, and there are families and individuals who are not doing well because they are new or not able to move beyond settlement challenges.
> *Participant 18, 30-year-old female, 15 years in Australia*

Integration occurs when refugees participate in the mainstream community, attain rights similar to those enjoyed by others in their country of settlement, obtain citizenship or permanent residence, as well as access to employment that matches their skill level. There are many challenges to local integration for both refugees and host communities. Sometimes there is tension between refugees and local communities who compete for scarce resources, including land and food. However, there are steps that need to be taken to support both groups to make integration succeed. These steps include raising community awareness and promotion of the benefits that refugees can bring to the local community.

The reason for the labelling of the South Sudanese community's failure to integrate – it's 'disintegration' – is the youth riots, including recent events in Melbourne related to the "Apex Gang". The perception within the community about the failure to integrate is that disengaged young people do things that go against societal expectations. However, participants believed that Sudanese crime is far smaller than that of other community groups.

> If you compare the crimes committed by South Sudanese with other ethnic groups, you find that South Sudanese people have less crime. These could be things related to alcoholism and not like other ethnic communities, which may have major crimes. The South Sudanese people have not been in Australia for long; we are still working out how to establish ourselves as a community. (
> *Participant 6, 27-year-old male, 11 years in Australia*

There are always unmet needs for people to react negatively or cause disintegration into a mainstream. There must be a reason for someone to decide not to participate in the general community's activities. Lack of participation in the mainstream community's activities could be something beyond their control. Participants reported that those who were not settling into the community were facing social isolation and a lack of activities in which to participate.

> Those who are not settled are those who choose to remain to isolate themselves, disengaged from activities that can help them to move on.
> *Participant 15, 28-year-old male, 10 years in Australia*

The community is not happy with people – young people – who are burning bridges by causing some problems for the community. These young people are being blamed in the community and in their families.

> There are people within the community who avoid assimilating into society by choosing to engage in negative things or behaviours that do not help them to integrate better. These people refuse to learn English and refuse to look for work.
> *Participant 9, 30-year-old female, 12 years in Australia*

Participants acknowledge the challenges of coming from refugee backgrounds as a contributing factor to the disengagement of some people. Others see the South Sudanese community as doing well compared to the first few years after they arrived. Some were running their small business and driving cars. However, participants recalled tough life experiences for some people in their community not integrating well.

> Yes, we came from refugee backgrounds and tough life experiences, but I think we are doing well. We have people who have done well within 10 years of their time in Australia in both education and participation in the workforce. We have people who are driving good cars and people who have shops in Footscray – running their small businesses like other communities.
> *Participant 6, 27-year-old male, 11 years in Australia*

Participants believed that mainstream media treated issues of integration and disengagement in their community poorly. They believed that there were positive stories of integration, but the media has not reported them. A young man stated that there was fear of unknown people affecting the South Sudanese, and this makes their integration more difficult at some points. The interaction of young people with police was one of the difficulties this young man experienced.

> I had difficult reactions with police and the system. There is a fear of unknown people, which always affected people from

the South Sudanese community because their positive part is not known in the media. These make our settlement experiences more challenging and hard for some of us to integrate.
Participant 5, 20-year-old male, 10 years in Australia

Lack of integration comes when a conflict occurs between host community groups and refugee groups, and this causal factor can be why some refugee groups such as the South Sudanese become disengaged. In this case, disengagement is viewed as a major issue for young people who are struggling with settlement issues. They are more likely to disengage from community activities or school. However, the community wants to teach these young people – particularly boys who become disengaged from school – to work hard for their future. The South Sudanese traditional family taught young people to work hard by starting with their tasks within the family. This tradition appeared to be useful when a person grew up and entered the workforce.

When we came to Australia, my mum pushed us to work hard on learning and interacting with people in a different community as a way of improving our English and connections because we were in a place where there were not many Africans. Our family was the only family from an African background. Mum believed that it was important for her children to integrate and not to be left out of the wider community. Pushing myself helped me to connect with people from different groups. To integrate well, you need to go beyond your comfort zone. You can be rejected, but you need to be ready for rejection or disappointment. Integration needs you to be courageous enough to face challenges and you will succeed after you try many times, with some disappointments. (
Participant 18, 30-year-old female, 15 years in Australia

A NEW LIFE WITH OPPORTUNITIES AND CHALLENGES

The need for advocacy services on behalf of South Sudanese-Australians.

There is a great need for support services and advocacy in order to allow refugees to settle better and be accepted with fewer prejudices. Advocacy can be one way of supporting the community in order for other people within the mainstream community and politicians to understand the critical issues facing refugee communities like the South Sudanese community. Australia is well known for embracing multicultural policies, meaning that all people are given a fair go, regardless of their cultural backgrounds and practices. Many in the South Sudanese community appreciate the generous opportunities and multicultural policy of Australia. Despite this multicultural policy and spirit, some members have encountered difficult challenges or think that they have been side-lined by being treated unfairly in the workplace, and in other areas such as education, and may not always speak out about their experiences. As such, participants in this study have called for support from the government to help their community by creating jobs and awareness among employers and agencies in order to accommodate those from their community in the workforce. They believes that this may reduce some challenges and could provide them and their community with opportunities, which may lead to better settlement outcomes for families and individuals.

> We believe that Australia is a fair nation as we sing the words of the national anthem. We should be treated equally in the workplace and given the opportunity to work. The government should pressure those agencies who have denied jobs to refugees and people from non-English backgrounds. Jobs should not be given because you are white or black. I think people should be given jobs according to their willingness and capabilities to work.
> *Participant 13, 39-year-old male, 10 years in Australia*

The importance of advocacy on behalf of vulnerable families and individuals was emphasised by participants. Advocacy can be carried out by anybody, including service providers who work with community groups such as the South Sudanese community. Sometimes a lack of skillsets or English-language problems can make it more difficult for the non-English community groups to express their views well. They need assistance from policymakers and individuals who can advocate on their behalf in areas of employment, housing, and sport, and to combat racism and discrimination.

> The community should stand up for its members' rights and advocate on critical issues that are affecting the community and its young people. We are part of Australian society, we cannot be [mis]treated or told, "go back to where you come from," without challenging such attitudes.
> Participant 5, 20-year-old male, 10 years in Australia

Support services are critical for newly arrived families and individuals. All participants requested more support services for their community from government agencies and for agencies to work with the community in order to identify issues affecting the community. They raised issues of youth and elderly people needing some support. They stated that the main reason for the negative reports and social issues in their community was the lack of support services.

> The government needs to work with community leaders to identify issues affecting the community socially, particularly young people and old people. They [refugees] need government support services as well as community support, but at the moment, they don't have such support, and that is why all these social issues that come out of the media are present. Young South Sudanese are struggling with a number of issues including where they belong. They don't fit into their community and not in the Australian community because

their friends still tell them, "You are from the South Sudanese community and don't know much about Australia". This is really holding people back at the moment and making them feel isolated. There is no aspiration as they don't get jobs and some of their friends tell them, "Well, it is a piece of paper which you have, but the reality is it will not get jobs"
Participant 9, 30-year-old female, 12 years in Australia

Empowerment through training is one of the supports that the South Sudanese community needs in order to participate in the wider community. All participants requested specific support to undertake job training in order to assist them to get into the workforce.

I think we still need more support from the government: training and engaging in work can be good for the community or people who are not working. The government needs to promote and support refugees and migrants [to get] more jobs.
Participant 1, 24-year-old male, 8 years in Australia

Increased resources and support were reported as something that the government could do to assist vulnerable members within the South Sudanese community.

It would be nice if a government supports those people who are not able to support themselves by providing resources to assist them [to] move on with their lives.
Participant 14, 23-year-old male, 9 years in Australia

There are specific issues facing young people as part of their settlement challenges. Participants have pleaded for recognition of the need for support services specific to young people. They have asked for support services from government organisations and non-government organisations (NGOs) to engage young people in productive activities, which can help them to grow as good citizens instead of living without well-planned and directed activities.

> I think there should be more support services for the community and young people who are new to Australia. The government needs to provide enough services to help people settle better. Without proper support, our young people and the community will continue to struggle with many issues.
>
> *Participant 11, 28-year-old female, 11 years in Australia*

Programs for young people can assist in engaging young people in the South Sudanese community. Participants request government assistance for their community by creating programs for youths to engage them. They suggested that sporting programs are good for their young people.

> I think our young people need support and to actively engage in the activities that can assist them to grow as good citizens. The government should also provide better services and support for the newly arrived community groups to settle better by listening to their needs and help them grow as good citizens.
>
> *Participant 8, 25-year-old female, 14 years in Australia*

Lack of transparency and partnership from settlement agencies and the South Sudanese community were reported as issues. Some of the participants were critical of settlement support services. They felt that some settlement agencies received funding from the government to provide support services to the newly arrived, however, some providers failed to assist the community.

> People face tough issues sometimes when they are in a new environment. The critical aspect of being in the new system is that when they react, they can suffer more. They can be put in the difficult position of being victims while people who are critical seek to prove they [refugees] are not able to participate. The community feel they contribute less to the system while its young people are struggling with settle-

ment-related issues, which reflect back on the community as its own failure. This is not true. The community should be serviced by organisations which are funded for that purpose. Those organisations need to work for the community rather than spending a very small proportion of those funds on the community.

Participant 19, 27-year-old female, 11 years in Australia

Working with refugee communities such as the South Sudanese community in partnership can help build relationships with service providers. Partnership can empower people through mentoring programs and advocacy; raise awareness on behalf of the vulnerable community of issues such as employment; and empower them to address racism and discrimination issues.

I think there is a need for people to move into partnerships of working with new community groups, which are very vulnerable. The partnerships should bring in comprehensive programs to improve ways of understanding how settlement issues affected the refugee issues. For example, family violence can affect a child's education or employment, and it has affected the possibilities of how parents can support their children at school and sports. I think there is a need for a comprehensive understanding of social issues; a short consultation of 30 minutes is not enough to capture all social issues that people are facing.

Participant 19, 27-year-old female, 11 years in Australia

Involving community members in the process of planning or even including them on a board of management can be an empowering process for them. Participants stated that community organisations should work collaboratively with the community to better understand the social issues affecting families and the community.

The community organisations should work collaboratively

with community groups. For example, by having community members represent their community groups in organisations such as on a board can bring a better understanding of social issues and better ways of working collaboratively.
Participant 19, 27-year-old female, 11 years in Australia

Community role and support for vulnerable families and young people

Families and young people are more likely to be affected by the complex settlement issues, and sometimes they do need assistance from community members and community leaders to help them with social issues related to the settlement. Having discussed what the community expected from government and non-governmental organisations, there is also a significant role for community members to play in helping and supporting each other in order to overcome some of the settlement challenges. During interviews, participants identified problems and requested community members play their part in addressing social issues affecting families and young people. They stated that the social issues affecting young people and families in their community could not be addressed by the supporting organisations without the involvement of community leaders or well-educated community members. They believed that these members had more understanding of the critical social issues affecting young people and families.

> The community needs to come up with some plans that can help them and young people. People who have more experience in understanding settlement issues can advise others who are stressed because of social issues with families and children.
> *Participant 11, 28-year-old female, 8 years in Australia*

Community leadership is needed when there are difficult issues facing families and young people. Participants reported that their community leadership should act quickly on issues affecting their community members.

> I think there are issues that a community needs to work on very quickly. Without addressing those issues, it is hard to move on. Once the community knows the real matter, people can move on quickly. People need to prepare themselves to deal with those issues. I want to see the community flourishing and to see community prosperity in Australia. I don't want to see it failing and not [be] able to move on and beyond.
> *Participant 18, 30-year-old female, 15 years in Australia*

Some people, if not all people, do need encouragement and support in order to realise their potentials or work harder to reach their potentials.

> I would encourage people within my community to take things seriously and not take them for granted. We need to work hard and contribute to society as good citizens and not as a bad image for those who cannot contribute. Our community leaders and educated people should help those on the streets to understand and learn good things for the benefit of all.
> *Participant 14, 23-year male, 9 years in Australia*

People suggested 'Prevention is better than cure', with some participants offering advice to their community members to help those who needed help before it was too late. They wanted South Sudanese community members to come together and help each other with settlement issues. They also wanted to see their community leaving tribal issues behind and making positive contributions for each other in Australia.

> I think it is important that people get help in times of need: help from your community, agencies and friends in particular during their settlement time. The community needs to work hard and support each other, to leave their tribal

conflicts [behind] when they arrive in Australia and work as one South Sudanese community. If we support each other, we can overcome settlement difficulties. We can also contribute well to society. It is not good for those young people on the streets if community leaders do not engage with them, to think positively instead of having problems with the system all the time.

Participant 8, 25-year-old female, 14 years in Australia

The importance and benefits of community programs were raised during interviews by participants who stated that it is helpful if there are family members and community members who can take the initiative to support programs for young people, such as organising sports days or other events for young people. All Participants stated that their community members could play a crucial role in supporting young people to engage in sports programs. They want their community members to become role models for young people and get them involved in meaningful social activities.

> I would like us to become involved in sports programs as an example to young people. Sport can break down social isolation and help them to meet other people from different ethnic backgrounds. There are more opportunities in sport by which they can overcome their weakness because the South Sudanese are very athletic. They need to show their talents through sport. I joined basketball when I was not a good player, but I managed to learn my skills within a short time. Sport is all about dedication and you commit yourself and practice. Therefore, I encourage young people to be active in sport and see sport as a good thing for them to grow and discover.

Participant 14, 23-year-old male, 9 years in Australia

Lack of collective views and vision in the South Sudanese community was identified as an issue. It is not a bad idea at times to have collective views as a community, but it is also difficult to have collective views in

A NEW LIFE WITH OPPORTUNITIES AND CHALLENGES

a community affected by so many issues. During interviews, participants suggested that their community collectively come up with clear goals and visions for their community and create some programs. They believed that their community should have goals about what they want to achieve as well as what they could contribute to society. Success can only come when people work hard on their goals and have a wider vision for their community and families.

> The community must work hard with clear goals. People need to work hard by defining their goals, why they are here, what they really want to achieve or contribute in a positive way [pause for reflection]. There are people with a mind-set that they will go back to South Sudan and have better lives. Yes, but it is a problem if you don't work hard here to establish yourself well. People need to think about things like, "If I do this now, it will help me in the next few years there and here, or if I do this now it will help my child in future. I am using sport now as something that I will be remembered for and I think it will also be easy for children to remember if I do well."' People will be saying, 'Oh, he is the son of so and so; she is a daughter of so and so," in sport.
> *Participant 10, 21-year-old male, 8 years in Australia*

Getting advice from the right people was one useful way to assist families and individuals. Participants believe that people who are struggling with settlement issues need to seek support and advice from others. Indeed, talking with people with experience and a positive mind-set is something that can help some people realise what they need to do in order to address some of their settlement challenges.

> Those who are confused to work out their problems, do need to seek help and advice in order to assist themselves with their families' difficult issues
> *Participant 1, 24-year-old male, 8 years in Australia*

There is always a need to be wise and make the right choices in what we do as people in life. Making the right choices in life can come with experience and guidance from the right people with experience. It can be so easy for people to lose their cultural values in a multicultural society like Australian society.

> It is always easier to be wise enough to choose when you are in multicultural groups. I am more open to different cultures in Australia, but I am very cautious that some of those cultures are very toxic and can easily take your good vision away as a young person.
>
> *Participant 14, 23-year-old male, 9 years in Australia*

Engaging with other community members through mentoring was a great help in connecting with the mainstream community. All participants believed that mentoring and training as something that could assist the South Sudanese community to connect with host community members. They believed that their community members could obtain connections and other social skills through mentoring.

> I think the community needs support in mentoring and training to help them engage with mainstream community and learn to do things for themselves. I think training should be around health, employment or hunting for jobs and financial counselling to address financial stress
>
> *Participant 18, 30-year-old female, 15 years in Australia*

Participants had clear views of what about their community needed to do in order to support each other with difficult issues. However, the community had no resources to operate those support services for families and individuals. Their calls for support from government and other non-governmental organisations may be one of the solutions if authorities could listen to their voices.

CHAPTER 4

Racism is still a War in our Modern Time

The most dangerous thing that politicians can do is to divide society by singling out a particular community because of their cultural backgrounds and directed resentment towards general community members due to the action small number of young people who involved in criminal activities. African community groups were racially vilified by Australian –Medias and some racist politicians were too blinded to care about vulnerable and innocent young people and mums from African backgrounds who got nothing to do with some of the poor choices and behaviours displayed by few young people who were involved in criminal activities in Melbourne. These racist politicians failed to maintain the values and principles of multiculturalism in many aspects as some of them called out open for African community groups to be vilified in the Medias.

There are some stories where African young people or individuals were vilified for, but later emerged out from police investigation to be fabricated stories by individuals who either have no ethical values for some reasons or have personal problems with African people. For instance, one of the fake stories included the case of a Fijian-born mother who murdered baby girl, and "told police her baby had been snatched from her pram by a barefoot man of African appearance who smelt of alcohol".

Another example for situation, is a case of autistic boy in Werribee area told media that "African gang" has pushed him. This case well covered in media because his parent were outraged and demanding answer from the Government about "African Gang" or African community as bad apples in Melbourne.

Again, the investigation was done and concluded that it was not genuine story. Police later accused the boy and say they were going to charge him of telling lie. This is not to say there are no bad apples in African community groups in Melbourne or in Australia by pointing out the above fabricated examples in media African community. Absolutely, there are many African young people with poor behaviours or make some poor choices. These young people sometimes don't realise the image they are portraying in society about their families and African community at large in Australia when they are engaging in negative activities or behaviours.

We know that Australia is multicultural society with many migrants from different parts of the world. However, I did not expect some can be extremely racist in Australia. I did not expect some politicians in Australia to use derogatory and irresponsible language against minority groups and people of colour. I did not expect talking about racism and discrimination can be viewed as divisive and therefore, it should not be discussed. I did not expect some people can be treated in Australia as less human in our society. I did not children of African migrants can be called animal or gorillas in school. I did not expect people of colour of can be boobed in the sport field such as Adam Goodies. I did not expect some of can be denied of decent jobs because their background coming from minority groups. I did not expect hate speech and racist ideologies can kill 50 innocents' women, children and men in Christchurch in New Zealand. I did not expect our first people; indigenous and Torres Strait Islanders are still treated unfairly by some racist individuals in Australia. I did not expect national media can be unfair or promote racism and discrimination in Australia. I did not expect white supremacists and racist people can be descripted as a concern citizen by the media

We know that Australia is multicultural society with many migrants from different parts of the world. However, racism is still an ongoing war in our modern history in Australia. It is happening everywhere, in schools, workplaces, shopping centres and in media. For instance,

A NEW LIFE WITH OPPORTUNITIES AND CHALLENGES

when I choose to migrate to Australia, I did not expect some people were or are still holding extreme racist views in Australia about minority groups, but it is happening. I did not expect some politicians in Australia to be using derogatory and irresponsible language against minority groups and people of colour. I did not expect talking about racism and discrimination can be viewed as divisive and therefore, it should not be discussed. I did not expect some people can be treated in Australia as less human in our society. I did not children of African migrants can be called animal or gorillas in school. I did not expect people of colour of can be boobed in the sport field such as Adam Goodies. I did not expect some of can be denied of decent jobs because their background coming from minority groups. I did not expect hate speech and racist ideologies can kill 50 innocents' women, children and men in Christchurch in New Zealand. I did not expect our first people; indigenous and Torres Strait Islanders are still treated unfairly by some racist individuals in Australia. I did not expect national media can be unfair or promote racism and discrimination in Australia. I did not expect white supremacists and racist people can be described as a concern citizen by the media

Therefore, this book addresses a question of racism and discrimination in Australia. Does racism and discrimination exist in Australian and it is impacting on victim? Racism is a threat to national security and is undermining many ways of democracy by placing silence voice to people from minority groups. Jacinda Ardern, beautifully put it her addressed to the national when New Zealanders and many other people in the world were mourning for people who were killed during Christchurch's mosques shooting. "Racism is not welcome here" meaning racism and discrimination is welcome in New Zealand.

Racism and discrimination is one of the problems facing people from the South Sudanese community, including in the employment sector and in schools, because of negative media reporting on this community. This racism and racial verification has been identified in research context as unfair in which some of these research argues for how members of the South Sudanese and recent African communities have become part of a broader system of racism and racialisation in Australia. (Ang & Stratton 2001; Baak 2016; Due 2008; Majavu 2017; Walton et al. 2016). The impact of racial vilification has been largely felt by African community groups in public places such as schools, shopping centres, and bus and train stations. The comments made by politicians such as Peter Dutton have promoted hatred and encouraged a great deal of racism toward the South Sudanese community and other African groups, such as the Somalian community. There is no doubt that Australia is a fair-go country, but it has an interesting record about racism and discrimination toward minor groups such as African communities and the Aboriginal community. Racial vilification can be a damaging issue for young people and for minority community groups if there are no policies in places to protect them from such vilification (Baak, 2018). There are policies such as the Racial Discrimination Act but this doesn't protect people from experiences of every day racism. In 2017 and 2018, the South Sudanese community in Victoria was faced with serious attacks by media and some politicians, such as Peter Dutton, who made the outraged comment that "Victorians are "scared to go out to restaurants" because of "African gang violence" (Karp, 2018, p 1) His outraged statement was later backed up by the Prime Minister by warning the Australian of "the threats posed by supposed criminal gangs of African descent in Melbourne" (Farid, 2018, p 1). This was viewed as a racist remark within African community. Also, members of the South Sudanese and other African communities were victims on streets and in shopping centres, facing abusive language from some members of the public who disliked African people. Young people from the South Sudanese community had been in media spotlights due to some poor choices they had made that led to crimes. These youth choose their own ways of integrating into mainstream society, without considering advice from their own families and other community members.

Settlement has been generally difficult for the families from the South Sudanese community or other African community groups in Australia. For example, one of the challenging issues facing African families in Australia is how to find ways to engage young people (Abur, 2012). It is true that young African people are like other young people with migrant backgrounds in Australia who have faced common settlement challenges. In many instances, young people with migrant backgrounds are misunderstood and, as a result, their potential for creativity and innovation in resolving their settlement problems are not recognised. Like all refugees, young refugees bring with them useful skills and experiences that they can employ to negotiate the settlement process.

For minority community groups such as the South Sudanese or other Africans, racism is a serious matter as it affects their ability and confidence to integrate into the mainstream community. It is a problem within minority groups that have limited ways of voicing their concerns due to a number of barriers such as language and the confidence to speak up. Speaking up about racism and discrimination in the workforce and in schools appears to be a greater offence then practising racism and discrimination (Abur & Spaaij, 2016). The current trend of racial vilification in Melbourne, Australia, targeting the African community as "African gangs" has generated interesting discourses within both the African community and mainstream community groups, including the media (Farid, 2018; Karp, 2018). The negative news reported by media outlets is disturbing and damaging to society. It is important for media outlets to understand that the poor behaviours displayed by some young African people or by Sudanese people in Melbourne are not a part of Sudanese or African heritage or culture. It is an entirely home-grown culture within Melbourne and in Australia. Many African parents are dismayed and fear for their young children. History tells us that Australian immigration has a bad record of practising racist policy, known as the "White Australia Policy", under the *Restriction Act 1901* (Abur, 2012; Atem,

2011). This immigration policy was designed to allow particular races and exclude others. After Federation, the new Australian nation continued to allow refugees to settle as unassisted migrants, as long as they met the restrictions imposed by the White Australia Policy. Later, small numbers of German, Russian, Greek, Bulgarian, Armenian and Assyrian refugees—including Jewish refugees—were permitted to settle after demonstrating that they met Australia's immigration criteria (Refugee Council of Australia, 2010). Between 1933 and 1939, for example, more than 7,000 Jews fleeing Nazi Germany were settled (Neuman, 2006). In 1937, the Australian Jewish Welfare Society pioneered the first refugee settlement support services, with financial assistance from the Australian Government. This settlement program was cut short by the outbreak of World War II (see Refugee Council of Australia, 2012).

Although multiculturalism is celebrated and used to strengthen citizenship and nation-building programs, it is difficult for refugees to access employment and build their earnings. In fact, evidence shows that refugees tend to experience a higher rate of unemployment and lower earnings than other migrants (Abdelkerim & Grace, 2012; Abur & Spaaij, 2016). In some workplaces, an equal employment policy needs to be adopted as recognition of social inclusion (Abur & Spaaij, 2016; Siddiquee & Faroqi, 2010). This proposal is a measure to address discrimination and inequality in workplaces. In both academic and professional circles, it is strongly felt that a dynamic and effective administrative system cannot be created unless it is based on the principle of merit, where people get a "fair go". Discrimination occurs when an individual is adversely excluded from employment opportunities on the basis of race, colour, sex, religion, age, nationality, ethnicity, political opinion or other factors; these acts are not lawful in many countries, including Australia (Abur & Spaaij, 2016; Siddiquee & Faroqi, 2010). Globally, many governments have legislated to seek to end discrimination and promote fairness in employment. Therefore, equal opportunity is a concept that seeks to ensure that all individuals have equal opportunity for employment, regardless of characteristics such as race, colour, or religion (Abur & Spaaij, 2016).

The settlement of refugees in a new country is a complex and ongoing process that requires support from the host community, government, and non-government agencies to address different challenges. The questions of what represents successful settlement and what this means for refugees are still debatable. However, there are various understandings of what it means to be "well settled" in a new country (Atem 2011; Abur & Spaaij, 2016). These include feeling safe from racism and discrimination, obtaining secure and well-paid employment, buying a home, children feeling well supported at school and in the community, and playing sport within the host community, all without experiencing aggressive or abusive language (Abur & Spaaij, 2016). Sometimes, settlement can be a two-way process of mutual understanding of cultural expectations, with the host community working in partnership with refugees.

Settlement experiences can be challenging and difficult for refugee communities and individuals. People often experience feelings of homesickness, isolation, exposure to unfamiliar systems, culture shock and many other feelings, which compound their inability to start a new life in a new country. Newly-arrived refugee communities from non-English speaking countries in Africa have to face these issues regularly (Abur & Spaaij, 2016). Their settlement situation can be miserable, particularly for those who have no networks or support services from relatives and friends. Australia has a history of resettling refugees and people in humanitarian need. It is a signatory to the United Nations 1951 Convention relating to the Status of Refugees and to the subsequent 1967 Protocol (Abur & Spaaij, 2016, Atem, 2011, Humphrey & Steven, 1984). Since 1947, more than 800,000 refugees from a broad range of nationalities have been resettled and have rebuilt their lives in Australia (Atem, 2011; Humphrey & Steven, 1984, Refugee Council of Australia, 2010).

Australia's Humanitarian Resettlement Program began in 1947, with the resettlement of people displaced by World War II (Abur & Spaaij, 2016, Atem, 2011, Refugee Council of Australia, 2010). However, the first asylum seeker groups landed in Australia during the 1890s, comprising Lutherans, a Christian group escaping restrictions on their right to worship within Prussia. They settled in South Australia, and their contribution to that State's subsequent progress was significant (Hugo, G. (2014, Refugee Council of Australia, 2010). Australian resettlement efforts were most pronounced in the late 1940s and early 1950s, when hundreds of thousands of European Displaced Persons were brought to and accommodated in Australia under the auspices of the International Refugee Organization (IRO), the immediate precursor of the UNHCR. In 1949 alone, Australia resettled 75,486 Displaced Persons sponsored by the IRO (Humphrey & Steven, 1984).

Racism is a national hazard in face of multicultural society.

We know that consequences of discrimination and racism can be harmful to individuals and community if there are not detected early enough and address properly. The question of why racism can be national hazard in multicultural society? There is nothing that can explains the harmful and danger exposed by racism to the society or innocent people than what happened on 15th of March, 2019 in New Zealand. The killing of innocent worshipers is just one of the simple examples of how racism and discrimination is threatening the multicultural values in the western world. There is nothing that a society can gain by subjecting minority community groups to a high level of discrimination and racial vilification. We know that children from minority groups suffer badly from bullying and other forms of abuse in schools, families can be scared to seek assistance or complain about what happen to their children at schools, and workers from minority communities suffer psychological harm due to abuse and racial vilification and can lose their jobs easily. Australia's Race Discrimination Commissioner, Dr Tim Soutphommasane, has argued that "the panic about African youth crime has undoubtedly done significant damage to racial harmony in Melbourne and Australian society more generally" (Baak, 2018, Millar, 2018).

In many cases, mainstream Medias have played negative role in fuelling racial debates about vulnerable and minority groups. African community groups and particularly Sudanese/South Sudanese community was targeted by the mainstream Medias due to the poor behaviours of some few young people. In some cases, some journalists failed to understand the negative impact of Medias in community when issues are reported in Medias. We know that the important role performed by media in the politics of belonging, unifying and dividing society. This has been a serious matter in recent debates about what so-called African gang in Melbourne (Marjoribanks, 2016). Politics of race was seriously played by the Malcolm Turnbull's government before he was ousted out from his Ministership role. Young people from South Sudanese community were persistently being called gangs, lawless group, thugs and offenders when they are hanging out in group for social reason.

Racism and discrimination form just one element of the settlement issues faced by the South Sudanese people in Australia. Both international and local reports have indicated that negative settlement experiences are likely to cause more trauma for refugees if there is not strong support from governments and local community groups (Abur, 2012; Correa-Velez, Spaaij, & Upham, 2013). Australia's Humanitarian Programme is reportedly experiencing pressing issues with the integration of new refugees (Abur & Spaaij, 2016; Refugee Council of Australia, 2012). There are many settlement initiatives, but it seems that many recently arrived refugees are often failed by these, especially in the area of employment (Correa-Velez et al., 2013). Also, students in secondary schools are struggling with serious issues, including bullying and discrimination, because of their social and cultural backgrounds (Abur, 2012).

The research findings of this study indicate that the settlement experiences of South Sudanese Australians have been extremely difficult during the last few years, due to negative reporting by different media groups. The impact of this negative reporting has led to high levels of unemployment and youth dropping out from schools because of bullying and discrimination. Furthermore, the negative experiences of unemployment and other settlement issues has led to many families experiencing family conflict and separations. Studies suggest that South Sudanese community members are experiencing a greater sense of exclusion from mainstream Australian society as their children are experiencing higher levels of discrimination and racism. They are also experiencing high levels of unemployment, and many who are employed are experiencing underemployment. All these have affected their level of social and economic participation. For example, the level of participation of young people in sporting clubs is affected.

The findings of this study have policy implications in the areas of resettlement and employment assistance for all people from refugee backgrounds, and particularly for South Sudanese Australians. One of the most important implications of this study is the need to tackle barriers to employment and discrimination to promote better settlement outcomes for refugees. The findings suggest that a more targeted approach may be required to facilitate refugees' access to the labour market; this will require going beyond building the capacity of South Sudanese Australians to also critically reflecting on and transforming organisational and professional practices (Abur, 2012; Marlowe, 2014). The narratives of participants in this study reinforced the findings of Colic-Peisker and Tilbury (2007, p. 2), who argued that "discrimination on the basis of race, religion and ethnic origin plays a role in creating unsatisfactory employment outcomes", in particular through discrimination on the part of employers on the basis of "soft skills" such as Australian cultural knowledge. Discrimination in the workforce cannot be seen in isolation from discrimination in other societal domains: systematic discrimination appears to have also been meted out against refugees in other areas, such as the housing sector, with negative effects on settlement outcomes (Dandya & Pe-Puab, 2015).

There is a great need to formulate strategies to address racism in schools and discrimination in the workforce. The strategies could include vocational education and training programs linked with English language learning, streamlining the qualification recognition process, introducing specialised job networks, challenging stereotypes and discrimination, promoting diversity awareness among employers, providing greater opportunities for refugees to gain work experience, introducing incentives to undertake volunteer work, and mentoring programs (e.g. Abdelkerim & Grace, 2012; Colic-Peisker & Tilbury, 2007b; Correa-Velez et al., 2013; Refugee Council of Australia, 2010). Some existing strategies, such as the provision of tangible work experience opportunities through traineeships and apprenticeships (e.g. Brotherhood of St Laurence, 2016), have had proven success in addressing employment barriers for refugees. Another potentially effective yet currently under-utilised strategy in assisting people from refugee backgrounds to access employment is the provision of professional connection and mentoring programs for job seekers.

There is a clear need for continuing pressure in both the workforce and schools to address discrimination issues affecting people from refugee backgrounds and their children. This could involve educating employers about workplace diversity and supporting them in developing relevant workplace programs and practices, while also challenging stereotypes and bias (which is often unconscious) and holding employers accountable for discriminatory practices. Recognition of the benefits of diversity in the workforce, and promoting the view that many South Sudanese Australians are hardworking and want to work, are important elements of this approach. In conjunction, these strategies could contribute to a labour market that better enables people from refugee backgrounds, and South Sudanese Australians in particular, to realise their full potential as productive citizens.

There are evidences in research which suggest that the benefits of employment include financial, social and mental wellbeing. Some of these benefits for people from refugee backgrounds are well documented (Abur & Spaaij, 2016; Hugo, 2014; Refugee Council of Australia, 2010). Unemployment and discrimination in any form brings psychological suffering and despair in the community. The identified barriers resonate strongly with previous research undertaken with people from refugee backgrounds (Abur, 2012; Abur & Spaaij, 2016; Correa-Velez & Onsando, 2009; Correa-Velez et al., 2013; Dandya & Pe-Puab, 2015) and newly emerging African communities in Australia (Abdelkerim & Grace, 2012). The institutional racism is also something which is still existing in Australia. The settlement experiences of the South Sudanese or African community groups tell the difficulties and fear from these African community groups to access mainstream services.

Subtle racism and discrimination

Subtle racism and discrimination is very common and often people become confused on how to react with such subtle racism and discrimination when someone is subjected to. During my research work with the community, it is very clear from participants' views that some of them or their closed family members were subjected to racism and discrimination in workplace, schools, shopping centres and so forth. Some of the specific issues of racism and discrimination in relation to participation in employment and sport are discussed under each section later. It appears that racism and discrimination have been widely experienced in institutional settings as well as random occurrences in community neighbourhoods.

> My sister who started her primary school at Year 5 here was told she would not do her VCE because she came from a non-English background. This was really bad for her and for her family because we believe that the school let her down. There was not enough support given to her at school. They know she came from a non-English speaking background. The school should have supported her to learn English and not say she cannot do this and that because of her poor English.
> *Participant 11, 28-year-old female, 8 years in Australia*

Participants reported some issues of racism and discrimination based on their experiences or experiences of their family members.

> Racism exists in schools and workplaces. Some people let their personal opinions overarch their professional responsibilities and a duty of care by becoming racist. It is not good for people to be racist to other cultures and let their professionalism down. It is not good to be emotionally negative to other people or cultures because you are adding to their emotional sorrow and you are discouraging them from growing as good citizens. I think people need to do things based on the ethical and moral duty of the schools or organisations they are working for.
> *Participant 14, 23-year-old male, 9 years in Australia*

Consequences of racism and discrimination do affect people psychologically and limit their free moment in public places. Some participants in South Sudanese community reported that those who experienced racism and discrimination in public were fearful of going out and beyond their comfort zone again because the experiences remained with them.

> People who experience racism remained closed and were not ready enough to go beyond their comfort zone. This is a hard thing for many of our people. It is unfortunate that racism still

exists: the important message is not to let racism hold you back. When I came to Australia, I went through racism and discrimination. People used to say to us on the street, "Go back to your country," and people said to mum, "She comes from banana land; go back to your banana land". People used to spit at me and sometimes I went home crying and thinking, "Why did people treat me like this? What is wrong with me?" However, later I learnt that racism and discrimination should not hold me back. I have studied as much as I wanted to. I learned quickly that there are good people out there; there are good and bad people in every society.

Participant 18, 30-year-old female, 15 years in Australia

The negative interactions between young people from the South Sudanese or African backgrounds with police in Melbourne have created a lack of trust in the community. This created a perception that the police officers are racially targeting young people from African community groups

> I am concerned with the way police interact with young people from the African community while they expect you to integrate successfully in Australia. Police are punitive on young people, they treat them badly even when the young people have done nothing wrong and were just socialising as a group. Police can interview them as if they committed a crime. Such attitudes make it hard for young people to trust and believe that police are there to protect people – including them. Many young people from South Sudanese and other community groups believe that police treat them as a gang while they are not, but once they are treated as a gang by the authorities, they turn against the authorities and do not trust them anymore. Now many of young people are in prison and this shows the system does not support newly arrived refugees and migrants to settle better. Small issues

can fuel them and if they react negatively, they will end up facing gaol.

Participant 9, 30-year-old female, 12 years in Australia

Participants believed that not all South Sudanese young people were bad when it comes to poor behaviours. Some participants stated that they decided to get involved in advocacy because of young people being targeted by police officers and treating them badly.

> I was involved in an advocacy group because I did not like the police targeting refugee young people, particularly black young people from Africa who are often treated or targeted by police as criminal. Look at me; I am a South Sudanese and I have never fought in my life but guess what? The police or some people think that all the South Sudanese young people are bad because they fight lots on the streets. This is not true to generalise and treat the whole community as bad people.
>
> *Participant 12, 22-year-old female, 11 years in Australia*

A lack of empowerment and skills to deal with some racial issues was highlighted by participants as something affecting their community members. However, some participants had strong feelings toward claiming their rights as an Australian citizen.

> There is no doubt in my mind and the minds of other South Sudanese that we are citizens of Australia. Although there are discrimination and racism here and there, we need to claim we are South Sudanese Australians. Nobody is going to give them that; we needed to claim this for ourselves. Many people in South Sudan respected the system; they respected the judicial system and laws. However, this does not mean people cannot be critical of some things. I do think that people eventually feel as citizens of Australia, not by holding passports, but by asking the question: "How long is it going to take?" The real point is this: People are going to go;

people do need to be given opportunities in the workforce to feel that they are contributing to this society and not depend on welfare payments. When people enter the workforce and become taxpayers, involved in the army, police force, studying and so on. I think people do need to respond to racism: I am an Australian citizen as much as anyone else who thinks they are an Australian citizen.

Participant 19, 27-year-old female, 11 years in Australia

Participants believed that there was a negative stereotyping of South Sudanese community. They believed that there are people who constantly stereotype them without knowing much about their backgrounds. They also believed that people in the South Sudanese community need to stand up and talk about racism and discrimination issues.

Some people can judge you when they see you without knowing your background. I think the issue of racism and discrimination needs to be discussed and challenged openly. Racism and discrimination are everywhere, but the problem is that people do not want to discuss this openly. This is what makes it alive in the community: people need to be encouraged to talk about racism and discrimination openly.

Participant 15, 28-year-old male, 10 years in Australia

Ignorance can lead people to make wrong comments about other peoples' cultures or backgrounds based on their situations. One of the participants described her experiences of growing up in Australia as a black child as very difficult because of the racism and discrimination she had witnessed.

I grew up in Australia as a black kid for over 15 years. People are often subjected to racism [pause] and the argument that Australia is not a racist country is not true. There is still racism in Australia compared to America. America has a long history of dealing with the black population and the black community

has emerged strongly in America, while in Australia indigenous black people have been marginalised and always treated as low-class citizens. The same attitudes have now been applied to African migrants. Their rights and dignity are often undermined or ignored. The thing is, there is an open or hidden racism in Australia, which is affecting people because people that experience racism always remain isolated from the rest of the community.
Participant 18, 30-year-old female, 15 years in Australia

Participants believed that casual racism is very common and is expressed in different ways such sarcastic expressions. Some participant believed that nobody liked to be talk down to, and people did not deserve to be treated in that way.

Settlement experiences can be bad sometimes when you meet people who have their personal issues with certain ethnic groups. They can try to talk you down because they don't like you or people from your background for some reason. Such people make settlement difficult because you always think; I don't deserve to be treated like this. I deserve an equal opportunity like others. It is unfortunate that there are people who aim to distract the others and deny them opportunities to grow and contribute to Australian society as good citizens.
Participant 14, 23-year-old male, 9 years in Australia

Institutional racism in school.

As far as we know that school is supposed to be a safe place for young people regardless of their backgrounds. Young people from minority groups and with skin colour different to the general population are often subjected with different types of racism. They can be called different names such apes, gorilla or animals. Some young people choose to dropout from school because of unfair treatment in school or racial verification subjected on them. Many interviewees believed that subtle forms of discrimination and racism have affected them and their family members, regardless of anti-discrimination law in Australia. Some reported that they had experienced firsthand what they considered to be unfair treatment in the workplace, schools or community shopping centres. Those participants who had encountered discrimination did not hesitate to relate their experiences and opinions, hinting at the effects of a "visible difference" on employment outcomes (Colic-Peisker & Tilbury, 2007a). Participants narrated the level of racism and discrimination that some of them had encountered in public places, for example:

> Racism and discrimination is high now in public places such as employment sector, schools and shopping centres, you do not know who could attack you because of being looks different among the majority of people. Also, people from the African community or with dark skins are more likely to be discriminated in employment. For example, you can be told straight when you are looking for work that you have no local experience. How would someone get local experience when you are not given a chance to voluntarily work with the company?
>
> *28-year-old female, 11 years in Australia*

The expectations in public places like schools can make it challenging for some students to maintain respect and positive behaviours when they are not being treated well by other people.

> There is always pressure and expectations at schools that you have to do well and be respectful to other people even though they are not respectful to you. Some people can try to put you down but you can only try your best to be polite

and remain disciplined and positive. But it is clearly unfair to treat people in a cruel manner because of their backgrounds or colour of skin.

28-year-old female, 10 years in Australia

Some participants reported that students from South Sudanese or Sudanese communities are often viewed in schools as though they are associated with the "Apex gang" or involved in other crimes committed by African youth. This has created some tension between parents and some schools: parents are not trusting the school because teachers are not trusting their students.

> In school, some racist teachers make inappropriate remarks sometimes toward our students. They also failed to investigate some racial vilifications directed to African students by the white students. Teachers are so quick in defending white students when bullying issues between students are reported.
>
> *26 year old male, 12 years in Australia*

Participants reported that some schools asked African students not to gather in groups during recess and lunch times, claiming that they intimidate other students when they are in groups of five or six students.

> Sometimes teachers don't want to see our students playing with other students; they say they are intimidating. A lot of stereotyping—the media is playing a significant part in how we're being treated here. For instance, whenever they congregate together, they are called names such as gangs, but when it is white students, nobody tells them to split up or calls them gangs. They are being treated differently. The media has done significant damage.
>
> *40 year old male, 15 years in Australia*

All participants believed that the negative reporting by media outlets about African people and the Apex gang in Melbourne has brought negative repercussions in the community and has affected African students in schools. The misrepresentation of news in the media often brings negative debates in society. This has been confirmed in both local and international research, showing that a negative media representation results in some people being portrayed as "bad"; these people often internalise it and that affects their health, wellbeing and self-esteem, and limits their education, employment and economic opportunities (Marjoribanks & Muller, 2014).

> Because of bad reporting in media, we are always seen like criminals, even our children are often suspected at schools while they are supposed to be treated like other students from mainstream community groups. Teachers show poor attitudes to innocent children as criminals. It is really bad to hear when students come home and report of incidents in school.
>
> *28 year old female, 14 years in Australia*

Some participants reported that schools have serious issues to answer when it comes to institutional racism and discrimination. Students with African heritage are sometimes treated differently because of their backgrounds. When a student shows negative behaviour, some teachers do not consider it as just the normal poor behaviour of a student and it is often taken to a different level.

> There is often high level of accountabilities expected on students from African backgrounds in schools, instead of treating them as normal students similarly to other white students, they are expected to show a high level of respect in class and to other students as well as teachers. If they don't show high level of respect, they are told what the hell you are or you are doing? You are brought here and expected

in school, but you are not appreciating the opportunity and support provided to you.

34 year old female, 12 years in Australia

Discrimination and racism in employment

When participants were asked about their experiences in the workplace, most of them reported encountering negative experiences. They narrated that discrimination in the workplace or in the process of seeking work was still an issue for them and their community members. They believed that it is a difficult problem for them and their community members to break through, as it is one of the common issues facing settlement in a new country.

> People are concerned about racism and discrimination in the workplace and schools. It is a major issue affecting young people from the South Sudanese or African communities. It is like many young people who face bullying at school: South Sudanese young people all face bullying and racism in Australia. It is part of community life now. People with black skins are easily victimised by racists.
>
> *30-year-old female, 14 years in Australia*

Some participants felt that their inability to gain employment was attributable in part to how employers judged their physical appearance or skin colour. For example, a 25-year-old female, who has been in Australia with her family for 12 years, recounted her experience when she was invited for an interview:

> I know this through my own experiences in looking for the jobs in Australia. I have been left out several times because of small things that should not hold me back, but because of my background as an African person, I was not able to get the job. Your physical appearance is a problem sometimes, especially

when you are looking for work. People can deny you because of your physical appearance. One time, I applied for a job and was invited for an interview. I went and waited at the reception for the interview. A lady who was doing the interview calls my name out and I responded. When she saw me, she said, "Oh!" and paused. I was, like, what was that pause about? It is because of my physical appearance of being black. I noticed the change in her face, felt uncomfortable and she felt uncomfortable with me. I straightaway knew that I was not going to get this job and it was true; I have not got it.

25-year-old female, 12 years in Australia

One of the participants gave two specific examples of his experience of discrimination in the workplace:

There is racism and discrimination in the workplace; this is still an issue in Australia. I have faced this in different ways. I remember at my work, I was told by one guy, "Hi mate, you should not wear black clothes because you are black." This is an example of how racist people behave. When I reported him, he claimed that he was talking about a safety issue and he refused to attend a meeting with me. He claimed that migrants and refugee people "should learn our ways".

25-year-old male, 13 years in Australia

I was abused by a drunken customer in public who said, "Go back to where you come from. You are not needed here. This is my country. My grandfather fought for it to keep black people away from this country." I ignored her because she was drunk but one of my colleagues did not like the way this particular customer was behaving. There was general discomfort from people who were listening to what she saying. She was later asked to leave.

25-year-old male, 13 years in Australia

Participants reported that some simple conversations make them a bit uneasy, for example when they meet with ignorant people who assume that you are not educated or do not speak or write English.

> Racism comes when people ask you during an interview or even when you are just socialising with people. They ask, "Where did you come from?", and if you say you come from South Sudan/Sudan, the next question is, "Where did you learn English?" These kinds of questions are annoying because people just prejudge that you have no English and you are not supposed to be here meeting me. I think the image of the South Sudanese community has been badly portrayed by the media because of young people. However, young people are young people everywhere; it doesn't matter whether you are a young person from America, Africa or Australia. They still have issues of young people. It is not fair when the whole community has been judged and labelled as bad because of a few people who are struggling with social issues. I feel that is racism and discrimination because I would like to be judged as individual and not as the community I come from.
>
> 28 year old female, 14 years in Australia

Supporting people from refugee backgrounds to understand their rights in the workplace and when they experience discrimination is critical. The importance of empowerment was discussed by several participants, and the following comment by one participant, who described how his colleague mistreated him but, through standing up for his rights, the problem was quickly resolved, is indicative of that:

> One of my colleagues used to undermine my work and treated me badly. She always brought her personal issues from home and behaved aggressively towards me. I tried putting up with her behaviour, ignoring her aggression and discrimi-

> nation, until I stood up for myself. She realised I was going to report the issue to the manager. She became friendly to me and worked with me in a respectful way. This came after I confronted her and told her she didn't need to talk to me like this and she needed to respect me as I respected her as a colleague. I said that should she continue in the same way, I would resign and there would be an investigation.
>
> 25-year-old male, 10 years in Australia

Lack of strong policies and disciplinary actions allow ignorant people to abuse their power and privileges by treating other employees poorly. Employees of colour or minority community groups are most likely to be subjected to a high level of abuse by their counterparts. Participants highlighted the need for organisational support and procedures to address workplace discrimination.

> Sometimes racism and discrimination in the workplace is not the organisation, it is a personal interest of those who have racist behaviours or attitudes learnt from other groups. I think the organisation needed to tighten up its policy to ensure that those who hold senior positions should not bring their racist behaviour into the workplace. Organisations should integrate a positive culture and cultural understanding to ensure that people from different cultures are given the opportunity to work in the organisation.
>
> 25-year-old female, 12 years in Australia

Relationship between police and youth of African backgrounds

The relationship between African young people and police is often perceived in community as being difficult. Some youth do complain to their families about the way the police had interacted with them. Participants explained how some people, especially young people, had suffered negative interactions with police, which had instilled in them a more generalised fear of discrimination that also extended to the labour market. The negative interactions between young people from South Sudanese backgrounds and police in Melbourne were believed to have created distrust in the community, including a perception that South Sudanese Australians and other African Australians were being racially targeted by law enforcement. This caused anxiety in the community, as the following comments suggest:

> I am concerned with the ways police interact with young people from the African community while they expect you to integrate successfully in Australia. Police are punitive on young people, they treat them badly even when the young people have done nothing wrong and were just socialising as a group. Police can interview them as if they committed a crime. Such attitudes make it hard for young people to trust and believe that police are there to protect people including them. Many young people from South Sudanese and other community groups believe that police treat them as a gang while they are not, but once they are treated as a gang by the authorities, they turn against the authority and do not trust them anymore. Now many of young people are in prison and this shows the system does not support newly-arrived refugees and migrants to settle better. They can be fuelled by small issues and if they react negatively they will end up facing jail.
>
> *30-year-old female, 14 years in Australia*

The specific issues surrounding youth are linked to parenting responsibilities and the lack of role models for young family members. Parenting is one of the challenging issues for South Sudanese families. For many parents, the task of single parenting is not easy. In South Sudan, war has resulted in there being many single parents, because many men lost their lives in conflict and some fathers were forced to separate from their families due to the conflict. Another cause of the increase in the number of single parents is cultural change or culture shock in Australia. These issues have torn many relationships apart and left the responsibility of caring for children with one parent, usually the mother. During interviews, single parenting emerged as one of the difficult issues in discussions about family matters. It is very clear that single parents in the South Sudanese community were struggling with their teenage children, who were taking different directions from their parenting.

> Many young people are lacking parenting discipline; many families or young people are being parented by single parents—particularly by mothers. Many of my friends and cousins are lacking male parenting or male role models because their fathers are not here in Australia. Some lost their fathers during the war in South Sudan/Sudan.
>
> *32-year-old male, 12 years in Australia*

CHAPTER 5

Employment and Unemployment for Refugees

This chapter provides general view of employment, benefits of employment for people from refugee backgrounds and more importantly, views of the South Sudanese-Australians in relation to benefits which people can get from employment. Modern employment theory argues that there is no single policy that carries more potential benefits than the full employment of individuals willing to work (Forstater 2006). Employment has important social benefits for individuals, families, neighbourhoods, and communities. Research has linked employment with through decreased crime rates, reduced drug and alcohol abuse, and stable healthy families (Cullen 1999; Forstater 2006). Employment is particularly significant for refugee communities as it assists in enabling people to integrate more easily into the host community. Financial independence, opportunities to enhance skills, build social networks and contribute to society all aid in the process of establishing a sense of home in a new country and creating a positive self-identity (Cholewinski 2010; Trewin 2001).

However, while multiculturalism is celebrated, and used to strengthen citizenship, and nation-building programs, there is a gap between the rhetoric and the actual lived experience of particular cultural communities and individuals. This can be seen in the experience of refugee communities in terms of difficulty in gaining employment and earning an income with which to establish themselves and their families. (Abur & Spaaij 2016). While obtaining, and being engaged in employment is an extremely important aspect of the integration process for refugees (Abur & Spaaij 2016; Colic-Peisker & Tilbury 2007), and a first priority for those who wish to support their families either overseas or where they have settled (Ager & Strang 2008), refugees tend to experience a high rate of unemployment and lower earnings compared to other migrants (Abdelkerim & Grace 2012, Abur & Spaaij 2016).

The meaning and impact of employment and unemployment are critical aspects of the study of refugee settlement and part of this research focuses on the benefits of employment both in regard to financial enablement and the important skills and social networks that people can gain through employment. Before reviewing previous research in this area, brief definitions of key terms are provided. Paid employment has been defined as a state of having a job or via providing a service for wages or salaries, in cash or via in kind support of some variety (Krahn, Howard & Galambos 2015). Employment provides potent functions such as a sense of societal structure and a meaningful life, as people are able to work and make a contribution to their families and community (Blustein, Medvide & Wan 2012). Employment may be full-time or part-time and range in stability from casual or contract to ongoing. Under-employment is when the hours of paid work may be casual or insufficient to meet living costs (Cullen 1999). Unemployment is a situation where a person has no paid work but is actively looking for paid work (Hussmanns 2007). In order for a person to register as unemployed and claim an unemployment benefit, they must be immediately available for paid employment (Cullen 1999)

In the context of settlement, there are many factors as to why refugees struggle with difficulties in obtaining employment (Abur & Spaaij 2016; Colic-Peisker & Tilbury 2007). These problems often include a shortage of jobs in the market, meaning that there is strong competition for positions. However, gaining employment is also hampered by a lack of fluency in English, lack of local experience and as well as lack of understanding sophisticated system in Australia (Abur & Spaaij 2016, Correa-Velez, Barnett & Gifford 2015). Additionally, people from refugee backgrounds are vulnerable to long-term unemployment and lower earning jobs because of the lack of required skills, non-transferability of skills and qualifications (Taylor 2004). Due to war and conflict and long periods spent in camps refugees frequently have low literacy and numeracy skills, which impact both on their ability to do some jobs and on their confidence. However, even those who are highly literate also face barriers as often their qualifications are not recognised and this causes difficulty in obtaining jobs (Abur & Spaaij 2016; Colic-Peisker & Tilbury 2007 Fozdar & Hartley 2013). These issues around qualifications mean that when refugees are able to find work it is often in low-paid jobs such as cleaning and seasonal fruit picking (Colic-Peisker & Tilbury 2007, Taylor 2004). It is also significant that, as new arrivals, refugees do not have the social networks of long-term residents, which can often be instrumental in assisting people find work.

These are the most obvious reasons for unemployment in refugee communities. However, there are a host of other reasons which are connected to, or a result of the post-trauma, loss and disruption refugees have experienced prior to their arriving in a country such as Australia. These post-traumatic experiences include physical and mental suffering. The experiences also some conflicts in families, caring responsibilities, and a feeling of hopelessness (Abdelkerim & Grace 2012; Colic-Peisker & Tilbury 2007, Lawlor & Perkins 2009, Ziguras & Kleidon 2005). Refugees who have spent a long time in refugee camps may also have substance abuse issues which can interfere with obtaining employment (Ziguras & Kleidon 2005). Families also find harder to access affordable rental houses which add on top of other pressuring issues. Lack of available and affordable rental properties and discrimination towards families and individuals from refugee backgrounds is some which has been experienced by the South Sudanese community in Australia (Abur 2012).

Racism and discrimination is another considerable barrier for refugees engaging with employment (Abur & Spaaij 2016, Colic-Peisker & Tilbury 2007, Taylor 2004). Refugees from African backgrounds are more likely to experience racism and stereotyping in the workplace because of their accent and physical appearance (Fozdar & Torezani 2008) as well as various forms of bullying and harassment (Abur & Spaaij 2016, Taylor 2004). Racism and discrimination can hurt, humiliate, enrage, confuse and ultimately prevent optimal growth and functioning of individuals and communities (Baker-Lewton, et al 2017; Fozdar & Torezani 2008). Refugees are also vulnerable to workplace exploitation due to lack of awareness about their legal rights. This mean they are paid less or have worse conditions than other workers because they don't know their legal rights (Colic-Peisker & Tilbury 2007).

Impacts of unemployment

Lack of employment is something very frustrating to people who are looking for work, but tend to be difficult to secure jobs due to many reasons. The high levels of unemployment and discrimination in the workplace can contribute to refugees feeling alienated and disconnected from mainstream society (Abur & Spaaij 2016). They may feel powerless to reach their potential in terms of work opportunities, are suffer from more financial stress than the rest of the population and, thus, feel that their quality of life, and general wellbeing is significantly lower than average (Fozdar & Torezani 2008). The personal and social costs of unemployment or lack of skilled employment are significant across all communities and can become an overarching issue for families and individuals impacting on many other areas of their lives (Forstater 2006; McClelland & Macdonald 1998). Psychological distress is high amongst unemployed people, who are far more vulnerable to poor states of mental health than those who are employed (Murphy &Athanasou 1999, Warr 1987). Arguably psychological distress and poor states of mental health is compounded for people from refugee backgrounds, by both their previous circumstance and the challenges of settlement. Research shows that settlement process is unlikely to be successful without sustainable employment, particularly for those who remain unemployed due to lack of employability skills (Colic-Peisker & Tilbury 2006; Correa-Velez, Barnett & Gifford 2015).

The impacts of long term unemployment include long-term financial hardship and poverty, housing stress, homelessness, family tension and breakdown, shame and stigma and increased social isolation, as well as increased crime, erosion of confidence and self-esteem, and a deteriorating ability to work (Abur & Spaaij 2016, McClelland & Macdonald 1998; MacDonald et al. 2004). The negative consequences of unemployment also include perceptions about unemployed people, as they are more likely to be stereotyped and ostracised by the public, service providers, and government officials as lazy people who do not want to work (Abur & Spaaij 2016, Cullen 1999).

Benefits of employment for a refugee community

The benefit of participation in employment is a key to refugees' wellbeing, both physical and mental, as it is the best weapon in eradicating poverty and reducing crime (Abur &Spaaij 2016, Colic-Peisker & Tilbury 2006). Children of employed parents can complete their schooling or spend more years in school (or university) compared to children of unemployed parents (Forstater 2006). Employment can bring real, tangible, and both direct and indirect social and economic benefits, not only for those employed, but for all members of the community. Employment for refugees can facilitate pathways to integration with the host community through positive interaction and learning of different cultures in workplace between employees (Abur &Spaaij 2016, Atem 2011a).

Participation in employment is a key to wellbeing, as employment provides income as well as socioeconomic status. In many cases, people do want to participate in employment to make them feel socially included and to make a contribution in society (Krahn, Howard & Galambos 2015; Wilson 2008). Participation of refugees in employment can make them contribute to the economic development of a nation while supporting their families financially and pay taxes to the government (Abur & Spaaij 2016). Refugees bring different levels of skill and experience. However, some refugees who have spent a long time moving from place to place, have not had the opportunity to attain qualifications and employment experience because of the nature of their migration experiences, including long periods spent in refugee camps can be supported to obtain skills for employability (Abdelkerim & Grace 2012; Abur 2012; Colic-Peisker & Tilbury 2007).

Participation in employment

The benefits of participation in employment include financial and social benefits through connecting with like-minded individuals who have positive attitudes to assist others, such as people from refugee backgrounds. Participation in employment is very important, particularly for people who are re-establishing themselves in a new country, such as the South Sudanese community in Melbourne. There are many factors holding people from refugee backgrounds back from participating in their host community. However, with greater support for those people to enter the workforce, it is likely that the settlement challenges confronting refugees can be reduced and employment can open more opportunities for them to integrate successfully. During interviews, participants raised the benefits of participation in employment, including providing financial benefits, social capital or social connection, and learning opportunities. Good learning experiences can occur when a person finds work. In addition, employment provides a platform for financial stability, which helps to reduce stress and other settlement pressures.

A NEW LIFE WITH OPPORTUNITIES AND CHALLENGES

> There are lot benefits of employment to all people. Employment can help people financially and with many [other] aspects. It helps a lot in making people settle better, particularly refugees or migrants like us. The financial benefit of employment is paramount, as we all need money to pay bills and make a living. This is one of the many reasons why people go to work; it is to get payment at the end of working days.
> *Participant 13, 39-year-old male, 10 years in Australia*

Employment brings both social and financial benefits for people who are working, particularly those who have no connections as they are new in the mainstream community.

> Employment is very important because you earn money and it gives you something to do routinely. You can also meet many people at work and have many friends who help lots. If you work in customer services, for example, you meet many people and talk with them on different issues, which you learn lots about, and it helps you lots as individuals. This can help newly arrived migrants or refugees to integrate easily, compared to people who are not employed.
> *Participant 3, 20-year-old male, 11 years in Australia*

Some people want to work and avoid being "parasites" by depending on social security. They also want to make contributions to the community through either paying tax or other means of contribution, including supporting family members. All participants believed that having work is extremely important in Australia.

> I don't think that anyone wants to be a parasite and stick to welfare benefits and suck government's money. Some people like to work and have a sense of identity, a sense of belonging as workers. Therefore, employment is extremely important to people.
> *Participant 19, 27-year-old female, 11 years in Australia*

Employment brings stability and independent life for people because of financial benefits. Participants believed that stability and independence from relatives were important aspects of employment. Learning and socialisation with friends comes when a person is stable and financially independent.

> Employment helped in many ways. First, you can support yourself if you don't have relatives or friends to support you when you want something. You can buy things that you want if you are employed, pay rent and other bills. You can also learn lots in workplaces by meeting friends, socialising with workmates, learning from workplace culture and English. It always helped to get employment. I enjoyed my time when working because I could buy what I want.
> *Participant 1, 24-year-old male, 8 years in Australia*

A sense of contributing to society was very important for some people because it gave them meaningful life within the community, helping people in their own community and beyond. Participants described how important employment is for them as they were able to make contributions and gain independence.

> Employment is essential, not only to provide income for yourself, but also you feel like you are meaningfully contributing to society through work and taxpaying. I don't think that anyone wants to be a parasite and stick to welfare benefits and suck government's money. Some people like to work and have a sense of identity, a sense of belonging as workers. To me, employment is extremely important as it can help people get and use money.
> *Participant 19, 27-year-old female, 11 years in Australia*

Responsibility for family and community is always strong when there is financial stability. Participants believed that when a person is employed, it comes with responsibility as well in terms of contributing to family and community.

A NEW LIFE WITH OPPORTUNITIES AND CHALLENGES

> You become a responsible person, because you know that you are contributing to yourself, family, community and government by paying taxes
> *Participant 12, 22-year-old female, 11 years in Australia*

Participation in employment brings encouragement and a sense of contributing to the community through tax paying. This makes some people feel special because they are making a contribution to society.

> When I was working, I got many benefits. I benefited from working as an individual and contributing to the community through paying taxes as a citizen of the country. One of the many benefits I got from work was an active engagement and routine focus on my work
> *Participant 15, 28-year-old male, 10 years in Australia*

There is always a strong feeling about assisting the community in the South Sudanese community. Some people do feel that they have a responsibility and duty of care to work for the community because it is great way of winning respect with the community. Feelings of respect and meaningful contribution are also benefits of employment, as one is able to make a contribution in society.

> Employment is essential, not only to provide income, for yourself, but also ... you felt like you are meaningful, respectable and contributing to society through work and tax paying
> *Participant 19, 27-year-old female, 11 years in Australia*

There was a recognition of participation in employment as something that assists people with social problems to stay away from their problems because they have no time. Participants also believed that employment was a great way to exclude other social problems. Those who were employed had no time to engage in negative activities. The negative activities South Sudanese people referred to included drinking heavily, and having no plans for the future, or not being involved in schooling and family issues as some men and women abandoned their responsibilities due to drinking problems.

> To me, employment controlled me and engaged me which helped me to avoid being with people who are not contributing positive things to the community.
> *Participant 15, 28-year-old male, 10 years in Australia*

Economic capital and financial benefits of employment

Economic capital is simply refers to economic resources, such as money and assets. Any financial benefit of employment is regarded as economic capital, which can assist individuals to access other important capitals such psychological, social, cultural, and physical capital. Economic capital is a resource because employment provides economic stability, reduces psychological stress, and assists in gaining inner peace and psychological satisfaction. During interviews, participants described financial benefits through employment providing a great deal of psychological and economic stability. People who have work seemed to be happy and more settled than those who depended on social security benefits.

> It is good to be engaged in work to get a financial benefit and experience of working. This helps people to move on with their lives and grow as good citizens rather than depending on welfare payments, which are not enough to cover their living costs.
> *Participant 14, 23-year-old male, 9 years in Australia*

Accessing employment brings benefits to people who secured employment and their family members. Participants believed that when a person is working, she/he can gain independence from the family in terms of financial support. They also believe that if one is working, the financial benefit is extended to the family by providing financial support to family members.

A NEW LIFE WITH OPPORTUNITIES AND CHALLENGES

> When you are working, you don't need financial help from your family or friends. Your financial benefits from work can be extended to your family members who need your help. I believe when you are working, you are working for your own good at the end of the day, because when you don't have money you cannot buy things that you need or want for yourself and your family. Working is a good thing because you benefit lots for yourself from employment.
> *Participant 8, 25-year-old female, 14 years in Australia*

Financial resources and stability come from employment, which assists people to be independent from welfare. Managing one's own needs, such as buying a car and paying bills, were examples of the financial benefits.

> Work is beneficial to me because I am able to pay bills, my car's fuel and buy things that I wanted to buy for myself. This is helpful lots compared to someone who is living on welfare security benefit. It is difficult to meet your needs due to financial difficulties
> *Participant 17, 25-year-old female, 12 years in Australia*

Employment assists people to access different opportunities and support themselves financially

> I am currently working part time and enjoy my work while studying at the same time. Being employed, you have many opportunities. I am able to support myself, buy things that I want; buy a car for myself, as I was not able to buy a car before.
> *Participant 6, 27-year-old male, 11 years in Australia*

Participants believed that the financial benefit of employment compared to the time they were unemployed, were the financial freedom to support himself and assist their family members overseas.

> I am employed in one of the factory companies in Melbourne. I do factory work and I have benefited a lot from my work because I am paid fortnightly and I am able to support myself financially compared to the time I was not working. When you are employed, you depend on yourself and are not depending on social security Centrelink payments. You can afford to rent a house, buy a car for yourself and afford to support your relatives or family members. Especially as we, South Sudanese or Africans, have our relatives/family members back home in Africa: we send money to support them. In my workplace, I have a good relationship with my team in which I have learned lots because we work as a team, not as individuals or in isolation. Because of my hard work, I was promoted to an assistant supervisor. I know my role well and it was hard for people to put me down for what I was doing.
> *Participant 7, 38-year-old male, 10 years in Australia*

Participants had a similar view that employment gives them the benefit of financial stability, which allows them to access other resources. Participants who had employment experiences also agreed that there is a great learning opportunity in the workplace.

> Employment is also good for the individual when you are employed; you have a sense of stability and you can learn lots about employing new knowledge and skills
> *Participant 19, 27-year-old female, 9 years in Australia*

Participants believed that the importance of financial stability, associating it with better lives, purchasing a house, and less stress.

> The benefits of employment are many and can range from making a better living, pay[ing] the mortgage when you have money or are employed. Employment brings many benefits including a financial benefit that helps people enjoy a better life in general. When you are employed, you can have less

financial stress as well as having a decent life because of financial stability.

Participant 9, 30-year-old female, 12 years in Australia

Financial benefits are just one of the many benefits that people get through employment. All participants believed that people can meet great friends through employment.

> The financial benefit is one of the benefits that I got from my work as an individual and connecting with people in my workplace. You can meet some great people who can support you and socialise with them
>
> *Participant 16, 28-year-old female, 10 years in Australia*

Psychological capital

Having a positive state of mind can assist individuals to participate widely in many activities, such as education and work. During interviews, participants believed that employment could bring benefits such as a positive life, peace of mind, and happiness. People with a positive state of mind similarly made positive contributions in the workplace and in connections with others.

> Employment is good for me because it gives me a positive life experience, peace and happiness for myself with my job, as I was able to do something productive. I was able to sponsor my family and support them to come to Australia through my job. I feel like I was able to contribute back to the community because I was able pay taxes and support family and relatives. I had a positive relationship with my workmates and manager and I learned lots from them and through my work. I was able also to inspire my friends because they always meet me and say, "You have done a good job at your work and career wise".
>
> *Participant 6, 27-year-old male, 11 years in Australia*

Having positive emotional wellbeing and good health are associated with psychological capital. Participants believed that having employment was good for their emotional wellbeing because it reduced financial stress.

> The benefit of employment is financial and health because of emotional wellbeing attached to employment or finances. So, employment improves your psychological and physical wellbeing. With work, one could support himself or herself with finance or you could support your family members who are going through financial hardship.
> *Participant 18, 30-year-old female, 15 years in Australia*

Living expenses are growing higher and higher in cities such as Melbourne. People have to pay a variety of bills as part of city life. Participants believed that having an income to pay these bills was a big relief of financial stress. Similarly, one could buy and maintain a car.

> The benefit of employment is that I am able to pay my bills, buy fuel to go to school and other expenses. It was difficult for me before when I was living on welfare payments, which are not enough. I was not able to pay for my schoolbooks, but now I can pay for my books for school
> *Participant 5, 20-year-old male, 10 years in Australia*

Providing financial support for family is one of the big issues that people from the South Sudanese community face daily, as many of their close relatives and friends live overseas. A lack of finance to support family members and friends could cause high levels of stress. Participants stated that many people in their community would like to get employment to earn income in order to provide some support to their close relatives and friends in Australia and back in Africa.

A NEW LIFE WITH OPPORTUNITIES AND CHALLENGES

> Employment helps you financially and reduces your financial stress because when you are employed, you can earn income and pay bills; buy things that you need for yourself or to support your family members when they need your help
> *Participant 4, 24-year-old male, 9 years in Australia*

Some people enjoy their lives when they know that they have something to do tomorrow or something they do daily. For some South Sudanese, having nothing to do every day is problematic.

> I am working; I got a job that helped me to get myself up and support myself financially. When I got a job, I know that I have money coming in and know that I am working for myself and not being in Australia for nothing.
> *Participant 10, 21-year-old male, 8 years in Australia*

The power of financial freedom cannot be taken lightly for people with refugee backgrounds such as people from the South Sudanese community. For some, becoming independent can be a significant achievement for people who have never had financial freedom and independence, as many refugees have been dependent on UNHCR food and other provisions. Some participants reported that employment assisted them to obtain financial freedom and reduce other stresses.

> The financial benefit of employment for me is that when I was employed, I became independent because I have financial freedom; I buy things that I want and pay rent on time. I was not having stress because I was employed
> *Participant 15, 28-year-old male, 10 years in Australia*

Feeling valued and included in society are associated with psychological capital for some people. Participants believe that participation in employment made them feel that they were contributing to their wellbeing and community. Similarly, employment gave people a sense of inclusion, compared to some of their community members who had no jobs.

> I'm not a psychologist, but I think there is more than what I just said as social and psychological benefits of employment; it is important that people feel included in employment to participate and contribute to society. You feel valued when you are employed, which is opposite to when you are not employed.
>
> *Participant 18, 30-year-old female, 15 years in Australia*

Employment assists people to have a better routine and something meaningful to focus on in their lives.

> Talking about employment, it is a good thing because when you are working it keeps you out of trouble as you come home exhausted and there is no time to go and see something that may take you in a different direction. Work keeps you busy and you come home a bit tired, but it helps you because you know what is coming in, in your account and that is a good thing to have. You don't have to stress any more when you need finance because money helps you settle down quickly too. [Pause] When you have a job, you have no time to engage with people who can cause you problems. You can only do your job and go home, go back to work tomorrow. But when you are not working, you are more likely to encounter bad people on the streets because you are more likely to walk around when you have nothing to do. When you have a job, you are safe in both psychological [terms] and even from other physical problems on the streets
>
> *Participant 10, 21-year-old male, 8 years in Australia*

Having less financial stress, buying yourself things you want and not needing to seek financial assistance have a positive impact on people's lives. Participants reported that some young people in their community who were not working and had financial problems caused themselves trouble by stealing, which is a crime.

You have less financial stress when you are working and you are able to spend your income on the things you wanted to have instead of waiting and asking someone to assist. Employment helps you to stay away from committing crimes because people who are [not] working, particularly young people, some can attempt to steal or do stealing which is a crime and not good for their future. To me, employment is so important to anyone's life.
    Participant 19, 27-year-old female, 11 years in Australia

I like to work and contribute to the community and myself and in that way, I can feel good about myself.
    Participant 12, 22-year-old female, 11 years in Australia

Social capital

Meeting friends and colleagues in the workplace and outside work are associated with social capital. People from the South Sudanese community with refugee backgrounds often have little or no social network due to a lack of connection with people in Australia. Participants believed that connections in the workplace were one of the benefits that assisted them to integrate into the mainstream community.

Employment can help refugees to integrate easily because it is a great way of connecting people. With refugee communities, employment is the first priority for them because they want to get work and assimilate quickly into the host community through a network. Without employment, how would one integrate and form networks? If as a refugee you are not employed, you feel that you are not given an opportunity to contribute and feel that you are part of the community. It is hard to form networks without employment.
    Participant 18, 30-year-old female, 15 years in Australia

Building social capital through networking with colleagues from the workforce is an incredibly powerful way of integrating for refugees. Major learning and job opportunities are often enhanced through networking with friends, and present and past work colleagues. Social networks are important for sharing formal and informal knowledge that enhances future opportunities and innovative thinking. They also provide learning opportunities for those involved in three main areas: knowledge transfer, support, and generation of ideas.

> When I started my job, I had a friend working in the same company with me. I got work for him there and we quickly became best friends. We always enjoyed our time together and that motivated us all the time to come to work. When you have good friends at work, you always think of going to work because weekends can even become boring for you and that is a benefit of work too, apart from financial benefits. We always had good break times socialising with each other and that was what made us love our work. Socialising at work is great as it makes you think on the weekend that Monday is to . . . I wanted to go to work and meet friends. I have great friends at work and in sport. They say, "Hey, how you are doing?" checking in with me all the time when I meet them, which is great for me.
>
> *Participant 10, 21-year-old male, 8 years in Australia*

Making local connections is very important for people who are new in the community, but it often takes time for people to establish themselves through making local connections. People need support and facilitation to join a local community network and to have the courage to involve themselves in local social activities. Without support and facilitation from the host society to work with people from refugee backgrounds, it is hard for the latter to get into the workforce. Therefore, lack of social capital and networks in the job market is a major issue holding people back from accessing employment.

A NEW LIFE WITH OPPORTUNITIES AND CHALLENGES

> At the moment, I am employed but it took me a long time to get employment. Getting a job is about networking, online cannot work when your names do not match English names, particularly with the South Sudanese people who are badly painted in the media. This makes things hard for us: some people deny us opportunities because we are South Sudanese or of African backgrounds.
>
> *Participant 5, 20-year-old male, 10 years in Australia*

Gaining connections with people outside your community group comes with some opportunities and social benefits. Participants believed that participation in employment brings networking with people outside of her community.

> The social network is very important in the workplace. Work contributes to your social life as you meet people in the workplace, some of these people can become your best social friends
>
> *Participant 16, 28-year-old female, 10 years in Australia*

Participants believed that employment assist people are socially isolated to break a cycle of social isolation in their lives.

> One of the benefits of employment is active engagement with people from work. Work helps to connect people or colleagues to network, which break social isolation and stress. Networking and socialising with friends helps refugees and migrants to integrate in Australia. There are some people in the South Sudanese community who choose to alienate themselves from engaging in active networks or community groups.
>
> *Participant 9, 30-year-old female, 12 years in Australia*

Participants believed that some people did obtain their employment through networking with different groups and different professional workers. They stated networking assisted those seeking employment to access useful information about jobs through their friends.

> Networking is critical because people get jobs through their networks. I would encourage people to seek networks as a way forward to get jobs.
> Participant 14, 23-year-old male, 9 years in Australia

Participants believed that readiness to take some challenges by participating in meetings outside comfort zones could eventually assist people. They stated that networking requires a person to leave his or her comfort zone and be willing to meet people.

> I attended many networks when I was looking for work. I am always ready to take a challenge. I got my job through networking and my personality. It is important for people to take available opportunities and not to be selective when hunting for work. Without that network, it is challenging for refugees to find employment. There is an unemployment problem with South Sudanese and other African migrants. The benefit of employment: there are many benefits when you are employed, especially within a refugee community; you learn a lot of work. Get experience; build your network with people you are working with. You learn about work and of course, get an income to pay bills and rent. It is very important to rent a place for yourself and family.
> Participant 2, 25-year-old male, 10 years in Australia

Participants believed that social connections with people in the workplace often assist people to break the cycle of social isolation, particularly those who are new in the country and have no connections.

> I met many friends through work and we all shared our experiences and cultural knowledge with each other. They learned lots from me and I learned lots from them. Work teaches

you to be responsible because you follow policies in the workplace and under the guidance of your boss.
Participant 15, 28-year-old male, 10 years in Australia

One participant got employment by discussing unemployment situation with friends through networking.

> I got my job because of an idea which I discussed with my friend; I applied for the job and was called for an interview. I was given the job because I had done well during the interview. When you are working, your living standards change because you can be in a better position financially, in which you have no worries about financial stress
> *Participant 19, 27-year-old female, 11 years in Australia*

Participants believed that lack of opportunity is a great barrier to participation in social connection. Having an opportunity to engage with professionals and other members of the community outside your own community group is important for people from refugee backgrounds such as the South Sudanese community members.

> A social benefit of employment is that it gives you an opportunity to engage with people from different community groups. At the same time, you can engage with professionals in the government and private sectors. My work is linked to both sectors, which helped me to understand their work and the way they engage community groups on different social and public policies.
> *Participant 18, 30-year-old female, 15 years in Australia*

Participants who were employed reported that they had accessed both social benefits and financial benefits as a result of their employment.

> It helped me to get financial benefits as well as meeting people and socialising with them. Some people became my friends; sometimes we catch up after work or even when

we are not working. There are huge benefits in working as you can wake in the morning knowing that you have got something you need to attend to, compared with those who are not working.
> Participant 11, 28-year-old female, 8 years in Australia

Cultural capital: learning experiences from employment

Cultural capital is refers to different forms of knowledge, educational credentials and skills acquired by a person which can assisted in life. Skills learned through work and experiences through work are associated with cultural capital. Cultural capital is important to people who are new to a country. The South Sudanese community in Melbourne is a case in point. It is vital to secure cultural capital in order to interact with host community members with confidence. Cultural capital consists of informal and formal learning that individuals obtain through social and educational knowledge within their new community by, for example, attending classes for English language, or learning from cultural orientation discussions with neighbours. Participants of this study believed that people built their knowledge through employment because of the experiences learnt at work. They believed that benefits of employment can also contribute to cultural capital.

> I like working with people; we do lots of teamwork in our team. When you are working you can learn about teamwork which is very crucial in the workplace because without teamwork skills, the workplace can be challenging and people cannot support themselves.
> Participant 8, 25-year-old female, 14 years in Australia

All participants believed that South Sudanese people have come from a protracted civil war, which has deprived them of accessing education, and they appreciate educational opportunities in Australia. They take education seriously as one of the best opportunities they have had, and they do not want to miss out.

> Education is very useful for us: we are benefiting lots from Australia's education. The only problem is that English is hard for some of us because it is the third or fourth language. It is also hard for those who never went to school because there were none or because of conflict, which made them run from place to place.
> *Participant 20, 19-year-old female, 9 years in Australia*

Participants believed that interaction in the workplace with different professionals can be a great learning opportunity for people from refugee backgrounds who want to learn new ways of working in their new country. People from the South Sudanese community are a great example of this.

> Participation in the workplace is a good way of meeting people with different backgrounds and learning from their cultures, and their stories from their previous work which can be so beneficial for you as a worker. It helps you to understand someone who is serious and someone who is rude to you. Work teaches us to leave your personality issues and collaborate with colleagues in respectful ways. You can meet people who are rude to you or to your race, but you learn much how to deal with such rude or racist people in professional ways.
> *Participant 4, 24-year-old male, 9 years in Australia*

Cultural capital can be obtained through work and study, all participants who were working shared their experiences that they had opportunities of interacting with different people through the work, which they described as a learning opportunity for them.

> I am currently working in retail and I have been enjoying working there; something different every day, which I love.

> Something different every day is to meet customers; some customers talk with you on different topics every day. Some talk about the things they want; some talk about the things that are going on in their lives, which are very interesting for me. Yes, there are many learnings at work through interacting with people. Socially, it is a great benefit meeting people, talking with them can be therapy for some people, and it carries a great learning. For example, you could meet an elderly person who can tell you about some of the things he or she has done or talk about their children or grandchildren.
> *Participant 17, 25-year-old female, 12 years in Australia*

Participants viewed education as a fundamental need for their community. They believed that education shapes their future directions, as well improving their social situation, health, and wellbeing. Many have taken the opportunity to engage in education as a way of learning about the Australian system and culture. It is also a pathway to employment, and improves the level of English and social interaction with host community members.

> It was hard for people a few years ago because they were struggling to understand English and to communicate well with others. This is not the case anymore because most are able to communicate in English and have more understanding of social issues and things that are critical in terms of the settlement.
> *Participant 16, 28-year-old female, 10 years in Australia*

In addition

> South Sudanese value education more than other things because education comes with many modernisations such as working for good money. It is good to integrate or be around people who can help you and avoid people who talk you down in terms of education. Education is a way of changing a

A NEW LIFE WITH OPPORTUNITIES AND CHALLENGES

life; South Sudanese want to be educated better and change their lives.

Participant 14, 23-year-old male, 9 years in Australia

Participants acknowledged and appreciated the education opportunities in Australia – to which many of them would not have had access in South Sudan.

> A good thing in Australia is education: you can learn through government payment, although you later pay it back when you get work. I think it would be difficult for many people in Australia [to] participate in education if the government was not able to support people through [the] educational loan scheme.
>
> *Participant 7, 38-year male, 10 years in Australia*

Participants believed that participation in employment can provide skills and experiences. For people with refugee backgrounds, such as the South Sudanese, these learning experiences and skills are very important in understanding Australian culture and workplace policies, including understanding the systems and policies of organisations, workplace politics, and general behaviours of employers, as well as employees.

> I used to work with people from different community groups and I have learned lots of their ways of doing the work and their cultures. For example, I worked with Chinese and Indians in my company. We talked to each other about food and culture, which was good for me in terms of learning.
>
> *Participant 12, 22-year-old female, 11 years in Australia*

In addition.

> There [is] lots of learning in employment depending on your field of work, your role or job description. You can learn about the system, policy in the workplace, connecting with

people. You can always meet new faces at work that may want to know a bit about you or share their own stories with you, which you really benefit from in terms of learning. It depends on the industry: in some, you can learn so much about work and many other responsibilities, which can be used for future responsibilities. Some industries are just about going there, and make money and go [home] at the end of the day.
Participant 16, 28-year-old female, 10 years in Australia

Securing employment mean a lot and can be game changing for someone who have been looking for work. During interview, participants believed that finding employment means a great deal for those have been struggling with unemployment issues for a long time.

> Having a job means a lot to me because I learned lots from work; it is a bit tougher with expectations and responsibilities.
> *Participant 5, 20-year-old male, 10 years in Australia*

Some participants who were exposed to leadership skills believed that leadership can be learned in workplaces.

> I was managing a team and there was a senior manager who came to oversee our works. It was a great time for me working with a team, although I was in charge of making sure things were done in an orderly manner. I always communicated openly and clearly with my team about teamwork and we all got on well. We supported each other in working as a team when someone needed help and you had finished your task for the day. You can help a person who needed help at that particular moment.
> *Participant 12, 22-year-old female, 11 years in Australia*

Participants believed that teamwork and social skills are some of the skills expected from workers in workplaces. Those with very limited experience and skills can benefit from their colleagues by working together and learning from each other.

A NEW LIFE WITH OPPORTUNITIES AND CHALLENGES

> I work in a small environment with a great team; we know ourselves well in terms of skills and strengths. Work can expose you to meet people from different backgrounds and some can be so helpful.
> *Participant 14, 23-year-old male, 9 years in Australia*

Participants described their first jobs as an important step towards their future jobs because of the experience they could obtain. They also believed that a lack of local employment experience is one of the problems affecting people from the South Sudanese community.

> There are many benefits when you are working including the fact that people get skills through work, which they can use for their next job. As someone who worked previously and continues working part-time, I have better employability skills, which help me to engage with people from different backgrounds.
> *Participant 14, 23-year-old male, 9 years in Australia*

Participants believed that dealing with people in the workplace does comes with interesting challenges in terms of behaviours. For someone who is new, it can be a learning opportunity when interacting with people.

> Working is very interesting because sometimes you can find grumpy people and good people, and you learn from both sides. For example, with grumpy people, you can learn to understand that they may have had a bad night and "cannot be bothered." Let me deal with this in a positive way and let them play their grumpy way if they want to continue being grumpy for a day. Sometimes you can treat such grumpy people in a nice way that can change their day and see it in a positive way. In my opinion, it is good to work and meet all different people with different behaviours, which can assist you understanding society better.
> *Participant 8, 25-year-old female, 14 years in Australia*

Participants believed that working in a good organisation (i.e. one with a positive attitude) can be rewarding with professional development that can assist in the next job. They believed that work experience for them is about both personal and professional development.

> Personal development is one of the big benefits that you get from employment because you can learn from people and people learn from you as well. There is a lot of learning in which you can be a teacher at some points and be a student at some points.
> *Participant 18, 30-year-old female, 15 years in Australia*

Participants believed that for people who have never worked in professional organisations, obtaining employment is a good way of learning about policies and workplace communications.

> When you work, you can learn about workplace policy and communication. Your boss can ask you to deal with some issues that need more understanding before you approach it. You may not fully understand it, but learn or read about it until you understand the policy or procedures to manage tasks. People can tell you what you had never heard before and you ask what it means. This can be a learning moment for you at work.
> *Participant 8, 25-year-old female, 14 years in Australia*

Participants described their experience of meeting different people in the workplace as enjoyable because it provides a great learning opportunity for them.

> One of the benefits of working with people is the learning and experience that I got from talking and handling some challenging issues which people seek help for. I enjoyed working and meeting people from different walks of life. Some with great social skills and some with hard or challenging issues in their lives
> *Participant 11, 28-year-old female, 8 years in Australia*

Some participants stated that financial management was another skill gained by those who are working by budgeting their own incomes accordingly. This skill is not necessarily to be learned through working in the finance section, but by being in charge of one's own finances.

> When you are working, you learn how to manage your finances and be in charge of your life. If you are not working, you feel like you are dependent on someone else or government and not contributing.
> *Participant 12, 22-year-old female, 11 years in Australia*

Unemployment, social and psychological impacts

This section presents social and psychological impacts of unemployment from participants 'findings Unemployment is one of the major challenges of settlement for refugee community groups, particular people from the South Sudanese community. Unemployment carries the burden of psychological stress and despair among those who want to work, but are unable get to jobs. During interviews, participants described unemployment as a factor affecting their community because unemployed people were not able to support their families financially.

> Unemployment is an issue facing many people in this community. The government needs to help people to get a job and settle better. People struggle from time to time with many settlement related issues
> *Participant 20, 19-year-old female, 9 years in Australia*

In addition

> When I was not working, I struggled a lot with many things. I was not able to pay bills and books for my course. My living standard was not good; I was not able to buy food sometimes if I wanted particular food and had no money to buy it

Participant 14, 23-year-old male, 9 years in Australia

Participants believed that the psychological impacts of unemployment are largely felt in the South Sudanese community. They believed that people who have been trying their best for a long time to find work without success face a major psychological setback. A lack of sustainable employment has a critical effect on individuals and families from refugee backgrounds.

> To get employment is one of the many settlement challenges with people from the South Sudanese community. There are people who have finished their schooling, but still have difficulties in getting employment because there are no jobs or employers refuse to give them [work] because of some racist attitudes. These people have isolated themselves from the community because they see themselves as failures and others are doing better than they are.
> *Participant 9, 30-year-old female, 12 years in Australia*

Participants viewed lack of employment as a problem preventing the South Sudanese community from progressing. They believed that unemployment comes with feelings of frustration, hopelessness and desperation.

> Lack of employment is a problem that can hold people back and not integrate [into the community], and this can later be seen by small groups of people with negative perceptions about the South Sudanese as a failed or bad community. In my opinion, we are not bad people; every community has bad people and good people and that is how we are, as the South Sudanese community in Australia.
> *Participant 6, 27-year-old male, 11 years in Australia*

Participants believed that gaining employment is a relief for people such as the South Sudanese people in Australia. They believed that unemployment can be associated with mental health problems, such as depression and low self-esteem, because people are not able to help themselves and their family with financial issues.

> Unemployment issue is a problem – holding people back from settling better. When things are difficult or hard for refugees, it affects them psychologically because it was not their intention to face all the challenging issues. They had already had enough from where they came from; they just want to rebuild their lives. Some people cried; they became depressed not knowing what to do, as things got harder and harder for them. Some tended to engage in negative activities such as drinking heavily or experimenting with drugs. This is a result of being unhappy and not settling well. To make settlement easier for refugees, the government needs to provide jobs for them to avoid stress and mental health issues. People who have families and children are stressed because they cannot afford to take their children out for entertainment due to financial hardship. This can cause a worry within families and can sometimes create conflicts.
> *Participant 13, 39-year-old male, 10 years in Australia*

Participants believed that lack of local skills and experiences were among the factors making it difficult for people from the South Sudanese community to be employed. They believed that people should be given the opportunity to gain local experience, rather than employers refusing them work because they have no local experience.

> People are denied employment because they don't have local experience. How would someone get local experience in Australia when they are not given the opportunity to participate? Government and policymakers need to understand and help refugees or people from refugee backgrounds to access employment opportunities. Some people in the South Sudanese community have higher education now, I mean a good degree, but they have no jobs.
> *Participant 2, 25-year-old male, 10 years in Australia*

Participants believed that a lack of employment caused many problems, such as the disengagement of youth in their community. They believed that when young people were employed, their problems decreased because they became responsible people.

> Lack of employment caused many problems including disengagement. Disengaged young people are always viewed as troublemakers, and that is how many African or South Sudanese people are perceived. I know someone who used to have problems here and there when he was unemployed. As soon as he got a job, all his problems disappeared and he became a great man in the family. He is looking after his family very well.
> *Participant 17, 25-year-old female, 12 years in Australia*

The social impact of unemployment ranges from social breakdown, family break-up, and lack of self-care to abuse of alcohol and other drugs as ways of managing the stress of unemployment. Being unemployed does have long-term effects on an individual's ability to support the family and one's own needs and wellbeing. For the South Sudanese, it is almost a duty of each individual to contribute to the family when reaching a reasonable working age. This expectation is weakened by the lack of employment, which leads to dependence on welfare. Participants believed that living on social security payments is problematic, because there were not enough incomes to meet the daily cost of living.

> The impact of unemployment is that it makes people live on the social security benefit, which is not enough for family and individuals. Sometimes people think those who are not working are lazy; they don't want to work. That is not true for many people. People do want to work, but there are no jobs for them.
> *Participant 13, 39-year-old male, 10 years in Australia*

Participants believed that unemployment is linked with homelessness,

A NEW LIFE WITH OPPORTUNITIES AND CHALLENGES

as some experienced homelessness due to the fact they were not able to pay for rent. Young people and some adults have experienced homelessness because of financial problems.

> So, joblessness and homelessness are the key challenging issues in the settlement. People can suffer psychological stress; lack of psychological freedom can lead to self-destruction such as causing people to drink heavily, which is because their minds are not free. They have to find something that can help to deal with psychological stress and drinking is unfortunately not a solution because alcohol is a depressive and habit-forming. It becomes a habit to drink and is hard to get out once you get used to it.
> *Participant 14, 23-year-old male, 9 years in Australia*

Participants believed that financial stress is associating with drinking problems and other social issues such as disengagement and homeless.

> If you are not working, you can face many challenges, including financial stress, disengagement, or engaging in negative activities like drinking heavily. You can become homeless if you are not managing your social security payments. Sometimes, those are not enough for the things you want to buy for a living. Unemployment can lead to crime, especially for young people who are looking for jobs but cannot find them; they tend to do negative activities.
> *Participant 15, 28-year-old male, 10 years in Australia*

Participants described how some refugees arrived with expectations that they could return to South Sudan, even after much suffering because of the war, through earning income. Therefore, when people remain unemployed for long periods, other social and psychological issues kicked in. This could make settlement increasingly hard for both families and individuals.

> Unemployment is not a good thing for people when they are looking for work but don't get it. I know there are many people in the South Sudanese community who are looking for employment. It is unfortunate that people have tried their best to look for work, but there is no work for them. This makes their lives miserable in many ways. Unemployment makes people feel depressed, hopeless about future and wonder why they are in a beautiful country like Australia and still suffer so much from being unemployed. Unemployment is destroying the whole community at the moment because people who are not employed tend to be depressed, get involved in heavy drinking, which holds many of them back from achieving their goal of coming here to have a better life.
> *Participant 14, 23-year-old male, 9 years in Australia*

Participants believed that some causes of family breakdown in their community are associating with financial distress and conflict over finances. They believed that lack of employment in the South Sudanese community led to unhealthy relationships within the community.

> Unemployment creates a lot of psychological stress and tension in families when there is no work and no income. It creates anxiety. Lack of employment has led to unhealthy relationships within the community. There is a high level of family breakdown and financial stress.
> *Participant 13, 39-year-old male, 11 years in Australia*

Participants believed that people from refugee backgrounds, such as the South Sudanese, must seek ways to deal with unemployment. They believed that long-term unemployment has affected individuals, families, and the South Sudanese community at large. For instance, people with a long-term issue of unemployment are more likely to have social and psychological problems.

> The problem is that people don't know how to deal with

social issues. Unemployment is a challenge for us: if people are not employed for a long time, they are more likely to do things that are not good for themselves and community. Lack of work is very discouraging to many people from refugee and migrant backgrounds. People desperately want to work, but there is no work for them. One of the reasons why young people or adults drink heavily is because there is nothing for them to do. They tried their best to find employment, but always failed. They stress and then tend to begin drinking as a way of managing psychologically.
Participant 2, 25-year-old male, 10 years in Australia

Participants see unemployment as the "end of the world", particularly those who have been to school, hoping that when they finished their studies they would be able to find work and earn an income for a better life. When it seems to have become an unreachable dream, it becomes hurtful and difficult to normalise.

Unemployment is challenging and it can be like the end of the world for some people who are looking for employment and not able to get work. In modern society, people go to school hoping that they will find employment when they finish school, or even before finishing. Life cannot make sense sometimes when you are not employed. You cannot make new friends if you are unemployed because you miss out seeing many friends that you would meet at work.
Participant 5, 20-year-old male, 10 years in Australia

Participants raised financial stress as something that could lead to serious issues, such as despair and suicidal thoughts. They expressed that social isolation was related to unemployment in their community.

The main issue facing people who are not employed is stress. Stress is a big factor because people from refugee backgrounds had already experienced many issues in their

lives, and stress of unemployment can lead to depression and suicidal thoughts. People feel isolated and lack of employment can lead to criminal activities. Unemployment brings or causes a lack of self-esteem and confidence.
Participant 18, 30-year-old female, 15 years in Australia

Participants described unemployment as having a devastating psychological impact on families, because people had a very limited choice of where to live and where to educate their children.

The psychological impacts of unemployment are devastating. Find yourself with no income and the Centrelink payment is not enough. People who depend on Centrelink income are struggling. I'm talking from my own perspective relating to the South Sudanese community here. People are struggling with financial issues because they are depending on Centrelink payments, which [are] not enough to address their financial needs. When you have such financial resources, you also have very limited resources; you can have very limited choices of where you can live and where you can educate your children.
Participant 19, 27-year-old female, 11 years in Australia

Participants have described the general difficulties when they were looking for work and their applications are continually rejected. Becoming unsuccessfully when applied for employment is painful and can force some people to consider going back for further studies as a way of preparing for employment.

Unemployment is very difficult and I would encourage people to help those who are looking for employment. For example, you know that there is a job available at your place of work: forward it to your friends and encourage them to apply. I think it is difficult for the South Sudanese, but they need to continue trying by looking around and applying for jobs. When you are looking, you also need to be organised

and ready to knock on doors because work will not come to you without working really hard at it.
>
> *Participant 8, 25-year-old female, 14 years in Australia*

In addition

> Unemployment is a difficult thing to live with, and especially when you are looking for a job and always get nothing as your application is rejected. It is a heart-breaking time when you apply for a job and sometimes receive no acknowledgement. You begin wondering why they have not even acknowledged the application. What is wrong with the application and my luck? Sometimes you learn to be open to any criticism when you are looking for the job. Sometimes you try to contact people from where you submitted your application. They will tell you your application is with a human resource officer and you will be contacted by the officer in charge but that never happens.
>
> *Participant 16, 28-year-old female, 10 years in Australia*

Participants believed that competition in the job market is a particular problem for non-English speakers and especially for the South Sudanese community. They often have not acquired enough or sufficient skills to compete with people who have achieved a high level of skills and education.

> There is also a high competition in the job market. It is hard for someone from non-English speaking backgrounds to compete with an Aussie who's English is their first language. South Sudanese people are easily knocked back in the job market because of English being their second, third or fourth language. I think there is no fairness and justice: people should not be denied work because English is not their first language.
>
> *Participant 13, 39-year-old male, 10 years in Australia*

Participants also believed that job scarcity forced people to take jobs that do not match their skills.

> When I was looking for a job, it took me a while because of the high competition in the job market. It is always disheartening to see people from refugee and migrant backgrounds looking for work and there is nothing for them in the field. Sometimes, conditions force them to take jobs that are not equivalent to their skills. Many have higher education, but they have no jobs in their fields of study.
> *Participant 14, 23-year-old male, 9 years in Australia*

Participants believed that lack of English language and lack of understanding the process of job hunting and networking with the right people in the labour market were among factors impeding employment.

> Factors that cause unemployment within the South Sudanese community are many; they include the lack of skills, lack of English language and not knowing the process of looking for jobs. For example, most work requires you to apply online, which is a major issue for those who have not enough skills in computing or do not know how to apply online. People who came to Australia as adults also have a language issue: their education is very low and it requires a lot of support to learn English to be able to look for work.
> *Participant 13, 39-year-old male, 10 years in Australia*

In addition

> Employment is difficult for our community because of high competition in skills demanded as well as lots of pressure and expectations that our community is not ready for, in term of skills and experience.
> *Participant 16, 28-year-old female, 10 years in Australia*

As evidences of the social and psychological presented in preceding section, it is critical to understand that a community where there is a high level of unemployment, there are always many social problems, such as crime, family breakdown, a high level of drug and alcohol consumption, mental health issues, and lack of education for the younger generations. These are facts in the South Sudanese community in Melbourne, Australia.

There are people who are willing to work and looking for work but are not employed. The historical record of the labour market shows that people from refugee and migrant backgrounds are less engaged in the employment sector. This leads to their community suffering from the risk of exclusion. There are factors behind this that would warrant serious consideration from a policy perspective. These problematic aspects of employment or barriers to employment include lack of local skills and experience, racism, and discrimination.

Discrimination and racism in employment

This section presented issues of racism and discrimination in workforce based on the findings from participants from the South Sudanese community. Their experiences and voices on the discrimination and racism is very important in contribution to knowledge. Employment is fundamental to peoples' lives in the contemporary world with many people hunting for employment opportunities.

In terms of racism and discrimination, it can be very challenging and daunting for people when they encounter discrimination and racism in the workplace. Many workplace laws and policies recognise that discrimination and racism in the workplace are unlawful. Discrimination happens when a person from a different race, culture, or religious background is treated unfavourably or unfairly because of that difference. It also occurs when employees experience unequal treatment due to their possession of specific characteristics, such as associating with certain races or cultural groups. During interviews, participants believed that many people are still experiencing these issues in the workplace in Australia

> People are concerned about racism and discrimination in the workplace and schools. It is a major issue affecting young people from the South Sudanese or African communities. It is like many young people face bullying at school: South Sudanese young people all faced all bullying and racism in Australia. It is part of community life now. People with black skins are easily victimised by racists.
> *Participant 9, 30-year-old female, 12 years in Australia*

In addition.

> There are racism and discrimination in the workplace; this is still an issue in Australia. I have faced this in different ways. I remember at my work, I was told by one guy, "Hi mate, you should not wear black cloth because you are black". This is an example of how racist people behave. When I reported him, he claimed that he was talking about a safety issue and he refused to attend a meeting with me. He claimed that migrants and refugee people "should learn our ways".
> *Participant 2, 25-year-old male, 10 years in Australia*

Participants believed that people some of them have encountered different types of discrimination at work or in the community.

> Racism and discrimination are high in employment. People from the African community or with dark skins are more likely to be discriminated in employment. For example, you can be told straight when you are looking for work that you have no local experience. How would someone get local experience when you are not given a chance to voluntarily work with the company?
> *Participant 11, 28-year-old female, 8 years in Australia*

A NEW LIFE WITH OPPORTUNITIES AND CHALLENGES

In addition

> Racism is one of the issues blocking people from getting employment in Australia. You can easily be rejected, or your application can be rejected because the foreign name does not belong to Australian society. It is easy to blend into American society because there are many more black people in America. Australia has a bad history of black people being treated as unsuccessful in terms of community, bringing up the next generation, leadership ambitions and so forth. Anglo people in America cannot see black people in a racial way because Americans have got used to all black populations.
> *Participant 18, 30-year-old female, 15 years in Australia*

Participants believed that issues of racism and discrimination in organisations existed because some senior managers bring their personal interests in terms of racist behaviours and attitudes. They suggested that some organisations should consider tightening up some of their policies in order to address discrimination and racist behaviours.

> Sometimes racism and discrimination in the workforce is not the organisation, it is a personal interest of those who have racist behaviours or attitudes learnt from other groups. I think the organisation needs to tighten up its policy to ensure that those who hold senior positions should not bring their racist behaviour into the workplace. Organisations should integrate a positive culture and cultural understanding to ensure that people from different cultures are given the opportunity to work [there].
> *Participant 17, 25-year-old female, 12 years in Australia*

Participants believed that some of their community members who managed to graduate from universities and colleges were not able to get jobs according to their qualifications.

> We have graduates among our South Sudanese community who graduated from Australian universities, yet they have no jobs. Sometimes we don't know why people don't get jobs related to their studies, or sometimes we feel like asking the state government why they invest in our youth by accepting them at universities, but in the end, they seldom get jobs in the state sector. This is an important matter [that] needs to be discussed with the government to find ways of helping us.
>
> *Participant 13, 39-year-old male, 10 years in Australia*

In addition

> There is racism in Australia, we hear this word lots; you make some mistake, there are people who say, "Go back to where you come from". There was a time I applied for a job and I was invited for an interview. The guy who was conducting the interview, saw me and got my resume out, called my name and asked me, "Are you sure this is your resume?", I replied "Yes". He said lots of young people from your South Sudanese or African communities cannot work because they are lazy and they don't have experience. I felt upset and left because it was not a good start for someone looking for work to be asked questions like that in the interview.
>
> *Participant 5, 20-year-old male, 10 years in Australia*

Participants believed that some casual conversations could be annoying and upsetting because of an ignorance questions.

> Racism comes when people ask you during an interview or even when you are just socialising with people. "Where did you come from?", and if you say you come from South Sudan or Sudan, the next question is, "Where did you learn English?" These kinds of questions are annoying because people just prejudge that you have no English and you are not supposed to be here meeting me. I think the image of

the South Sudanese community has been badly portrayed by the media because of young people. However, young people are young people everywhere; it doesn't matter whether you are a young person from America, Africa or Australia. They still have issues of young people. It is not fair when the whole community has been judged and labelled as bad because of a few people who are struggling with social issues. I feel that is racism and discrimination because I would like to be judged as an individual and not as the community, I come from.

Participant 16, 28-year-old female, 10 years in Australia

Participants believed that people who face discrimination in the workplace or in public are often left in vulnerable position and confused about what to do in such a situation. They believed that some have no power or knowledge to protect themselves from people who treat them unfairly. They tend to carry a feeling of rejection or being unwelcome in the workplace or in school with them.

I was abused by a drunken customer in public who said, "Go back to where you come from. You are not needed here. This is my country. My grandfather fought for this country to keep black people away from this country." I ignored her because she was drunk, but one my colleagues did not like the way this particular customer [was] behaving. There was general discomfort from people who were listening to what she is saying. She was later asked to leave.

Participant 2, 25-year-old male, 10 years in Australia

Participant believed that people from refugee backgrounds, like the South Sudanese, need support and empowerment in the workplace to know their rights and know how to fight discrimination and racism. Lack of empowerment is an issue. Empowerment helps members of the community to stand up for their rights and to challenge those who are racist in public places.

> One of my colleagues used to undermine my work and treated me badly. She always brought her personal issues from home and behaved aggressively towards me. I tried putting up with her behaviour, ignoring her aggression and discrimination until I stood up for myself. She realised I was going to report issues to the manager. She became friendly to me and worked with me in a respectful way. This came after I confronted her and told her she didn't need to talk to me like this and she needed to respect me as I respected her as a colleague. I said that should she continue in the same way, I would resign and there would be an investigation.
> *Participant 2, 25-year-old male, 10 years in Australia*

Participants stated they have experienced being put down in the workplace by their colleagues.

> Nobody appreciates being talked down to and it is a big thing in African communities when someone puts you down; you have to fight being talked down. It is bad; it is better to be lashed because talking down can always affect you psychologically and can be there in your mind for a long time, while lashing is a pain for a short time and [you] get over it when the pain finishes. Therefore, there is racism in Australia. It is about being honest here; some people cannot be honest by denying that there is racism.
> *Participant 14, 23-year-old male, 9 years in Australia*

As numerous narratives of how participants described racism and discrimination in the employment, as disempowerment and disheartened feelings when people experienced, some participants acknowledged that not all people are racist in the workplace. They believed that only a few people who cause problems to minority groups or people with different cultural backgrounds. They believed also that there are wonderful people who work with refugees and the South Sudanese community and who are not racist, but always want to support people from refugee backgrounds.

CHAPTER 6

Participation of South Sudanese Australians in Sport

Sport is an activity involving physical exertion and skill in which an individual or team competes for entertainment and winning reasons. The current view of sport is generally understood to extend beyond competitive games. Coalter (2005) suggests that sport is a platform for all forms of physical activity including casual and organised participation with an aim at improving physical fitness and mental well-being, forming social relationships or obtaining results in competition at all levels. The Australian Sports Commission views sport as a human activity capable of achieving a result requiring physical exertion and/or physical skill, which, by its nature and organisation, is competitive and is generally accepted as being a sport (see Refugee Council of Australia, 2010). These definitions are also supported by the "United Nations Inter-agency Taskforce on Sport for Development and Peace" that defined sport as all forms of physical activity that contribute to physical fitness, mental well-being and social interaction. These include activities such as play; recreation; competitive sport and indigenous sports and other forms of games (see Right to Play, 2008). Sport is regarded as universal to all cultures regardless of socio-economic and political boundaries. People enjoy sport when it is done in a right way which is free of violence, corruption and other forms of aggression.

There are many types of sports played around the world. For example, there are 8,000 indigenous sports and sporting games listed in the World Sports Encyclopaedia. However, sports commonly enjoyed by refugees with African backgrounds include soccer, basketball, running, wrestling and Australian football (Abur 2016.). What is important in this study is that people benefit when they engage in sport. Sport provides physical benefits and opportunities to network. The benefits of participation in sporting activities include: physical capital, social capital, psychological capital and cultural capital. Refugees often face barriers in both sport and employment. Lack of participation in sport as well as in many other community programmes such as employment and education have contributed too many problems, including dissatisfaction within refugee groups. Lack of empowerment and engagement in strategic activities often result in both refugees and their local communities failing to decide how best to move forward (Abur, and Spaaij. 2016). Young people can drop out from school and become aggressive as a result of not being engaged in relevant activities. This is a clear gap for young people but particularly for those with refugee backgrounds.

Playing sport can be a rewarding experience, particularly for young people. In some cultures, games and contests are grounded in folklore and religious beliefs. The focus is on the young men from wealthy families and society (Abur 2016 and Jay, 2011). Participating in sport is purposeful in many ways. It carries many benefits for the participants. Sport is a great way to have fun with friends, be productively competitive and stay in physical shape. Players can improve skills, make friends and learn how to be part of a team. It is a meaningful and pleasurable activity for anybody that engages in or follows sport. Physical activities and sports are integrally related to their social contexts. As social meanings and power shift in society, the purpose of organised sport activities and games also change (Bunde-Birouste. et al. 2012).

In theory, people choose to engage in sport because of three main factors: (1) a person's abilities, characteristics and resources; (2) influence of significance including parents, siblings, teachers, peers and role models, and (3) the availability of opportunities to play sports in ways that are personally satisfying. Participants may be given an opportunity to take personal responsibility for the creation of a quality lifestyle (Leeann et al. 2013). Participating in sport has been shown to have other benefits, such as gaining employment through sporting networks. Networking is important because individuals in sports organisations often hire those they know personally. This is extremely important in many ways (Alan and Michael, 2013) and can be a great help for refugees and other migrants. This social capital cannot be ignored: it is also meeting people in the field who can be a great help as well as a networking opportunity (Leeann et al, 2013).

Social networking is important in obtaining employment and career advancement. Recent studies have shown that networking is an important management skill that helps professionals to advance their careers (Abur, 2016, Alan and Michael, 2013.). While the theory of practical experience continues in full force as the core of the educational experience, it has become increasingly apparent that an understanding of the power of networking must complement this traditional model (Alan and Michael, 2013). Social networking activities allow opportunities for sports participants to expand their network. Leeann et al. (2013) suggested a positive, direct relationship between social support and the beneficial effects of the intervention in networking. Looking beyond the physical benefits of sports, it also provides opportunities for networking and engaging in a process which can be beyond one's existing social capital or network.

Thus, participating in sport can help refugees and other migrants to overcome critical settlement issues and to integrate into mainstream communities. Sport is among the activities that can promote social inclusion for the newly arrived, disadvantaged groups. Sports provide benefits and greater opportunities for all, regardless of race, colour, religion, age, physical ability and economic circumstance, by connecting people with each other locally, nationally and internationally. Sporting programmes can be one-to-one, in a group, structured with rules and set outcomes or take on a freestyle approach. Structured programmes allow participants to experience consistency and to build trusting relationships within a team as well as extending their level of confidence in connecting with different, mainstream groups.

Benefits of Sport for the Refugee Community

Sport is one of the areas in which young refugees have not been well engaged in relation to settlement strategies, yet there are potential benefits which those young people miss as a result of that lack of engagement. The benefits of sport for refugee community groups are not only through participation by its individual members and a more general inclusiveness; participants and their community groups can increase their social connectedness with people from mainstream communities and such social connections can provide them with different opportunities. Connecting with friends through sporting programmes is a simple but important part of integration. Sport and recreation represent a practical and accessible entry point for addressing the needs of those young people in need. Sport provides links between and within communities (Centre for Multicultural Youth, 2008; Bunde-Birouste et al. 2012)

Sport is well known for its potential in promoting positive societal outcomes and healthy living in term of leisure benefits and connections. Healthy communities are those in which people have physical and mental health fitness. Sport can address some well-being issues faced by socially-isolated individuals and communities as it can provide them with opportunities for doing something productive in their daily lives compared with being couch potatoes all day. Young people want to be part of productive activities such as sport. Therefore, the benefits of sport and recreation programmes in relation to their effects on supporting and building healthy communities cannot be underestimated (Ware et al. 2013).

In some countries, sport is highly valued for its ability to bring people together from diverse backgrounds and to create a strong sense of community and national identity. Sport has many positive attributes in uniting people in diverse communities. Therefore, it has been frequently used by social policy makers and by those involved in community development as a source of engaging the community, particularly young people. These outcomes cover a multitude of policy areas including health, community cohesion and integration of minorities, urban regeneration and crime prevention (Spaaij, 2009; Coalter, 2007). The beneficial effects of participating in community sport programmes and employment for any person (including refugees) are wide-ranging (Refugee Council of Australia, 2010). "Participating in sport can improve the quality of life of individuals and communities, promote social inclusion, improve health, counter anti-social behaviour, raise individual self-esteem and confidence, and widen horizons." (Coalter, 2005: p 4) Sport has been a powerful tool in tackling social issues of anti-social behaviour and cultural exclusion. In some countries, sport is used to integrate ethnic groups and reduce youth disengagement and crime (Spaaij, 2009; Coalter, 2007). Lack of engagement by those in refugee communities in meaningful leisure activities is a major barrier to achieving successful resettlement. Thus, refugees and their community groups can benefit from participation in sporting activities with host community groups. There is a need to engage the former in sport for social development beyond their personal, social connections; it can lead to relationship building with the host community. Engaging participants from diverse backgrounds can provide better integration, building abilities both personal and groups, and links to the host community (Bunde-Birouste. et al. 2012)

Community Sport here means involvement in local sport centres and community centres, and participating in team sports. Some community sports programmes have aimed to bring local people together and provide physical activities and relevant information and advice on a wide range of sports and physical activities to make it easier for locals to get involved and engage in a more active and healthier lifestyle. Physical benefits include improving fitness and decreasing the risk of chronic health issues such as cardiovascular diseases, high blood pressure, obesity, osteoporosis and some cancers (Coalter, 2005). Psychological benefits include building self-esteem, increasing mental alertness and counteracting stress and depression. Participation in sport also assists building social cohesion and reduces isolation, antisocial behaviour and crime (Refugee Council of Australia, 2010). In general, sports programmes can help counteract psychosocial problems and environmental and health issues as well as stress and loneliness. They contribute to physical fitness, mental well-being and social integration by providing a safe forum in which anyone can develop physically, emotionally and mentally.

Gaps in Sport for Refugees and their Community

Refugees carry a number of experiences and significant barriers to sports participation at different levels. Those experiences, and lack of English, can hold them back from engaging in wider activities. This effectively diminishes their civil rights to participate in different levels of sporting programmes and reduces their chances of full integration (Cough; 2007). Participation is often regarded as a good thing as it is embraced by non-governmental organisations which work with refugee community groups, but most of the work focuses on the Anglo-Australian community and overlooks minority groups like refugee groups from African nations and other ethnic minority groups. This trend has been identified by minority community groups but nothing has been planned to champion engaging the refugee communities in participation in meaningful programmes and activities that could help them elevate settlement challenges and integrate with fewer difficulties. Participation can also be an important tool for empowering refugees because this can help them to understand and change negative perceptions which they carry, as well as providing opportunities for increasing self-esteem.

Participation often includes the involvement in planning and decision-making in community development (Cough, 2007). If this is the definition of participation, then refugee community groups are often excluded from such an important process of working with host communities. In many cases, a lack of initiative to engage with the refugee community may be a major reason for their lack of participation. This makes it easy to blame them, the community feeling the refugees are not willing or ready to participate in programmes. Lack of participation and engagement of refugees in meaningful programmes contradict the proud statement of the Government, "Australia has a long and proud history of resettling people in humanitarian need and the Australian Government is committed to helping new arrivals become active participants in the community as soon as possible." (Buckmaster, 2012: p6) Refugees from humanitarian programmes often face challenges additional to those faced by other migrants, which can be underestimated by the agencies working with them or which can sometimes cause misunderstandings.

Refugee community groups are under-represented in organised sport including local sporting programmes. This has not been recognised as an issue by formal sporting associations. The level of involvement in sport by young people or youth groups correlates with their countries of birth. Those born in Australia had participation rates of 27%, compared to about 10% for people born in non-English speaking countries (Centre for Multicultural Youth, 2008). Sport and recreation can assist young people and individuals with language acquisition, provide a positive point of connection with other members of the community and support a sense of purpose and direction for young refugees recovering from the traumas of their experiences or the impact of racism as they are re-settling. At some levels, new refugees show an interest in sport and recreation as a major priority along with housing, employment and education (Centre for Multicultural Youth, 2008).

Research has indicated that young refugees and migrants often choose to participate in informal, unstructured games of badminton, soccer, table tennis and basketball because they have no connection with existing clubs. These sports have often been played by them before coming to Australia and are already familiar to them. (Buckmaster, 2012) It is important to understand that migrants from other cultural backgrounds are more likely to participate in sport in familiar and supportive environments such as schools and ethnic organisations, rather than through unfamiliar environments such as mainstream sporting clubs, associations and competitions. There is a clear gap between club associations and refugee community groups when it comes to general engagement of youth in sport. Therefore, there is a need to engage diverse community groups at all levels, including management. Diversity management is not being adopted widely among local sports clubs and this reduces the idea of a moral imperative to cater to people from different backgrounds (Spaaij, et al, 2014). In terms of diversity management in sport, there is still a long way to go before reasonable and inclusive participation of disadvantaged communities occur in organised and structured sports programmes. Sports clubs and associations should consider safe and inclusive practice by embracing all community groups in their local areas regardless of their ethnicity, gender, sexuality and religion (Spaaij, et al 2014). Sometimes ethnic communities have ongoing concerns about the challenges facing them in areas of social justice, developing diversity policies and implementation. This is an open discourse that needs consideration in both private and government sectors, especially when people are experiencing unfair treatment in sports programmes because of their cultural backgrounds. It is acknowledged that the language barrier is a probable, but not insurmountable, reason for the lack of engagement by community leaders in the management structure of more formal sports associations.

Buckmaster (2012) argued that emerging communities are consistently identified as communities requiring high levels of support and would need specialised services to support them with enough resources. Such groups, often lacking earlier generations of settlers or an Australian-born second generation, generally lack organised advocacy or social networks, have difficulty in accessing government services and may require substantial assistance and time to settle effectively.

For refugee communities, sport can ease their integration during settlement processes. It can be an avenue for creating and building trust with mainstream community groups if they are welcomed and treated fairly. Participants from the mainstream community can be role-models by offering positive mentoring programmes for young refugees. The latter also have opportunities to meet and socialise with other participants which can break social isolation (Birouste et al. 2014). Sport activities are well known to be one the many activities that can bring different people and community groups together through celebration. Regardless of age, people can be involved in organised sport and physical activity as players, participants or competitors, and also in non-playing roles. The latter include: coach, instructor or teacher; referee or umpire; committee member or administrator; scorer or timekeeper, and medical support.

The Centre for Multicultural Youth (2008) suggested that sport and recreation can assist young people and individuals lacking English to build their self-esteem and improve their communication in English through interacting with other participants from English-speaking groups. It can also provide a positive point of connection with others and support a sense of purpose and direction for young refugees recovering from the traumas of the refugee experiences or the impact of racism as they are re-settling.

Sport for Social Change

Sport can ring social changes in the community and in particular the disadvantaged community can benefit much from sport in terms of development and engagement of youth in healthy ways. Sport has become an attractive mode of delivery for community and individual development around the world; however, there is a dearth of research into the provision and management of sport for social change programs.

Sport is a catalyst for change to build capacity and develop healthy and inclusive communities (Sherry et al. 2013). However, one doubts that sufficient efforts in sports management are being made for social change in order to create more opportunities to work collectively with disadvantaged community groups. It is important for organisations to take sport seriously as an avenue to provide those changes. With sport, community programmes can be developed and delivered to marginalised community groups by the sporting organisations as part of their effective engagement with the community.

The only critical issue holding back this social change in sport is the lack of recognition of diversity in sport at the management level. There is no strong approach to the engagement of culturally diverse communities in sport. Australia has a multicultural society: Victoria is Australia's most culturally diverse State with over 23% of Victorians born overseas, coming from over 200 different countries, and about 72% were born in non-English speaking countries. This makes a significant proportion of the population (Centre for Culture Ethnicity & Health, 2006). Thus, there is a great need for changes in sport to accommodate the needs of community groups, including fair recruitment and positive engagement of refugee and migrant community groups in sport. Sports clubs and associations should reflect the communities they are representing. Mobilising resources with a multicultural portfolio may help to meet those challenges and facilitate engagement to assist sports organisations in reaching out to people from diverse backgrounds. (Ware and Meredith, 2013; Sherry, et al. 2013) Good sports programmes can provide safety and protection to vulnerable youth from diverse community groups that are at risk of isolation. The programmes can also provide a welcome relief from daily struggle. For people who have been displaced, who become disaffected or simply disengaged from their community, belonging to a continuing sporting programme or team can be a lifeline, especially in times of chaos where routine and stability are desperately needed and hard to find (Abur, 2018).

The level of social changes that sport can bring to people from refugee and migrant backgrounds includes real life issues and challenges that relate to the dislocation and tensions in the settlement process. These social issues can sometimes be misunderstood as a microcosm of life's issues, but they are serious issues that seriously hold back the progress and potential development of people with refugee and migrant backgrounds (Abur and Spaaij, 2016). Sports clubs can help by providing an environment where people from many backgrounds are welcomed, heard and supported when struggling with social issues (Ware and Meredith, 2013). The good news is that structured sporting programmes can unite people from different language groups and backgrounds by using activities with a common goal. This allows participants to engage at a higher level of participation who could otherwise face social isolation or disengagement (Abur, 2018).

Problems of Sport for Refugee Community

Sport is not the only way of engaging refugee communities to settle more easily: it has limitations which require some understanding and awareness when promoting engagement of sport for refugee communities. Sport can bring different views in communities, both positive and negative. In terms of negativity in sport, racism, violence, doping, corruption and sexism are part of the sporting world and cannot be ignored. Sometimes, there are some visible expressions of aggression and violence in the field (Spaaij, 2013). For refugees, there are risks that too much focus will be given to sport, neglecting other important activities such as education, employment and family. These risks are often perceived by parents who want their young people to focus on education more than other activities. These views are equally important and need to be discussed when it comes to the latter's engagement in sport in order to avoid conflict.

On a positive note, young refugees often show their enthusiasm for sport as their desire is always driven by an aspiration to express themselves, to connect with their peers and to become professional players. Such enthusiasm and desires can be an indication of their selective adjustments of family cultural values to accommodate personal preferences (Spaaij, 2013). Using a sports program to facilitate the integration of young refugees into host communities' is relatively innovative as an intervention strategy. However, it is essential to acknowledge that engaging them in sporting activities can be a hindrance through some practical issues such as transport and costs. These issues can be barriers to participation in sports (Hancock, et al, 200).

Brown et al. (2006) argued that sport should be viewed as a good way to meet people and to establish new friendships, but often their ability to participate is limited by many other responsibilities including school work. Some parents have a strong desire that their children perform well in education and can view sport as a distraction from academic directions. Also, some players have encountered negative experiences in sport clubs, including discriminatory attitudes which have caused some refugees to establish their own, mono-ethnic clubs. This experience of discrimination, aggression and violence on the field can create negative implications for community engagement and resettlement. Spaaij (2013) observed challenges in sport such as discrimination and aggression are some of the many concerns which are holding refugees back from engaging effectively in mainstream sporting clubs.

In 2014, there were many issues with many clubs. It was not a surprise, but it was a big shock for some. Once the game starts, opposing players or spectators respond by name calling: racial abuse was and still is an issue and, although you really want to move on, sometimes it holds you back. (Spaaij, 2013) Apart from discrimination and racial affiliation of minority groups in sport, it can be detrimental to disadvantaged groups because it exacerbates their disadvantage. This critical view is in line with the perception that regards sports as a false front which reproduces inequality by trapping young people from disadvantaged backgrounds into a belief that sport is the ticket to a better life, diverting their attention and energies away from more likely pathways to upward mobility (Messner, 2007; Spaaij, 2013). Although family attitudes to sporting participation are slowly changing as more parents come to value its potential social and health benefits, their reservations indicate how recent migrants and refugees tend to prioritise other means of successful settlement: education and employment. Sport can be perceived as a distraction from these pursuits (Spaaij, 2013).

The downside in some sports includes financial problems. Sports clubs can be very expensive, particularly for disadvantaged groups. While there has been some shift in recruiting better players from lower socio-economic classes to be paid and participate at a high level, there are still implications of violence, discrimination and racism, the effects of bureaucracy, religion and gender implications. Social bonds and bridges can be developed in the sporting context and assist in rebuilding networks in the community that have been eroded by war and displacement. However, bridging social capital in sport is relatively weak between refugee community groups and the host community. It is often hijacked by negative social encounters such as discrimination and aggression which cause and reinforce group boundaries. This makes it hard to access and use linking social capital, which is unequally distributed across gender, age, ethnic, and socio-economic lines (Spaaij, 2012).

The issues of discrimination and racism for minority and ethnic groups still exist in today's sporting activities and cannot be denied. Players from certain socio-economic groups were under-represented in some sports because of economic and neighbourhood differences as well as racial/ethnic tension (Kanters et al. 2012). Young players also encounter challenging experiences which are not always beneficial: they can get hooked up with coaches who are more interested in their own egos than helping young players to grow. Ideally, coaches should be there to facilitate and provide direction for those who work closely with young players and not to practice their individuality which may seem difficult to young players.

Gender Division in Sport Sociology

When it comes to the gender issue in sport, one can see a clear division in terms of the roles that are played. Gender identity is a critical part of sociology understanding in sport. Thinking about gender differences in sport, it is clear that many sporting activities are dominated by men. There are many unexplained reasons why women are often excluded in organised sports. Kanters (2012) observed that women from African, American and low-income backgrounds were more likely than their male counterparts to be left out of participating in sports. At some sports clubs, women are treated more harshly and ridiculed by boys and coaches. In addition, male coaches do more coaching while female coaches are more involved in organisational duties. These are examples of how gender plays different roles in community sports. Thus, participation in masculine sport creates gender identity conflict for females, while participation in feminine sports creates gender identity conflict for males. This is a systemic problem in different cultures in many parts of the world. There are sports typically dominated by boys/men in the contemporary sporting system. This is due to the influences of cultural values and beliefs in society. Families and institutional sports clubs often decide who is best to play in their teams while the family can think about the resources required to support those wanting to participate in sport at a high level. In some countries, some sports are often dominated by males, such as basketball in America and football or footy in Australia. This is an example of how sport has created a division in gender. The level of participation for females is often higher in athletics, gymnastics, figure-skating, netball, and tennis and diving.

A NEW LIFE WITH OPPORTUNITIES AND CHALLENGES

Young people from South Sudanese-Australians love to participate. Sport is a powerful tool for engaging young people in any community. When South Sudanese people arrived in Australia, some had no idea if they would play or see some of their generations playing in the Australian Football League (AFL). Many of South Sudanese people and parents knew about sport was soccer, basketball, and running. However, it was not too long before some young South Sudanese entered the sporting arena and showed their skills.

Over the past few years, the following players from the South Sudanese community joined the AFL with help from their Australian friends who saw their sporting talent and ability. These players include Majak Daw who plays for North Melbourne, and Aliir Aliir who plays for the Sydney Swans. Other young players followed, such as Gach Nyuon who was drafted by the Essendon Bombers, Reuben William of the Brisbane Lions, and Mabior Chol of the Richmond Tigers.

There is no doubt that the settlement of these young people had been very different from those young people in the South Sudanese community who have not been involved in sport. This raise hopes within the community that more of its young men will join the AFL. During interviews, participants who play sport stated that sport has assisted them to settle better and to integrate into the Australian community.

> Sport has assisted me to integrate and settle better because when I came to Australia things were very different until I joined sport. I had no friends before, but now I have a lot of Australian friends and that helps me to settle better and relax. People have supported me in terms of sport and I feel good because of that. I love sport as something that I want to do for a career as I don't want to finish with sport. Seeing good people supporting me makes me feel good and I play better.
> *Participant 10, 21-year-old male, 8 years in Australia*

Participants noticed the progress made by some of their community members in participation in sport. They believed that it is only a matter of time; many young people in their community will eventually become AFL players because of the benefits they have seen through those who are involved in sport. They also stated that some young people in their community are already very talented in athletics and in basketball.

> We have a few young South Sudanese that play Australian football at the moment and it is only a matter of time until we have more young people from the African communities in Australian football. My young brother plays both Australian football and basketball at the moment.
> *Participant 14, 23-year-old male, 9 years in Australia*

Participants believed that participation in sport assisted young people from the South Sudanese community as they were going through settlement challenges.

> I played lots of sports – soccer, martial arts and gymnastics – which made me a sporty person; every day I play sport. Talking about sport, it has helped me as a person in many ways. It is not just about going there to get fit and healthy, it is more than that for me
> *Participant 4, 24-year-old male, 9 years in Australia*

In addition.

> I see sport as an important activity for young people because I have seen the benefits of sport as a person from a refugee background that had no such connections. I was involved in basketball as a young person and became a coach for young people because I know the benefit of sport as an individual.
> *Participant 6, 27-year-old male, 11 years in Australia*

Participants who were involved stated that sport assisted them to define themselves and focus for their future directions.

> Sport assisted me to define myself because sport is very vocal and I was not a vocal person, but I became vocal through sport – basketball now. Sport has put my personality together; you know what I mean: I am now myself. I believe young people with a refugee background can benefit lots if they participate in sports programs. South Sudanese are very athletic people naturally, and what they really need to do is focus a little bit while engaging in sport. I know lots of South Sudanese young people in Australia who now play basketball, which helps them stay off the streets and away from other problems.
> *Participant 3, 20-year-old male, 11 years in Australia*

These preceding narratives demonstrated the benefits of sport for the South Sudanese community, especially social benefits including playing with friends, teammates, and meeting new friends. Those who play or engage in sport make friends, which enhances the positive feelings of belonging to a group or team (social capital). Similarly, active participation in physical activities can come with health benefits, be fun and provide other rewarding benefits (physical capital). People who play sport can achieve different levels of skills and knowledge in the sport field (cultural capital). Finally, those who are involved in sport can develop self-confidence and self-esteem through gaining a sense of achievement (psychological capital). These capitals are discussed in the followings sections.

Physical capital

As discussed in Chapter 4 of this thesis, Bourdieu (1986) refers to physical capital as a production of the social formation, which individuals develop through participation in the field of sport. Participation in sport assists people to develop their bodies and acquiring physical capital is convertible into different forms of capital.

All participants of this study believed that young people in their community who did not engage in sport are more likely have issues, including health issues. They also believed that young people in their community had physical power and the ability to compete at high levels of sport.

> African young people and their communities have physical power and ability to become involved with sport
> *Participant 13, 39-year-old male, 10 years in Australia*

Participants see sport as a great vehicle for fitness and health. They believed that the reason why some people run or walk in the morning and evening is to get fit and gain good health through exercise.

> I used to play basketball when I was at school. What I do now is running and walking every morning just to keep healthy and fit. I believe physical exercise is so important for me and of course to people who want to keep their fitness and health. I think sport is good and there are a lot of physical benefits as well as psychological benefits from engaging in a sport. I believe the South Sudanese young people can benefit a lot, as well as the community and families seeing their sons and daughters playing at any level of sport.
> *Participant 11, 28-year-old female, 8 years in Australia*

Getting fit and healthy are associates of physical capital and many people work hard to secure these benefits. Some participants believed that the benefits of sport were fitness, health, and friendship or connection with people, which helped them in many ways.

> Sport helped me to remain fit and healthy as well as helping me to connect with people whom I built a friendship with. When I came to Australia, I started to play basketball, although I was not good at it at first. I chose to play basketball because I'm tall and my basketball coach recommended that

A NEW LIFE WITH OPPORTUNITIES AND CHALLENGES

> I join this sport. I was a bit unsure of myself at first, but eventually I became a dominant player in the team. I really enjoy this and I have built many friendships through sport.
> *Participant 14, 23-year-old male, 9 years in Australia*

Being physically active and healthy are associated with physical capital and these can be acquired through participation in sport. All participants reported that participation in sport is good for health benefits and social benefits.

> Sport is a good thing that helps people health-wise, engages people by bringing them together and enjoying their time. You could also see some politicians running or going to sporting events because sport is good for everybody. I think our people should engage in sport, young people and grownups, because it keeps them active and we can also contribute to Australian society because we are very athletic when it comes to sport.
> *Participant 13, 39-year-old male, 10 years in Australia*

Participants believed that participation in sport assisted some people to have something to do daily as part of their lives. Many people do sport for reasons like physical fitness and for career reasons.

> Those who engage in sport have many benefits because sport keeps them active. Sport becomes one of the important tasks in their daily routine. Sport helps you personally because you remain physically fit and healthy. You also have a fresh mind when you play. I think young people can benefit a lot if they are engaged in sport.
> *Participant 15, 28-year-old male, 10 years in Australia*

In addition.

> Sport is very important for young people and adults, physically, mentally and even career-wise. When I started

playing basketball, I was not intending to do it as a career, but my main goal was fit, healthy and to encourage other young people who were isolated to do something meaningful
>> Participant 6, 27-year-old male, 11 years in Australia

Participants reported that those who plays basketball and accesses similar benefits, such as physical, psychological and social benefits.

> I play basketball and my brother plays basketball too. We like sport because there are many benefits when it comes to sport, physically and psychologically. First, we know many friends through sport. We hang out together and socialise after and before games.
>> Participant 19, 27-year-old female, 11 years in Australia

Psychological capital

Psychological capital is the powerful combination of resilience, hope, optimism, and confidence to approach daily issues without fearing consequences. This assists individuals or community groups to cope with demanding or difficult situations. The most common way of describing psychological capital for people from refugee backgrounds is resilience: the resilience to cope with displacement, lost, settlement issues and the resilience to hope for a better life in the future. These individuals and families are more resilient psychologically as they have endured enormous challenges and struggles in their journeys as refugees.

However, it is important to acknowledge some level of trauma due to hardship and events that refugees like the South Sudanese have experienced or witnessed. Thus, being a refugee can include long periods of suffering before reaching a destination they may call their new home. Many refugees face desperate challenges when running from their country and in refugee camps. When they have resettled, traumatic experiences often remain unaddressed, which makes settlement more difficult. These are the experiences of many people in the South Sudanese community, if not all of them.

> Settlement is challenging, [and] often adds to the previous challenges of conflict as many of these families and individuals came from conflict with no healing [process]. In some cases, they are extremely disadvantaged compared to normal, mainstream families. Some have no skills or financial capacity to rent a house; they may choose to rely on public housing, which is not enough for large families of six to seven children.
> *Participant 19, 27-year-old female, 11 years in Australia*

Psychological stress and trauma are part of the common issues experienced by some members within the South Sudanese community. The levels of resilience for people from the South Sudanese community with refugee backgrounds were varied. Some of them acknowledged their ability to manage stress, but others were acutely aware of their limitations. Some participants discussed mental health issues where some people break down, as they were not able to achieve their goals and expectations, such as getting employment.

> In recent years, there have been many who had mental breakdowns because of unemployment issues. They tried to look for work, but when they failed to get employment, they faced stress and mental breakdown. I have so many friends and relatives who have faced these [issues] seriously, as they see themselves not worthy after completing school but remain unemployed.
> *Participant 9, 30-year-old female, 12 years in Australia*

Participant believed that confusion and lack of connection with the right people to assist can cause high levels of frustration and stress in the new environment during the settlement journey. They also suggested that those community members who were struggling with settlement and mental health issues to seek help as a way of addressing those issues, including social issues.

> People need to seek help if they are confused and have nothing to engage with. Don't stay with confusion and mental health issues… it is important to seek advice that can help you. There are many people outside who are willing to be honest or help people to move on with their lives by providing advice.
> *Participant 15, 28-year-old male, 10 years in Australia*

Participants believed that participation in sport teaches people some exceptional skills, such as resilience, confidence, hope, and courage to compete with an aim to win. These skills add to the fun and joyful aspects of sport. All these come with positive feelings and courage to do more in sport.

> You must have a certain mind-set when you are playing sport because anything can happen to you, which can destroy your play. You can hear some racist comments directed at you when you are doing well in the field.
> *Participant 10, 21-year-old male, 8 years in Australia*

Remaining positive and motivated are associated with the psychological capital acquired through participation in sport. Some participants saw sporting opportunity as a tool that helped them to focus on their studies by learning challenges and hardworking skills.

> It has helped me in my studies; it is about challenging myself and not to give up. My course is not an easy one; it can be stressful and challenging sometimes. However, I have learnt sportsmanship where I treat everything as a challenge and do

A NEW LIFE WITH OPPORTUNITIES AND CHALLENGES

> not give up. For example, the way I look at my assignment is like when I am doing push-ups. If I can do 10 push-ups today, I will do more push-ups tomorrow; this is the same way I do my assignments. One might be difficult today, but I look at it and say, well, the next assignment may be easy; I cannot give up [on] doing this assignment today.
>
> *Participant 4, 24-year-old male, 9 years in Australia*

Having hope during a difficult time and being able to avoid becoming involved in something that may cause problems for the future are attributes of psychological capital. Participants believed that sport is something that can assist young people in their community to get out of trouble and gain positive thinking. They believed that young people who participate in sport have no time for consuming alcohol or getting involved in crime.

> I wanted those South Sudanese young people who were on the streets to get out of trouble, because sport can help to engage them actively, so they have no time for consuming alcohol or doing other things that are no good. I know sport has helped me to focus on my schoolwork because I know what I was doing when I joined basketball. I was able to think positively and focus on my work because I know that I am going to play when I finish my schoolwork. I had no time for other things except schoolwork and sport.
>
> *Participant 6, 27-year-old male, 11 years in Australia*

In addition

> Playing sport also helps you to be healthy and fit; when you exercise, you are improving your lifestyle and that is a huge benefit of engaging in sport. Also, it helps you avoid some of the unhealthy things such as drugs and alcohol because you become aware of your body's needs.
>
> *Participant 8, 25-year-old female, 14 years in Australia*

Participants believed that experiencing social isolation is heartbreaking for some people and can lead to serious mental health problems if there is no support put in place.

> Sport can break social isolation, which can lead to depression, and depression is a bad thing for those who are not engaged in social activities. You don't need to be the best player to engage [in] sport; you can still come and play for fun. What you get from sport is not just physical fitness or a healthy lifestyle; it connects you with people outside your community or family.
> *Participant 4, 24-year-old male, 9 years in Australia*

Cultural capital

There are a number of skills that people can learn through participating in sport which help them in other activities, such as at the workplace and in socially engaging. Skills such as teamwork, commitment, and personal organisation are some of the skills learnt from engaging in sport. These skills are transferable when one learns or adapts them well. Participants who plays sport stated that they have gained some skills through participation in sport which assisted them during their settlement in Australia.

> When I arrived in Australia, I fell in love with basketball; this engagement helped me to connect with many people. I still play both basketball and soccer. I represented my high school in basketball. I have benefited a lot because when I play sport I always feel that I have learned some new tricks. I have met many friends through sport including my best friend who has a Chinese background. We became best friends because we play together and sometimes talk about sport. I learnt a bit about his culture, he learnt about my culture, and we respect each other as best mates.
> *Participant 5, 20-year-old male, 10 years in Australia*

A NEW LIFE WITH OPPORTUNITIES AND CHALLENGES

Participation in sport assists people such as the South Sudanese to learn skills such as cooperation, teamwork, commitment, and discipline. These skills are attributes of cultural capital obtained through sport.

> I used to play soccer and our friends played better because there was a lot of cooperation, teamwork, commitment and discipline in their team. We learned from those experiences that I need to be committed, get organised, manage my time and be able to work with others.
> *Participant 8, 25-year-old female, 14 years in Australia*

Participants believed that sport provides some opportunities to build cultural capital through participation and young people can meet others from different cultures and learn from them.

> I met some of my friends through sport and we learned from each other. You can also learn lots about different cultures from friends as part of your social network rather than your own community members, because sport is very multicultural and you can meet people and build friendships with different people from different cultures. These friends are very inspiring in many ways because they tell you their stories, and how they manage some challenging issues.
> *Participant 19, 27-year-old female, 11 years in Australia*

Participants believed that there are some tough skills which people can learn through engaging in sport. These skills included collaboration with other people or teammates, leadership and time management; important skills for anybody, but more important for young people as learners.

> Sport can help you lots and you learn about leadership and teamwork skills. You can also learn lots from other players and build friendships. I have met and learned from many players

who played basketball in America. Any sport can help you to define yourself and your goal if you work hard for it. In my case, basketball has helped me lots. You can build your network and friendships through sport. Sport has helped me as a young boy who came to Australia early; I have been around different races, different cultures and spent much time learning about other people and not doing much about myself and where I want to be in the future

Participant 3, 20-year-old male, 11 years in Australia

Participants believed that participation in sport assisted them to gain a sense of belonging and identity as a sportsman.

Being in basketball has opened me up as a sportsman now, compared to the time I was not engaged actively in sport. I learned about teamwork because basketball is not like tennis where you play by yourself. It is something that requires teamwork and skills to work in a team. Sport helped me gain a sense of belonging and to find my identity as a sportsman. I find that I have a sense of being recognised in my team because of my skills and hard work in the team. For my height now, I see that I am not tall for nothing, but tall to contribute to the team and the community, as I would like to be a role model to other young people in sport.

Participant 14, 23-year-old male, 9 years in Australia

Participation in sport teaches young people to learn some technical skills that they can be proud of amongst their peers. All participants who play basketball believed that they learned some manoeuvring skills and rules of sport. They also believed that learning the rules of sport and following those rules does assist people in the long term in their lives.

Basketball is fun when you put the skill into practice. For example, dribble and manoeuvring in the field are fun.

A NEW LIFE WITH OPPORTUNITIES AND CHALLENGES

> Basketball helped me to learn skills and rules in a sport, which is great for me.
> *Participant 14, 23-year-old male, 9 years in Australia*

Participant believed that learning to work hard and take responsibility for what you are doing are positive skills and attributes to cultural capital.

> I come from a family where people viewed sport as a discipline that teaches people a lot of responsibilities and hard work. My mum played sport too. We love sport and I think young people can benefit lots from sport instead of loitering on the streets and causing problems due to lack of activities. Sport teaches you to be disciplined and it is something constructive for young people. I think sport is a great activity that can assist young people to integrate by meeting many other young people from different communities.
> *Participant 16, 28-year-old female, 10 years in Australia*

Participants who were involved in sport believed that sport helped them to learn things they may not have learned at home if they were not involved in sport. They believed that learning sport rules and regulations were positive things that players can use in life.

> I have learnt things in sport, things you cannot learn at home. You learn them when you participate or engage in sport. Sport can really help people to integrate successfully and know each other well. Sport can help young people to settle better. When I came to Australia, I had no friends because I didn't know many people, but I decided to engage in school sports, which helped me to connect with many friends. I got my first job through a friend whom I met through sport. We discussed work-related issues and I told him I wanted to work. Straight away, he advised me to submit my resume to him because he knew his manager was looking to employ someone.
> *Participant 4, 24-year-old male, 9 years in Australia*

Social capital

Sport is one of the ways in which people with no network can access social capital. A lack of social capital can be problematic for some people because it may lead to social isolation and mental health issues. Participation in sport can assist people from refugee backgrounds like the South Sudanese community members to make new friends and learn from the host community, while the latter can learn from refugees when they find a common interest through sport. People may play different types of sport based on their cultural background and the availability of local resources and support. During interviews, participants described the social benefits of sport as community cohesion because of the social connections sport brings to the community, citing the example of the World Cup and the community spirit derived from this event.

> Sport contributes lots in term of building a community. A good example is the World Cup sporting event, which is celebrated by many different cultures. It unites people and brings lots of enjoyment to young people and fans of the sport. Sport can bring people from different backgrounds together and I think if those in the South Sudanese community engage in sport, others will get used to them and the issue of racism in sport will diminish.
>
> *Participant 2, 25-year-old male, 10 years in Australia*

Many people do enjoy community events that bring people together and celebrate common interests. Sport is one of the events that bring people together in the community to watch players and enjoy socialising with friends and family members. All participants believed that when people come together for sport, they enjoy being together, regardless of their different backgrounds.

> Sport helps young people from refugee groups to gain a sense of belonging and participation. I know a group of

young people who play sport – soccer at the moment – and it helped them to form their own small community and enjoy their time together. To me, sport plays an important role in assisting young people to integrate with other community groups because players from different communities can come together and play sport together.

Participant 9, 30-year-old male, 8 years in Australia

Participants who involved in sport stated that the benefit of sport for them was connection with the right people in sports clubs.

The benefit of sport for me has been going around meeting other people from my community and beyond. I meet a lot of friends through sport and people who care about my sporting career, which is Australian footy. I also have many friends in the South Sudanese community who care for me because I play sport and they know me around Australia. I was supported and encouraged by one of the sporting legends; he helped me to join up and meet people with goodwill and encouragement.

Participant 10, 21-year-old male, 8 years in Australia

In addition

I am a great fan of sport; I play netball with girls of my age. We work hard for our team as players and learn lots as a team from our coach. The benefits of sport [are] many; when you play sport, you meet people, network with them and become friends. We always meet on Saturdays and sometimes after school to discuss sports plans and the skills we need in order to be the best players.

Participant 12, 22-year-old female, 11 years in Australia

Being new in the team and in the country required some support by people who are willing to assist and facilitate connection. A 23-year-old male stated that his coach connected him with the team and that helped him to connect quickly in Australia.

> When you join the team, there is always a person who can connect with you. There is always a person with whom your personalities click and this person has to be a coach. When I started, my coach was so supportive in introducing me to the team, and I quickly made friends within the team. All my friends in the team were so good for me; they always supported me and encouraged me to be myself when I am playing. I see myself now as a better player in the team. Having a network of friends is very important because you can help each other when one of you needs help. Friends always protect each other from unfriendly groups. I remember the time when I was a kid; we protected ourselves from other unfriendly groups or kids who were against us, for some unknown reason.
>
> Participant 14, 23-year-old male, 9 years in Australia

There are some an accidental evidences that come with a high level of participation in sport. In this research, participants who play sport believed that people who participate in sport at a high level become famous through their roles in sport. Participants gave an example of one of their community members who plays basketball in America.

> When you become a successful athlete, you can always go to different places, meet different people and become well known. I am thinking here about the South Sudanese basketball player, Luol Deng. He is well known now in the community and is respected because of his achievements in sport. If you become successful in sport, you can also help your community by establishing sport. I heard that Luol Deng has established his basketball academy in South Sudan to help that community. This is just one example of what sport can do.
>
> Participant 5, 20-year-old male, 10 years in Australia

A lack of engagement in some activities for young people can be problematic. Some young people can become involved in crime because there is nothing important for them to do. Participants believed that sport was good for the young people in their community because it kept them away from trouble. They stated that those young people who did not participate in fruitful activities, such as sport, were more likely to be caught up in crime.

> Young people from the South Sudanese community become disenfranchised because they do not engage in fruitful activities like sport. We know that if young people don't have anything to do, they can go out and do something against the law. I was involved in organising sporting activities for young people and basketball is my area of interest and skills with which I helped other young people who want to play.
> *Participant 6, 27-year-old male, 11 years in Australia*

In any society, people who have sustainable networks and relationships where they live and work support each other in different ways. People who have moved as refugees to another country often have little or no network, as they lose their connections when they leave for resettlement. Social capital is about relationships and networks among people, where they live, and where they work. Many people from the South Sudanese community clearly have had trouble in making connections during their settlement period. Participants were able to share both positive and negative settlement experiences. They acknowledged that positive settlement experiences can be achieved through social networks and support from the host community. It is essential that some of the small things that people take for granted can be recognised in order for good-spirited people to continue helping those refugees who are in need of their help. For example, teaching someone to cook rice can make a big difference.

> The settlement is quite different from person to person based on network and support that you get when you arrive in Australia. My settlement experience was good compared

to some people who were struggling with settlement issues. My friends helped me to settle better; I learned how to cook which was something I hadn't learnt when I was in Africa because the boys were not allowed to be in the kitchen as part of the South Sudanese culture.
  Participant 14, 23-year-old male, 9 years in Australia

Participation in community network in any society brings some positive outcomes to individuals in community. Some participants in the South Sudanese community were well aware of the importance of engaging in helpful activities as a way of accessing social capital.

> People can settle well when they put their minds to positive activities such as sport, work and school. Nothing could prevent you from settling better when you have such connections. Finding something that can help you here and beyond is very important for South Sudanese people, and doing something is very crucial for your settlement and general wellbeing. I am spending my time on such things. My involvement in sport will help me to achieve my goals.
>   *Participant 10, 21-year-old male, 8 years in Australia*

Economic capital

Economic capital is refers to money and resources which a person or family own. Participation in sport may bring financial rewards, particularly for those who reach a high level of sport. For example, some sports clubs have the financial capacity to pay their athletes when they are playing in professional sport. Participants who played sport stated that they had secured some financial benefits through participation in sport.

> I get financial benefits through sport because the club pays me and this helped me to get to the games. I had no worries about transport or things that I want to buy for training.

> Therefore, financial benefits in sport are so helpful. You don't have to be stressed when you have money, no worries about how I am going to get there, and whether I have money for the train and so on. I play VFL in Victoria, but I know there are some other South Sudanese who play sport in Australia, and these guys are really enjoying their time playing, meeting new friends and other supporters who like [to watch] their games. My dream is to make it to AFL level and for young South Sudanese people [to] see me and join in. I want to be like Majak Daw and Aliir Aliir. Majak plays for North Melbourne and Aliir plays for the Sydney Swans. This is a good thing for the community and for them too.
> *Participant 10, 21-year-old male, 8 years in Australia*

Participants believed that connecting with the right people through sport has helped some people to get work.

> I got my job through a sporting connection. My friend who played with me asked me to submit my resume. Within a few days, I was interviewed and I got the job because my friend had already discussed it with his manager, as he knew me well and believed in me: that I could do that job. I believe in sport because it challenges you and takes you to the next level. My sportsmanship assisted me to connect with many important people who come to games. I remember when I qualified for our soccer league; many important people came and talked to me.
> *Participant 4, 24-year-old male, 9 years in Australia*

Gaps in sport for the refugee community

There is a clear gap for people from refugee backgrounds in the general sporting community. One of the many issues holding back such people from engaging in sport is lack of connection with sports clubs. It is clear from the previous narratives that they see or know the benefits of sport, but they have no idea where to begin when they want to join.

> In terms of sport, I think the South Sudanese community needs to work hard to address their issues and engage young people in sport. I think parents are not supporting their young people to engage in sport. This is a two-way street; clubs need to do their part in welcoming newly arrived or young people from multicultural community groups in their clubs. Racist preconceptions are barriers to the engagement of young people in sport. People refuse to engage in clubs because of a preconception they will be rejected.
> *Participant 16, 28-year-old female, 10 years in Australia*

The lack of connection with clubs and support from the community as well as local organisations has been identified as something that is holding young people back from engaging in sport, particularly those from refugee backgrounds, such as the South Sudanese community. Participants expressed their concerns and wanted more support in order to engage their community members and young people in sport.

> I think clubs need to be open to welcome these young people from multicultural community groups and to be given a chance to try their best. If they don't perform well, the clubs have the right to refuse. Parents also need to support their young people to engage in sports programs.
> *Participant 16, 28-year-old female, 10 years in Australia*

Participants believed that lack of engagement and connection is a problem in their community of South Sudanese. They believed that their community members needed to engage in sport in order to have connection with other people beyond their South Sudanese community.

A NEW LIFE WITH OPPORTUNITIES AND CHALLENGES

> I think people need to be engaged in productive activities such as sport, work, and music and dance programs to help them get away from psychological stress and isolation. The community needs to stand up for itself and get involved in local activities to help them settle better.
> *Participant 12, 22-year-old female, 11 years in Australia*

Lack of resources is a problem for the South Sudanese community when it comes to participation in sport. Because of the lack of resources to support young people to participate in sport. Some participants stated that government organisations and non-governmental organisations should support their community members to participate in sporting activities.

> We need . . . support from agencies or the government to engage us in sport. Once we get in, we can show our skills and talents. We need to encourage our young people and introduce the sport to them without discouraging attitudes. I would like to see more South Sudanese young people actively engage in sport and work hard as good players in order to show their positive aspects and skills in sport.
> *Participant 13, 39-year-old male, 10 years in Australia*

In addition.

> Sport brings a community together and I want to see African or South Sudanese parents bring their children into the Australian Football League. There are lots of African young people with talent in sport; they can do well in sport. I want my South Sudanese people to participate in sport; we will not go back. This is our country; our contribution and participation are important.
> *Participant 2, 25-year-old male, 10 years in Australia*

Sport as a settlement strategy for refugees

While not the only settlement strategy, sport is one of the many strategies that can assist people from refugee backgrounds, such as the South Sudanese group, to secure some connection with mainstream community members. The findings from participants show that participation in sport assists people to connect with other people beyond their local community groups. Benefits of sport were discussed in different forms of capital. All participants believed that sport is good in controlling their young people who have nothing to engage in, and their participation in sport can lead to integration.

> Sport is so good in controlling young people and engaging them in terms of settlement services and integration. I know many young people who play basketball and soccer from the South Sudanese community: some play for pleasure and some take sport seriously as their career. I know some friends and family friends [who] went to America because of basketball. They are attending a basketball college there to become professional players. Basketball is very strong in America, but I want our young people to be supported here to become better basketball players instead of going to America.
> *Participant 11, 28-year-old female, 8 years in Australia*

Participants who involved in sport believed their participation in sport gave them something they always enjoyed, as well as keeping them busy as young people during their settlement journey.

> I used to play volleyball and I enjoy meeting all my friends that played sport with me. We would talk about sport and different issues as friends. But now I have brothers who play sport, and that has helped lots through their settlement. I also know some other young people from the South Sudanese community who are doing well because they have chosen to engage in sport. I strongly believe that sport is good for young people and is

a good activity to engage newly arrived young people from refugee backgrounds. My brothers play sport every weekend and attend weeknight training. It keeps them very busy and they all enjoy their time in sporting activities. One of my brothers plays rugby and he wants it to be his career. We are all supporting him in the family because sport keeps him busy and away from his wrong friends who are having some issues with drinking.

Participant 17, 25-year-old female, 12 years in Australia

In addition.

Sport has helped me to see things from different angles rather than seeing things from a one-sided view. It has taught me to remain calm, and to take time to challenge myself in a discipline. Sport also helped me to connect with the community, to meet and socialise with friends. Sometimes I may not understand what I am doing, but I can check with friends and talk with them and I learn or get some clarity from them. This is a good way of using your social network and friendships from sport. The friendships you make in sport are the friends who very often you see more than your family. This is really, because you regularly meet them through sport, play with them and spend time with them.

Participant 4, 24-year-old male, 9 years in Australia

Participants also acknowledged the fact settlement issues are very broad and that sport was not the only way of addressing settlement issues in Australia. However, it was good for those South Sudanese who had already decided to be involved in different types of sport.

I am not suggesting that sport is the only way to settle better in Australia; there are many other positive activities that people need to be involved in to make their settlement easier and better. I know many young people and friends from the South Sudanese community who play soccer and basketball.

> I and other South Sudanese Australians who play footy want people to come, join us, and love footy. I love footy so much now, but not when I started.
>
> *Participant 10, 21-year-old male, 8 years in Australia*

Participants provided some reasons for why they believed that sport assisted with settlement issues.

> Our young people should engage in sport to keep them away from problems such as drinking alcohol and using drugs. If they engage in sporting activities, they will not have time to think about negative things that put their lives in challenging situations.
>
> *Participant 19, 27-year-old female, 11 years in Australia*

In addition.

> People need to engage in activities that are good for their health and future. I do see some good young people engaging actively in sport such as basketball. These young people have no time for thinking or engaging in negative activities that have no benefit for their future. I would encourage South Sudanese people to look for work if they are doing studies and engage in sport to help them break social isolation.
>
> *Participant 8, 25-year-old female, 14 years in Australia*

Participants believed that sport helps young people by keeping them occupied and away from things that may distract them from their future direction.

> My cousin plays basketball and all the family are very proud of him. He does not have any time to think or spend with some of his peers who are not actively engaged in sport. I believe sport is a great thing that helps people to interact and learn lots from each other, and so become friends.
>
> *Participant 8, 25-year-old female, 14 years in Australia*

A NEW LIFE WITH OPPORTUNITIES AND CHALLENGES

Participants believed that they have seen an improvement with South Sudanese emerging basketball players being active in their local community. The South Sudanese basketball at Sunshine attracted many boys to play during weekends. This in turn has brought an observed improvement in the community, although some also want girls to play and not be left out.

> I have seen young boys from the South Sudanese community engage well in sport, which helped them in many ways, such as keeping them busy and off the streets. The only issue for me is that I want to see girls engage in sport and not only boys, because sport assists in creating networks and through networks people can get jobs
> *Participant 18, 30-year-old female, 15 years in Australia*

In addition.

> I used to play sport at school but not anymore; my brother still plays sport and he loves it because it has engaged him very well and kept him away from other destructive activities.
> *Participant 20, 19-year-old female, 9 years in Australia*

Participants who were involved in sport believed that sport was not just about playing with registered clubs. It was also about self-care and general wellbeing as people enjoy sport.

> Sport is important to me for reasons including health and psychological wellbeing because it provides opportunities for networking, meeting people who can be useful in terms of support and learning opportunities. My first job, which I got at a Safeway market, was because of a girl I went to school with, and whose sister used to work there and she played netball with us. She helped me to get the job. Anything that creates a network is helpful for people in many ways.
> *Participant 18, 30-year-old female, 15 years in Australia*

Problematic aspects of sports participation

When it comes to participation in sport for people from refugee backgrounds such as the South Sudanese community, there are problems to facing them. Some of these problems including fear of unknown groups, and a lack of financial resources to support those who want to participate. In addition, some parents lack understanding of the importance of sport, as they have not engaged in sport before. Participants believed that lack of support from parents, and an understanding and commitment to support young people to remain in sport was still a problem with some parents.

> Lack of support from parents and the community is a major barrier for many people to engage in sport. Young people, especially from refugee and migrant backgrounds, need lots of support and encouragement to get confidence. Those who are not engaged in sport are like people who are not employed. They have nothing to engage them socially and are more likely to be depressed or engage in drinking.
> *Participant 15, 28-year-old male, 10 years in Australia*

In addition

> There is not enough support in the community for people who play sport. Parents don't support their children to participate in sport and this is a big issue preventing us from being fully involved in sport.
> *Participant 20, 19-year-old female, 9 years in Australia*

Participants believed that young people in the South Sudanese community would like to participate in sport, but their parents at times refused to allow them to participate.

> I wanted to play sport, but my mother always said "no". The only person who used to support me was my uncle who was very young at the time and knew lots about sport. He always

argued with my mum that sport is good for her as a young person growing up. My mum, later on, put her case to me: "Okay, you can only play a sport if you find your way to the game and training; I will not be with you, drive you around to play sports all the time." She also added another condition that she would not pay the fees or for transport. Later I got a job for my sport, but I was also able to do housework, cleaning and washing dishes to keep my mum. Sport is two-way; it needs commitment from young players.

Participant 18, 30-year-old female, 15 years in Australia

Participants believed that the lack of support was linked to cultural attitudes, as some parents preferred their young people to do domestic duties at home. Some young people needed to remain at home to look after siblings, which meant that their time to participate in sport was often taken away from them.

With lack of support from parents and cultural attitudes about sport, some parents keep their young people doing domestic duties, which deny them the chance to engage in productive activities such as sport. The problem with some parents in the South Sudanese community is they never participated in sport and some of them don't even know what sport is or its benefits. Sport is a new thing for those parents who never engaged in sport and it is hard for them to understand and allow their children to participate. For example, when I was growing up, I wanted to be engaged actively in sport, but my mum wouldn't let me because she has no understanding of sport.

Participant 18, 30-year-old female, 15 years in Australia

In addition:

I used to play a lot of sport and my mother disagreed with me all the time because she believes in education not sport. I had

started playing soccer in Africa and I played in many soccer competitions or leagues.
Participant 5, 27-year-old male, 10 years in Australia

Participants believed that traveling to the sport locations was another problem that held young people back from participating in sport. Some South Sudanese parents were not able to drive young people to sport locations. Single parents also struggled to manage their children if they had a number of children in the family without support from other people.

> A lack of support from both parents to help young people travel to games was another issue. The disadvantage of single parenting seems to be holding some young people back from sport because their parent is busy with many other settlement issues. Some participants also mentioned financial obstacles as a reason as to why parents were not taking their young people to sports programs.
> *Participant 18, 30-year-old female, 15 years in Australia*

In addition to Transportation barriers for young people to attend sporting venues

> There is a lack of support from parents; some are single parents looking after a number of children. They find that they do everything for them, particularly those who want to engage in sport, but are often left out because of lack [of] support from their families. One of the barriers to sport is finance. Some [parents] are not able to pay the club fees. The young people from refugee backgrounds and their parents have no work. It is hard for them to pay fees including transport to training.
> *Participant 17, 25-year-old female, 12 years in Australia*

A lack of finance is one problem for South Sudanese parents. Participants believed that financial issues held some parents back, making them unable to support their young people in engaging in sport. At times, the cost was unbearable, as many parents depended on social security income through lack of employment.

> The financial issue is another problem holding our community back from participating in sport. Many people are not working and they cannot afford to pay the fees for clubs or gyms, so people cannot be bothered when they know that it is costing them money they don't have.
> *Participant 20, 19-year-old female, 9 years in Australia*

Racism and discrimination in Sport

The issue of racism and discrimination in sport is something many clubs and associations are recognising as a problem. The recognition began when serious debates were directed to club associations about their role in addressing racism in sport. The racism experienced by the indigenous former AFL player Adam Goodes, and Majak Daw, a North Melbourne footballer and member of the South Sudanese community, has raised the level of awareness on how deep the issue of racism runs in sport, particularly how racism can affect people of colour on sport fields in Australia. During interviews, participants provided examples of their friends who encountered some racist behaviour in sport.

> I have a friend who used to play basketball and he got into a fight with another player who called him a "black bastard". My friend got suspended for two months and the person who called him a black bastard was not punished.
> *Participant 14, 23-year-old male, 10 years in Australia*

People from the South Sudanese community who were involved in AFL have experienced negative language or abuse in sport. A player on the field may ignore the racist language, but the language could affect their supporters and other young people thinking of participating. A 21-year-old male who plays AFL at a junior level with the aim of reaching senior levels of the AFL told of his experience.

> I have been called a name that was not good in or [off] the field, but I just ignored them and kept playing because I was doing well and they knew that I was good and that was a reason for them to call me bad names. In sport, people can say things to you and if you react negatively and hit someone because of it, you will get suspended and delay your progress as a player while probably the name-caller may not lose anything. However, you will lose your game or [delay your] progress because you are focusing too much on negative things.
> *Participant 10, 21-year-old male, 8 years in Australia*

In addition

> I have seen indigenous black Australians being treated negatively in sport. People like Adam Goodes have been called [names] in a racist way while they were playing. This confirms that racism still exists in Australia. Some people hold negative thoughts in their minds, but they cannot say it openly as a matter of law. Australia is a multicultural society and racism cannot be allowed to destroy this beautiful nation.
> *Participant 20, 19-year-old female, 9 years in Australia*

Participants believed that racism will take time to go away in Australia. They believed that it reached to the level which it does not bother some of them anymore in the sport fields.

> I think there is racism, [pause] and racism is something that will not go away for a while yet in Australia. It has been there for years and I have encountered lots of racism in Australia. I have reached the point where it does not bother me when I am dealing with angry people. I just brush it

off and play my sport or do what I have to do. Racism is not about the South Sudanese or Sudanese: it applies to many other cultures, although Australia is a multicultural society. Still, people like me have experienced racism and discrimination. We need to think about the history of black people in Australia, which is not that good at all, but I think people should not react because our reactions can give racist people an opportunity to get what they want. I think you must not react to racists; they are not equal to you and that is why they are racist. There is something missing in their lives, which is why they play the racist card. You should not react to it at all.

Participant 3, 20-year-old male, 11 years in Australia

Participants believed that some sport associations were not open enough to support people from refugee backgrounds. They believed that a lack of engagement and racism were factors that made people from refugee backgrounds, such as the South Sudanese, choose not to participate in sport.

There are a few issues with sport clubs; they lack engagement with people from refugee or African backgrounds. Their talents are often played down and that is racism and discrimination. There is a need for strong advocacy to promote more engagement of young people from refugee community groups to participate in sport. I remember when I tried to engage in modelling; I was told by the agency worker that they don't work with dark-skinned people because it is hard to get jobs at the end [after graduation] with them. People don't take them for modelling shows.

Participant 11, 28-year-old female, 8 years in Australia

Participants recognised the work done in the sporting industry to reduce racism and discrimination. They believed that the government was working hard to reduce the issue, but still more work was needed to promote the positive image of sport in order to attract back those who were deterred by racist behaviour.

> There are some problems in sport, although the government is trying hard to prevent racism in public areas like sport. Still, young people from refugee and migrant backgrounds find it a bit difficult to engage in clubs because they find [it] hard to fit in [with] the big sports clubs. Sport needs to be promoted in a way that can attract young people from those backgrounds. Racist behaviour has deterred young people from participating in sports and this is a problem that needs to be addressed.
>
> *Participant 1, 24-year-old male, 8 years in Australia*

Some participants believed that some of their players in the South Sudanese community were assisted by their friends and coaches from the mainstream community who were aware of the challenges in sport when it comes to racism and discrimination.

> I was prepared by my best friend who advised me: "When you are in the game you must know that there will people who will say things to you, make you react and that is part of their strategy to destroy you or your game." I asked him what I could do to manage such a situation. He said: "If you are playing in the field and you know that you are doing well, do not listen to what they are saying to you. You keep playing well to beat them by seeing you do well in the field, and that is the best option for you to ensure that you hurt them by scoring goals or doing well. When you keep doing well or doing good things, you can hurt people who are racist to you by beating them. Some of them will give up and say, "Wow, this kid is doing well by ignoring negative aspects and does well in the field'."
>
> *Participant 10, 21-year-old male, 8 years in Australia*

A NEW LIFE WITH OPPORTUNITIES AND CHALLENGES

Participants believed that Australia is a multicultural nation with many people from cultural backgrounds, and that South Sudanese people should be allowed to participate in sport without facing some problems.

> We are a multicultural nation: I love multiculturalism. We should be allowed to engage in sport actively as part of this society without problems. It does not matter where you come from.
>
> *Participant 2, 25-year-old male, 10 years in Australia*

Concluding remark

The book has discussed a wide range of issues including settlement experiences, participation in employment and sport. It has provided in-depth detail about the settlement experiences of South Sudanese-Australians as participants shared their settlement stories and experiences as presented in the preceding narratives. Both positive and difficult experiences during the settlement journey have been clearly identified, ranging from difficulties to being in a new place without sufficient support and connection, to the positive experiences of available opportunities, such as education and freedom. South Sudan has suffered from the longest civil war of the Twentieth Century, driving many of its citizens into refugee camps and, given the horrors any war brings, many have fled to become refugees who have resettled in other countries. Australia is one nation that has opened its doors to them and several thousand now live there, chiefly in Melbourne. While Australia is a multi-ethnic nation, reportedly with about 200 different ethnicities represented, many from South Sudan continue to struggle to make Australia home. Because of the traumas suffered by them in war and in the first refugee camps in Kenya and other African nations (where thousands remain), South Sudanese-Australians merit and need further support from the State and Federal governmental agencies as well as from the mainstream communities and, in particular, a changed focus by the media. There are various factors that mean refugees may continue to be isolated and not to feel absorbed into the mainstream communities, even into subsequent generations of children of the original refugees. The results arising from the interviews can be summarised as follows:

Settlement experiences

Settling in new country different to one's own culture and systems is not easy in many cases. Settlement of refugees comes with many challenges including lack of language acquisition and understanding of system including one's right to support services. There was strong agreement that dealing with settlement issues required certain levels of skills and different forms of capital. For example, psychological capital is important for refugees to cope with settlement pressures, which include other issues such as racism and discrimination, as well as family breakdowns due to social and cultural change.

Language

One of the human capitals is language to communicate, skills, knowledge, and experience to engage well with general population. English is a second language to South Sudanese refugees and this applies to their children. South Sudanese languages continue to dominate in many homes because the parents do not have the same flexibility as the young in learning a new language. This difficulty leads to many problems such as barrier to employment and engagement with service providers. It is also leads to inter-generational conflicts between young people and parents. Some parents are more depending on their young people to assist them with English language and to understand the Western cultures and legal expectations.

Education

Perhaps this is first and foremost because it has a direct bearing on all the previous factors and is inevitably linked to them. A greater allowance and provision need to be made for further education that is cross-generational. And within the wider community. Misunderstandings arise between (particularly) "white" Australians and African refugees. This is not helped by blatantly incorrect and ill-researched media reports and statements from politicians who should know better if they are to live up to the claims that Australia is a truly multi-racial and multi-cultural nation. Education is thus a two-way necessity to promote understanding. Further, although some basic grounding in the Australian legal system may be provided to immigrants, there are often conflicts between the new and (South Sudanese) traditional customs and mores which lead to children being taken from their parents by the authorities? Again, if South Sudanese-Australian young people congregate in public areas, this does not mean they are a gang up to no good, but there is evidence that the police seem to target them simply "on suspicion".

Cultural conflict

Simply coming to a new country does not mean that ties to the former homeland are automatically cut. This particularly applies to South Sudanese-Australians. Many refugees originally lived in rural areas and now live in cities, wanting and needing to be supported by their own communities to provide some sense of continuation, particularly until the various traumas caused by war and the loss of loved ones are faced and resolved.

Accommodation

Housing is kindly provided by various authorities and communities, but that often has little regard to the sizes of refugee families which may include not just the parents and one or two children but also other family members and, seemingly due to traditional expectations based on that lifestyle, a greater number of children. More housing is thus needed to reduce the ills that come with over-crowding and unsuitable accommodation.

Participation in employment

Employment brings many benefits including financial benefits, learning and connection with new friends through work. Engagement in employment was seen as a potential source of economic capital, which assists people from refugee backgrounds to overcome settlement challenges surrounding them and their families. Employment was also a great source of cultural capital as work provides the opportunity for refugees to gain workplace experiences beneficial for their future work and for understanding workplace culture. On the other hand, a number of participants noted that a lack of employment had made things move from bad to worse. This was, in part, because refugees originally came with expectations of wanting to re-establish themselves after many years in war-torn areas and refugee camps. When they were processed through UNHCR, some hoped to enter the workforce to support their families financially, both in Australia and overseas, by sponsoring their relatives to join them. Some want to work and put their children in private schools. Some want to work to buy their own home as they are now in a stable country.

The barriers encountered through a lack of English were frequently identified as quite formidable. Other barriers included limited labour skills, lack of education, and racism and discrimination due to some reasons such as being an African or refugee backgrounds. In most cultures, including those in Africa, men are traditionally expected to be the bread-winner. But there was little training available or provided in the refugee camps for widening a skill base and, following their arrival in Australia, the traditional, often rural-based work, no longer served. Hence, training is needed but whether in factories or as apprentices or in schools or technical colleges, language is often a barrier to finding any employment. Further, even when employment is found, there is often some inherent or intrinsic racism, implicit or explicit (as demonstrated in this book) which makes it even more difficult for South Sudanese-Australians to find and keep work and to advance on merit. Also because of this, women will frequently become the major bread-winner and this reflects adversely on the emotional and psychological well-being of the menfolk.

Participation in sport

Many young boys in South Sudanese community love to participate in sport programs such as basketball, soccer and AFL. As part of engaging young people from refugee backgrounds towards settling better, sport can help to assimilate them into the mainstream community and build connections with others. Engaging in sports assists young people (in particular) to enhance social capital because it has a role in helping youth to integrate and break down social isolation. It is also a great source of connection and social interaction with the mainstream community. Sport also helps young people to enhance their psychological capital through gaining confidence and resilience skills from training and coaches. Thus, the benefits to refugee community groups in engaging in sport have been identified in this study through participant narratives. Some challenges were raised as issues of concern, such as lack of finances to access sport, lack of connection with sporting clubs, fear of getting involved with unknown groups, racism and discrimination, and lack of support from parents and organisations. Participation in Sport is not a barrier but will in fact break them down – if appropriate support from mainstream clubs can be provided and promoted. Concerns about language, employment, housing and even racial differences seem to become secondary considerations when participation is encouraged. This of course also leads to further benefits of assisting merging into the mainstream community, improved health, friendship and common goals. Of course, for much of this, financial assistance from the wider community, governmental bodies and NGOs is required but that is repaid many times over with the subsequent improvement in employment, community understanding and mental and physical health of citizens.

Institutional Racism

In this book, it is fundamentally important to acknowledge that there is high level of institutional racism which is currently affecting South Sudanese-Australians. There are common social, economic and political issues in Australia where minority groups are faced with inequality and injustice practices. These injustice practices are very common in areas of employment, sport, health services, schools and other institutions. Unfairly treatment often happens in these institutions to people from cultural background such as African people and indigenous Australians.

As a critical social worker and researcher, I have attempted to raise issue of racism and discrimination in my research and in this book with a hope of raising awareness about issues relating to inequality and injustice. Participants told me that racism and discrimination is something which is inflicted on them or their family members/ African people in Australia very often. In research and academic space, the issues of racism and discrimination are well debated without fear and sometimes well recognised as problems in society which needed more work from both government and private institutions to address. However, there are people in society who used a platform of free speech to attack minority groups. We know that a person could only be recognising the problem with free of speech when you are the victim or close relative or child is become a victim of racism and discrimination.

Community leadership and weaknesses

There are many members in South Sudanese-Australian community who have taken education seriously. Some of these members have acquired high levels of tertiary education in which they attained bachelor degrees, master degrees and PhD degrees. This mean that South Sudanese-Australians are or they will be among highly qualified groups within African-Australian community. However, there are many downside for the South Sudanese –Australians in relation to community leadership. They are among dysfunctioning African community groups in term of community leadership. It is very unfortunate that some people with insecurity and personal problems tend to hijack the community leadership. These hijackers used a very strong negative language that deter capable individuals to consider leadership. We know that there are well qualified and capable leaders who does not want to engage with negative politics in community. Therefore, they have chosen to take backseats because they are discouraged from engaging in community actively.

The lack of good leadership in community also involved some service providers contributing to the leadership problem by failing to empower and strengthen community in better direction. Because of confusion in community and lack of direction, "some service providers" are viewed as they are promoting or playing dirty politics between different groups within the South Sudanese-Australian community. Also, another problem with service providers is that some of these service providers "deliberately" choose to avoid well informed or well qualified community members to guide them or to work with them. If you ask question why? The answer is simple, those who are qualified in community are ideally avoided because their qualifications. Their qualifications are perceived as threat to "some of service providers' workers". Thus, it is one of the weaknesses from these service providers. They probably have a weak leadership as well. We know that weak leadership does not often want to engage with capable or well informed community members. This is a not a criticism, but rather than highlighting some strange feelings about some service providers within the South Sudanese-Australian community in Melbourne and perhaps similar feeling other states in Australia.

References

Abdelkerim, A & Grace, M 2012, 'Challenges to employment in newly emerging African communities in Australia: A review of the literature', *Australian Social Work*, vol. 65, no. 1, pp. 104–119.

Abur, W 2012, 'A study of the South Sudanese refugees' perspectives of settlement in the western suburbs of Melbourne', Master's thesis, Victoria University, viewed April 2014, <http://vuir.vu.edu.au/22013/>.

Abur, W & Spaaij, R 2016, 'Settlement and employment experiences of South Sudanese people from refugee backgrounds in Melbourne, Australia. *Australasian Review of African Studies*, vol. 37, no. 2, pp. 107–128.

Ager, A & Strang, A 2004, *Indicators of integration: Final report*, Communication Development Unit of the Research, Development and Statistics Directorate, Home Office, London.

Ager, A & Strang, A 2008, 'Understanding integration: A conceptual framework', *Journal of Refugee Studies*, vol. 21, no. 2, pp. 166–191.

Ager, A 1999, 'Perspectives on the refugee experience', in A Ager (ed.), *Refugees: Perspectives on the experience of forced migration*, Continuum, New York NY, pp. 1–23.

Ajak, B, Deng, B, Deng, A & Bernstein, J 2015, 'They poured fire on us from the sky: The true story of three lost boys from Sudan', *Library Journal*, vol. 130, no. 6, pp. 107–108.

Akarah, E 2014, 'Sports marketing in Nigeria: Governments' funding and sports development recommendations', *Academic Journal of Interdisciplinary Studies*, vol. 3, no. 1, pp. 279–282.

Akindola, R 2009, 'Towards a definition of poverty, poor people's perspectives and implications for poverty reduction', *Journal of Developing Societies*, vol. 25, no. 2, pp. 121–150.

Aldrich, D & Meyer, M 2015, 'Social capital and community resilience', *American Behavioural Scientist*, vol. 59, no. 2, pp. 1–16.

Allen, R 2009, 'Benefit or burden? Social capital, gender, and the economic adaptation of refugees', *International Migration Review*, vol. 43, no. 2, pp. 332–365.

Allerdice, H 2011, 'The effects of settlement policy on refugee political activism: Sudanese refugees in Australia and the US', Doctoral thesis, Syracuse University, viewed May 2015, <http://surface.syr.edu/cgi/viewcontent.cgi?article=1100 &context=psc_etd>.

Altman, L 2012, 'What does your work mean to you? The international workplace transforming work one conversation at a time', viewed 5 March 2014, <http://intentionalworkplace.com/2012/03/01/what-does-your-work-mean-to-you/>.

American Alliance for Health, Physical Education, Recreation and Dance 2013, 'Maximising the benefits of youth sport, position statement', *The Journal of Physical Education, Recreation & Dance*, vol. 84, no. 7, pp. 8–13.

Anderson, L 2006 'Analytic auto-ethnography', *Journal of Contemporary Ethnography* vol. 35, no. 4, pp. 373–395

Andrews, T 2012 'What is social constructionism?', *Grounded Theory Review*, vol. 11, no. 1, pp. 39–46.

Andriani, L & Christoforou, A 2016, 'Social capital: A roadmap of theoretical and empirical contributions and limitations', *Journal of Economic Issues*, vol. 50, no. 1, pp. 4–22.

Arseven, I & Arseven A 2014, 'A study design using qualitative methods for program evaluation', *International Journal of Academic Research*, vol. 6, no. 1, pp. 417–422.

Asun, R, Rdz-Navarro, K & Alvarado, J 2015 'Developing multidimensional Likert scales using item factor analysis: The case of four-point items', *Sociological Methods & Research*, vol. 45, no. 1, pp. 109–133.

Atem, P 2011a, 'The challenges facing South Sudanese refugees in the Australia's housing sector', *Proceedings of State of Australian Cities National Conference*, Australia, Melbourne, viewed 17 April 2014, < http://soac.fbe.unsw.edu.au/2011/>.

Atem, P 2011b, 'Housing affordability and refugee settlement: A critical analysis of the housing experience of Sudanese refugees and their settlement in South Australia', Doctoral thesis, University of South Australia, viewed 17 April 2014, <http://search.ror.unisa.edu.au/record/UNISA_ALMA51111915410001831>.

Ater, R 1998, *Mental Health Issues of Resettled Refugees*, EthnoMed, viewed 20 August 2014, < https://ethnomed.org/clinical/mental-health/mental-health>.

Atwell, R, Gifford, S & McDonald-Wilmsen, B 2009, 'Resettled refugee families and their children's futures: Coherence, hope and support', *Journal of Comparative Family Studies*, vol. 40, no. 5, pp. 677–697.

Australian Government 2014, *The people of Australia – Australia's multicultural policy*, Australian Government, Department of Social Services, Canberra, viewed July 2015, <https://www.dss.gov.au/sites/default/files/documents/12_2013/people-of-australia-multicultural-policy-booklet_print.pdf>.

Australian Human Rights Commission 2010, *In our own words, African Australians: A review of human rights and social inclusion issues*, Australian Human Rights Commission, viewed 9 August 2014, <http://www.humanrights.gov.au/sites/default/files/content/africanaus/review/in_our_own_words.pdf>.

Australian Long-Term Unemployment Conference 2014, 'Migrant unemployment', *Proceedings of the Australian Long-Term Unemployment Conference*, Melbourne, viewed 27 October 2014, <http://longtermunemployment.org.au/>.

Babbie, E 2009, *The practice of social research*, 12th edn, Thomson Wadsworth, Belmont CT..

Baron, S, Field, J & Schuller, T (eds.) 2000, *Social capital: Critical perspectives*, Oxford University Press, New York NY.

Barutciski, M, 1996, 'The reinforcement of non-admission policies and the subversion of UNHCR: Displacement and internal assistance in Bosnia-Herzegovina (1992–94)', *International Journal of Refugee Law*, vol. 8, no. 1–2, pp. 49–110.

Basel Committee 2008, *Range of Practices and Issues in Economic Capital Modelling*, Bank for International Settlements Press & Communications, Switzerland, viewed May 2015, <http://www.bis.org/publ/bcbs143.pdf>.

Bauman, Z 2004, *Work, consumerism and the new poor*, McGraw-Hill Education, UK.

Beatty, C, Fothergill, S & Macmillan, R 2000, 'A theory of employment, unemployment and sickness', *Regional Studies*, vol. 34, no. 7, pp. 617–630.

Bennett, S & Adriel, C 2014, 'Resettled young Sudanese and Somali refugees have high vocational and educational ambitions despite experiences of school disruption and language difficulties', *Australian Occupational Therapy Journal*, vol. 61, no. 1, pp. 35–36.

Birouste, A 2014, 'Refugee Youth Soccer Development Program (Football United)', University of New South Wales School of Public Health and Community Medicine, Sydney, viewed March 2014, <https://www.dss.gov.au/sites/default/files/documents/ 01_2014/2-soccer-development-program.pdf>.

Bishop, R 2011, 'To be a family: Changes experienced within South Sudanese families in Australia', Masters thesis, University of Melbourne, viewed March 2014, <http://hdl.handle.net/11343/36321>.

Blanche, MT, Durrheim, K & Painter, D 2006, *Research in practice*, 2nd edn, UTC Press, Cape Town.

Bloch, A 2008, 'Refugees in the UK labour market: The conflict between economic integration and policy-led labour market restriction', *Journal of Social Policy*, vol. 37, no. 1, pp.21–36.

Blustein, DL 2008, 'The role of work in psychological health and well-being: A conceptual, historical, and public policy perspective', *American Journal of Psychology*, vol. 63, no. 4, pp. 228–240.

Blustein, DL, Medvide, M & Wan 2012, 'A critical perspective of contemporary unemployment policy and practices', *Journal of Career Development*, vol. 39, no. 4, pp. 341–356.

References

Bonner, A & Tolhurst, G 2002, 'Insider–outsider perspectives of participant observation', *Nurse Researcher*, vol. 9, no 4, pp. 7–19.

Borrero, M 2014, 'Psychological and emotional impact of unemployment', *The Journal of Sociology & Social Welfare*, vol. 7, no. 6, pp. 1–20.

Bourdieu, P 1986, 'The forms of capital'. In: JG Richardson (ed.), *Handbook of theory and research for sociology of education*, Greenwood Press, New York NY, pp. 241–258.

Bourdieu, P 1991, *Rethinking popular culture: Contemporary perspectives in cultural studies*. University of California Press, Berkeley, CA.

Bourque, L & Fielder, P 2013, *How to conduct self-administered and mail surveys*, 2nd edn, Sage, London.

Brannen, J 2005, 'Mixing methods: The entry of qualitative and quantitative approaches into the research process', *International Journal of Social Research Methodology*, vol. 8, no. 3, pp. 173–184.

Braun, V & Clarke, V 2006, 'Using thematic analysis in psychology', *Qualitative Research in Psychology*, vol. 3, no. 2, pp. 77–101.

Breen, LJ 2007 'The researcher "in the middle": Negotiating the insider/outsider dichotomy', *Special Edition Papers*, vol. 19, no. 1, pp. 163–174.

Brown, J, Miller, J & Mitchell, J 2006, 'Interrupted schooling and the acquisition of literacy: Experiences of Sudanese refugees in Victorian secondary schools', *Australian Journal of Language and Literacy*, vol. 29, no. 2, pp. 150–160.

Bryman, A 2006, 'Integrating quantitative and qualitative research: how is it done,' *Qualitative Research*, vol. 6, no. 1, pp. 97–113.

Bryman, A 2008, *Social research methods*, 3rd edn, Oxford University Press, Oxford.

Buckmaster, L & Guppy J 2014, *Australian Government assistance to refugees: Fact versus fiction*, Social Policy Section, Australian Parliamentary Library, Canberra,, viewed February 2014, <http://www.aph.gov.au/About_Parliament/Parliamentary_ Departments/Parliamentary_Library/pubs/rp/rp1415/AustGovAssist-refugees>

Bunde-Birouste A, Nathan, S, McCarroll, B, Kemp, L, Shwe T & Grand Ortega, M 2012, 'Playing for change: Improving people's lives through football', School of Public Health and Community Medicine, UNSW, Sydney, viewed June 2015, <http://www.sphcm.med.unsw.edu.au/sites/default/files/sphcm/About_SPHCM/Football_United_Report.pdf>.

Bunde-Birouste, A 2013, 'Kicking goals for social change: An auto-ethnographic study exploring the feasibility of developing a program that harnesses the passion for the World Game to help refugee youth settle into their new country', Doctoral thesis, University of New South Wales, viewed January, 2015, < http://unsworks.unsw.edu.au/fapi/datastream/unsworks:11520/SOURCE01?view=true>.

Bye, L & Alvarez, M 2007, *School social work: Theory to practice*, Wadsworth Publishing, Belmont CA.

Calma, T 2008, *Newly-arrived migrants and refugees and human rights in the Multicultural Council of the Northern Territory*, National Human Rights Consultation Framework, viewed October 2014, <http://www.human-rightsconsultation.gov.au/ www/nhrcc/submissions.nsf/list/.pdf>.

Camfield, L & Palmer-Jones, R 2013, 'Improving the quality of development research: What could archiving qualitative data for reanalysis and revisiting research sites contribute?', *Progress in Development Studies*, vol. 13, no. 4, pp. 323–338.

Camparo, J & Camparo, L 2012, 'The analysis of Likert scales using state multipoles: An application of quantum methods to behavioural sciences data', *Journal of Educational and Behavioural Statistics*, vol. 38, no.1, pp. 81–101.

Caperchione, C, Kolt, G & Mummery, W 2009, 'Physical activity in culturally and linguistically diverse migrant groups in Western society', *Sports Medicine*, vol. 39, no. 3, pp. 167–177.

Carter, N, Bryant-Lukosius, D, DiCenso, A, Blythe, J & Neville, AJ, 2014, 'The use of triangulation in qualitative research', *Oncology Nursing Forum*, vol. 41, no. 5, pp. 545–547.

Castillo, J 1997, 'Looking for the meaning of work', *European University Institute*, vol. 24, no. 4, pp. 413–425.

Castles, S, Korac, M, Vasta, E & Vertovec, S 2002, 'Integration: Mapping the field', *Home Office Online Report*, vol. 29, no. 3, pp. 115–118.

Chambliss, D & Schutt, R 2015, *Making sense of the social world: Methods of investigation*, 4th edn, Sage, Thousands Oaks CA.

Chau, J 2007, *Physical activity and building stronger communities, report prepared for the Premier's Council for Active Living, Centre for Physical Activity and Health*, Report No. CPAH07-001, NSW, Australia, viewed April 2015, <http://www.pcal.nsw. gov.au/data/assets/file/0004/27679/Physical_Activity_Building_Stronger_Communities.pdf >.

Cheong, PH, Edwards, R, Goulbourne, H & Solomos, J 2007, 'Immigration, social cohesion and social capital: A critical review', *Critical Social Policy*, vol. 27, no 1, pp. 24–49.

Cheung, C 2013, 'Public policies that help foster social inclusion', *Social Indicators Research*, vol. 112, no. 1, pp. 47–68.

Cholewinski, R 2010, 'Refugees, recent migrants and employment: Challenging barriers and exploring pathways', *International Journal of Refugee Law*, vol. 22, no. 4, pp. 683–685.

Chua, C, Lim, W, Soh, C & Sia, S 2012, 'Enacting clan control in complex IT projects: A social capital perspective', *MIS Quarterly-Management Information Systems*, vol. 36, no. 2, pp. 577–597.

Coakley, J, Hallinan, C & McDonald, B 2011, *Sports in society: Sociological issues and controversies*, McGraw-Hill Education, Sydney, Australia.

References

Coalter, F 2005, *The social benefits of sport: An overview to inform the community planning process*, Sport Scotland, Edinburgh..

Coalter, F 2007, *A wider social role for sport: Who's keeping the score?*, Routledge, London.

Codell, J, Hill, R, Woltz, D & Gore, P 2011, 'Predicting meaningful employment for refugees: The influence of personal characteristics and developmental factors on employment status and hourly wages', *International Journal for the Advancement of Counselling*, vol. 33, no. 3, pp. 216–224.

Codrington, R, Iqbal, A & Segal, J 2011, 'Lost in translation? Embracing the challenges of working with families from a refugee background', *Australian and New Zealand Journal of Family Therapy*, vol. 32, no. 2, pp. 129–143.

Coleman, J 1988, 'Social capital in the creation of human capital', *American Journal of Sociology*, vol. 94, no. 3, pp. 95–120.

Colic-Peisker, V & Tilbury, F 2006, 'Employment niches for recent refugees: Segmented labour market in twenty-first century Australia', *Journal of Refugee Studies*, vol. 19, no. 2, pp. 203–229.

Colic-Peisker, V & Tilbury, F 2007, *Refugees and employment: The effect of visible difference in discrimination*, Centre for Social and Community Research, Murdoch University, Australia, viewed January 2014, <http.//apmrn.anu.edu.au/publications/ WA%20refugee%20integration%20report.pdf>.

Collis, J & Hussey, R 2013, *Business research: A practical guide for undergraduate and postgraduate students*, 4th edn, Palgrave Macmillan, Basingstoke UK.

Cook, E & Dorsch, KD 2014, 'Monitoring in youth sport: A paradigm shift' *Surveillance & Society* vol. 11, no. 4, pp. 508–520, viewed February 2015 http://www.surveillance-and-society.org | ISSN: 1477-7487.

Cope, B & Kalantzis, M 1999, *Teaching and learning in the new world of literacy: A professional development program and classroom research project–Participants' resource book*. Faculty of Education, Language and Community Services, RMIT University, Melbourne, Australia.

Corley, K 2012, 'What's different about qualitative research', *Academy of Management Journal*, vol. 55, no. 3, pp. 509–513.

Correa Velez, I, Barnett, A & Gifford, S 2015, 'Working for a better life: Longitudinal evidence on the predictors of employment among recently arrived refugee migrant men living in Australia', *International Migration*, vol. 53, no. 2, pp. 321–337.

Correa-Velez, I, Gifford, S & Barnett, A 2010, 'Longing to belong: Social inclusion and wellbeing among youth with refugee backgrounds in the first three years in Melbourne, Australia', *Social Science & Medicine*, vol. 71, no. 8, pp. 1399–1408.

Correa-Velez, I, Spaaij, R & Upham, S 2013, '"We are not here to claim better services than any other": Social exclusion among men from refugee backgrounds in urban and regional Australia', *Journal of Refugee Studies*, vol. 26, no. 2, pp. 163–187.

Couch, J 2007, 'Mind the gap: Considering the participation of refugee young people', *Youth Studies Australia*, vol. 26, no. 4, p. 37.

Creswell, JW 2013, *Research design: Qualitative, quantitative, and mixed methods approaches*. 4th edn, Sage, Thousand Oaks CA.

Cullen, A 1999, *Unemployment: its meaning and impact on contemporary society*, Doctoral thesis, Massey University, Palmerston North, New Zealand.

Daly, MW 2004, *Empire on the Nile: The Anglo-Egyptian Sudan, 1898-1934*, Cambridge University Press, Cambridge, UK.

Dei Wal, N 2004, *Southern Sudanese culture*, Migrant Information Centre, East Melbourne, viewed 9 June 2015, <http://www.miceastmelb.com.au/documents/ SouthernSudaneseCrossCulturalTrainingReport.pdf>.

DeLyser, D 2001 '"Do you really live here?" Thoughts on insider research', *Geographical Review*, vol. 91, no. 1 pp. 441-453.

Deng, FM 2011, *War of visions: Conflict of identities in the Sudan*, Brookings Institution Press, Washington DC.

Deng, L 2005a, 'The challenge of cultural, ethnic and religious diversity in peace-building and constitution-making in post-conflict Sudan', *Civil Wars*, vol. 7, no. 3, pp. 258–269.

Deng, L 2005b, 'The Sudan comprehensive peace agreement: Will it be sustained?' *Civil Wars*, vol. 7, no. 3, pp. 244–257.

Department of Immigration and Citizenship (DIAC) 2012, *Australia's humanitarian program 2013–14 and beyond*, Department of Immigration and Citizenship, Canberra, Australia.

Department of Immigration and Citizenship (DIAC) 2013, *Community information summary South Sudan-born*, viewed 9 June 2015, <https://www.dss.gov.au/sites/default/files/documents/11_2013/community-profile-sudan.pdf>.

Department of Prime Minister and Cabinet 2012, *Social inclusion in Australia: How Australia is faring: 2012*, viewed 4 February 2014, <http://nsforum.org.au/files/images/files/HACC-Misc/Social%20Isolation/Social%20 Inclusion%20report%20Australia-2012.pdf>.

Department of Social Services 2014, *Settlement and Multicultural Affairs: 2014*, viewed 21 February 2015, <www.dss.gov.au/our-responsibilities/settlement-and-multicultural-affairs/programs-policy/a-multicultural-Australia/national-agenda-for-a-multicultural-Australia/what-is-multiculturalism>.

Dieckhoff, M & Gash, V 2012, *The social consequences of unemployment in Europe: A Two-stage multilevel analysis*, Cathie Marsh Centre for Consensus and Survey Research (CCSR), School of Social Sciences, University of Manchester, UK.

Dimitriadou, A 2006, 'The formation of social capital for refugee students: An exploration of ESOL settings in two further education colleges', *Educate*, vol. 4, no.1, pp. 31–45.

Duany, J & Duany, W 2005, 'War and women in the Sudan: Role change and adjustment to new responsibilities', *Northeast African Studies*, vol. 8, no 2, pp. 63–82.

Easterby-Smith, M, Thorpe, R & Jackson, P 2012, *Management research*, Sage, London, UK.

Eime, RM, Young, JA, Harvey, JT, Charity, MJ, & Payne, WR 2013, 'A systematic review of the psychological and social benefits of participation in sport for children and adolescents: Informing development of a conceptual model of health through sport', *International Journal of Behavioral Nutrition and Physical Activity*, vol. 10, no. 98.

Ethnic Council of Shepparton and District 2013, 'Sudanese Community Profile', *Ethnic Council of Shepparton and District,* Shepparton, Victoria, viewed July 2014, <http://ethniccouncilshepparton.com.au/T/Sudanese_Community_Profile_-_2015.pdf>.

Evans, GL 2013, 'A novice researcher's first walk through the maze of grounded theory: Rationalization for classical grounded theory', *Grounded Theory Review: An International Journal*, vol. 12, no 1.

Fanning, P, & McKay, M 2005, *Self-esteem: A proven program of cognitive techniques for assessing, improving and maintaining your self-esteem*, New Harbinger, Oakland CA..

Field, J 2003, *Social capital*, Routledge, London.

Fisher, C 2013, 'Changed and changing gender and family roles and domestic violence in African refugee background communities post-settlement in Perth, Australia', *Violence Against Women*, vol. 19, no. 7, pp. 833–847.

Forstater, M 2006, 'Green jobs: Public service employment and environmental sustainability', *Challenge*, vol. 49, no. 4, pp. 58–72.

Fox, S & Willis, M 2010, 'Dental restorations for Dinka and Nuer refugees: A confluence of culture and healing,' *Transcultural Psychiatry*, vol. 47, no. 3, pp. 452–472.

Fozdar, F & Hartley, L 2012, *Refugees in Western Australia: Settlement and integration*, Metropolitan Migrant Resource Centre, Perth, Australia, viewed August 2015, <http.//www.mmrcwa.org.au/wp-content/uploads/2013/Refugees-in-WA-Settlement-and-IntegrationFINAL.pdf >.

Fozdar, F & Hartley, L 2013, 'Refugee resettlement in Australia: What we know and need to know', *Refugee Survey Quarterly*, vol. 32, no. 3, pp. 23–51.

Fozdar, F & Torezani, S 2008, 'Discrimination and well being: Perceptions of refugees in Western Australia', *International Migration Review*, vol. 42, no. 1, pp. 30–63.

Fryers, T 2006, 'Work, identity and health', *Clinical Practice and Epidemiology in Mental Health*, vol. 2, no. 1, p. 12.

German, M 2008, 'Educational psychologists promoting the emotional wellbeing and resilience of refugee parents', *Educational & Child Psychology*, vol. 25, no. 2, p. 91.

Gerring, J & McDermott, R 2007, 'An experimental template for case study research', *American Journal of Political Science*, vol. 51, no. 3, pp. 688–701.

Giddins, A 1989, *Sociology*, Polity Press, Cambridge.

Goldsmith, A & Diette, T 2012, *Exploring the link between unemployment and mental health outcomes*, American Psychological Association, viewed 20 September 2015, <http://www.apa.org/pi/ses/resources/indicator/2012/04/unemployment.aspx>.

Graham, D 2015, *Violence Has Forced 60 Million People from Their Homes*, viewed August, 2015 <http://www.theatlantic.com/international/archive/2015/06/refugees-global-peace-index/396122/>.

Graziano, AM & Raulin, ML 2004, *Research methods: A process of inquiry*, Pearson Education Group Inc., Boston, MA.

Greene, J & Caracelli, V 1997, 'Defining and describing the paradigm issue in mixed method evaluation', *New Directions for Evaluation,* vol. 97, no. 74, pp. 5–17.

Habermas, J, Jeurgen, H & McCarthy, T 1985, *The theory of communicative action, Vol 2—Lifeword and system: A critique of functionalist reason*, Beacon Press, Boston MA.

Hadgkiss, E, Lethborg, C, Al-Mousa, A & Marck, C 2012, 'Asylum seeker health and wellbeing: Scoping study', St Vincent's Health Australia, Australia, viewed October 2014, <https://svha.org.au/wps/wcm/connect/cb7b96fc-6653-42ea-9683-749a184d3aed/Asylum_Seeker_Health_and_Wellbeing_Scoping_Study.pdf?MOD=AJPERES&CONVERT_TO=url&CACHEID=cb7b96fc-6653-42ea-9683-749a184d3aed >.

Hamilton, D 2002, 'Traditions, preferences, and postures in applied qualitative research', in N Denzin & Y Lincoln (eds.), *Handbook of qualitative research*, Sage, Thousand Oaks CA, pp. 60–69.

Hammarström, A & Janiert, U 2000, 'Do early unemployment and health status among young men and women affect their chances of later employment?', *Scandinavian Journal of Public Health*, vol. 28, no. 1, pp. 10–15.

Hancock, P, Cooper, T & Bahn, S 2009, 'Evaluation of a youth CALD (culturally and linguistically diverse) sports program in Western Australia: Resettling refugees using sport as a conduit to integration', *Tamara Journal of Critical Organisation Inquiry*, vol. 8, no. 2, pp. 159–173.

References

Harris, A 2010, 'Cross-marked: Sudanese-Australian young women talk education', Doctoral thesis, Victoria University, Australia, viewed June 2014, <http://vuir.vu.edu.au/15544/>.

Harte, W, Childs, I & Hastings, P 2009, 'Settlement patterns of African refugee communities in Southeast Queensland', *Australian Geographer*, vol. 40, no. 1, pp. 51–67.

Hasmath, R 2012, *The ethnic penalty: Immigration, education and the labour market*, Ashgate Publishing, Aldershot, UK.

Hayes, N. 2000, *Doing psychological research. Gathering and analysing data*, Open University Press, Buckingham UK, pp. 134.

Hebbani, A., McNamara, J & McCallum, K 2010, *Examining the impact of 'visible differences' on multiple marginalization of Somali and Sudanese former refugees in Australia*, viewed June 2014, < http://espace.library.uq.edu.au/view/UQ:237420>.

Henning, E, Van Rensburg, W & Smit, B 2004, *Finding your way in qualitative research: A beginner's guide*, Van Schaik Publishers, South Africa.

Henry-Waring, M 2008. 'Multiculturalism and visible migrants and refugees: Exploring the yawning gap between rhetoric and policy in Australia', in *Reimagining Sociology*, Annual Conference of the Australian Sociological Association Conference. Melbourne: TASA.

Hiruy, K. 2009, *Finding home far away from home: Place attachment, place-identity, belonging and resettlement among African-Australians in Hobart*, Masters thesis, University of Tasmania, Australia, viewed October 2014, <http.//eprints.utas.edu.au/8592/>.

Humphrey, L, Kulich, K, Deschaseaux, C, Blackburn, S, Maguire, L & Strömberg, A 2013, 'The caregiver burden questionnaire for heart failure (CBQ-HF): Face and content validity', *Health and Quality of Life Outcomes*, vol. 11, no. 1, pp. 1–12.

Humphrey, M & Steven, H 1984, *Family, work and unemployment: A Study of Lebanese settlement in Sydney*, Department of Immigration and Ethnic Affairs, Australian Government Publishing Service, Canberra.

Hurstfield, J, Pearson, R, Hooker, H, Ritchie, H & Sinclair, A 2004, *Employing refugees: Some organisations' experience*, Institute for Employment Studies, Brighton, UK.

Hussmanns, R 2007, 'Measurement of employment, unemployment and under-employment—current international standards and issues in their application', *Bulletin of Labour Statistics*, vol. 2, no. 1, pp. 1–23.

Inkpen, A & Tsang, E 2005, 'Social capital, networks, and knowledge transfer', *Academy of Management Review*, vol. 30, no. 1, pp. 146–165.

Jick, T 1979, 'Mixing qualitative and quantitative methods: Triangulation in action', *Administrative Science Quarterly*, vol. 24, no. 4, pp. 602–611.

Juuk, B 2013, 'South Sudanese Dinka customary law in comparison with Australian family law: Legal implications for Dinka families', *Australasian Review of African Studies*, vol. 34, no. 2, pp. 1–14.

Kanters, M, Bocarro, J, Edwards, M, Casper, J & Floyd, M 2013, 'School sport participation under two school sport policies: Comparisons by race/ethnicity, gender, and socioeconomic status', *Annals of Behavioural Medicine*, vol. 45, no. 1, pp. 113–121.

Kebbede, G 1997, 'Sudan: The north-south conflict in historical perspective', *Contributions in Black Studies*, vol. 15, no. 1, pp. 1–31.

Keogh, V. 2002. *Multicultural sport: Sustaining a level playing field*. Centre for Multicultural Youth Issues, Melbourne, Victoria.

Kevlihan, R 2013, 'Providing health services during a civil war: The experience of a garrison town in South Sudan', *Disasters*, vol. 37, no. 4, pp. 579–603.

Kornspan, A & Duve, M 2013, 'Networking in sport management: Ideas and activities to enhance student engagement and career development', *Sport Management International Journal*, vol. 9, no. 1, pp. 1–19.

Krahn, H, Howard, A & Galambos, N 2015, 'Exploring or floundering? The meaning of employment and educational fluctuations in emerging adulthood', *Youth and Society*, vol. 47, no. 2, pp. 245–266.

Krulfeld, R 1994, *Reconstructing lives, recapturing meaning: Refugee identity, gender, and cultural change*, Taylor & Francis, Amsterdam.

Lambert, C, Jomeen, J & McSherry, W 2010, 'Reflexivity: a review of the literature in the context of midwifery research', *British Journal of Midwifery*, vol. 18, no. 5, pp. 321.

Lamont, M & Lareau, A 1988, 'Cultural capital: Allusions, gaps and glissandos in recent theoretical developments', *Sociological Theory*, vol. 6, no. 2, pp. 153–168.

Lawlor, J & Perkins, D 2009, 'Integrated support to overcome severe employment barriers: adapting the IPS approach', Brotherhood of St Laurence, Melbourne, Australia, viewed October 2014, < http://library.bsl.org.au/jspui/bitstream/1/1367/1/ Lawlor&Perkins_Integrated_support_employment_barriers.pdf>.

Lejukole, J 2008, '"We will do it our own way": A perspective of Southern Sudanese refugees resettlement experiences in Australian society', Doctoral thesis, The University of Adelaide, South Australia, viewed September 2014, <http://hdl.handle.net/2440/57097>.

Lewig, K, Arney, F & Salveron, M 2010, 'Challenges of parenting in a new culture: Implications for child and family welfare', *Evaluation and Program Planning*, vol. 33, no. 3, pp. 324–332.

Lichtman, M 2013, *Qualitative research in education: A user's guide*, Sage, Thousand Oaks CA.

Lin, N, 1999, 'Building a network theory of social capital', *Connections*, vol. 22, no. 1, pp. 28–51.

References

Lin, N. 2002, *Social capital: A theory of social structure and action*, Cambridge University Press, UK.

Lindley, A 2006, 'Researching conflict in Africa: Insights and experiences, edited by Elisabeth Porter, Gillian Robinson, Marie Smyth, Albrecht Schnabel and Eghosa Osaghae – review', *Journal of Refugee Studies*, vol. 19, no. 2, pp. 260–262.

Luthans F, Youssef, CM 2004, 'Human, social, and now positive psychological capital management', *Organizational Dynamics*, vol. 33, no. 1, pp. 143–160.

Luthans, F, Youssef, C & Avolio, B 2007, *Psychological capital: Developing the human competitive edge*, Oxford University Press, New York NY.

Luthans, F, Avolio, BJ, Avey, JB & Norman, SM 2007 *Positive psychological capital: Measurement and relationship with performance and satisfaction*, Leadership Institute Faculty Publications, Paper 11. Viewed 24 January 2017 <http://digitalcommons.unl.edu/leadershipfacpub/11>.

MacDonald, F, Kyle, L, Doughney, J & Pyke, J 2004, 'Refugees in the labour market: Looking for cost-effective models of assistance', *Migration Action*, vol. 26, no. 1, pp. 18–24.

Madden, R 2010, *Being ethnographic: A guide to the theory and practice of ethnography*, Sage, London UK.

Major, J, Wilkinson, J, Langat, K & Santoro, N 2013, 'Sudanese young people of refugee background in rural and regional Australia: Social capital and education success', *Australian and International Journal of Rural Education*, vol. 23, no. 3, pp. 95–105.

Makol, J 2012, *The Dinka Twï: Who is this tribe really? 48HrBooks*, New York, US.

Mamer, A 2010, 'Sudanese refugee, lived experiences: impact on their resettlement outcomes in New Zealand,' Masters thesis, Auckland University of Technology, New Zealand, viewed April 2014, < http://hdl.handle.net/10292/4697>.

Marivoet, S 2014, 'Challenge of sport towards social inclusion and awareness-raising against any discrimination', *Physical Culture and Sport, Studies and Research*, vol. 63, no. 1, pp. 3–11.

Marlowe, J 2010, '"Walking the line": Southern Sudanese narratives and responding to trauma', Doctoral thesis, Flinders University, South Australia, viewed March 2014, <http://hdl.handle.net/2292/21826 >.

Marlowe, J 2011a, 'South Sudanese diaspora in Australasia', *Australasian Review of African Studies*, vol. 32, no. 2, pp. 1–9.

Marlowe, J 2011b, '"Walking the line": Southern Sudanese masculinities and reconciling one's past with the present', *Ethnicities*, vol. 12, no. 1, pp. 50–66.

Marlowe, J, Harris, A & Lyons, T (eds.) 2014, *South Sudanese diaspora in Australia and New Zealand: Reconciling the past with the present*, Cambridge Scholars Publishing, Newcastle upon Tyne, UK.

McClelland, A & Macdonald, F 1998, 'The social consequences of unemployment', *Business Council of Australia*, Melbourne, Australia, viewed January 2014, <http://library.bsl.org.au/jspui/bitstream/1/266/1/social_consequences_of_unemployment_AMcClelland.pdf>.

McDonald, B, Gifford, S, Webster, K, Wiseman, J & Casey, S 2008, *Refugee resettlement in regional and rural Victoria: Impacts and policy issues*, Refugee Research Health Centre, La Trobe University, Australia, viewed May 2014, <http://library.bsl.org.au/jspui/bitstream/1/977/1/RefugeeResettlement_Report_Mar08.pdf >.

Mertens, D 1998, *Research methods in education and psychology: Integrating diversity with quantitative & qualitative approaches*, Sage, Thousand Oaks CA.

Messner, M 2007, *Out of play: Critical essays on gender and sport*, State University of New York Press, Albany, NY.

Mikkonen, J & Raphael, D 2010, *Social determinants of health: The Canadian facts*, York University, School of Health Policy and Management, Toronto, viewed April 2015, < http.//www.thecanadianfacts.org/the_canadian_facts.pdf>.

Mills, J, Bonner, A & Francis, K 2006, 'The development of constructivist grounded theory', *International Journal of Qualitative Methods*, vol. 5, no. 1, pp. 25–35.

Milos, D 2011, 'South Sudanese communities and Australian family law: A clash of systems', *Australasian Review of African Studies*, vol. 32, no. 2, p. 143–159.

Mohiuddin, M 2012, 'An empirical investigation into audit committee practices in Bangladesh: The case of companies listed on the Dhaka stock exchange (DSE),' Doctoral thesis, Cardiff University, United Kingdom, viewed August 2015, < http://orca.cf.ac.uk/18764/ >.

Morin, E 2004, 'The meaning of work in modern times', 10th World Congress on Human Resources Management, Rio de Janeiro, Brazil, <http://web.hec.ca/criteos/fichiers/upload/MOW_in_MTimes_EMM200804.pdf>.

Mungai, N 2008, 'Young Sudanese men experiences of racism in Melbourne', in *Building a common future – Africa and Australasia"*, African Studies Association of Australasia and the Pacific 31st Conference (AFSAAP), Melbourne, viewed February 2014, < http://afsaap.org.au/assets/Ndungi.pdf>.

Murphy, G & Athanasou, J 1999, 'The effect of unemployment on mental health', *Journal of Occupational and Organizational Psychology*, vol. 72, no. 1, pp. 83–99.

Nash, M, Wong, J & Trlin, A 2006, 'Civic and social integration: A new field of social work practice with immigrants, refugees and asylum seekers', *International Social Work*, vol. 49, no. 3, pp. 345–363.

Neuman, WL 2006, *Social research methods: Qualitative and quantitative approaches*, Pearson Education, New York NY.

Newman I & Benz, C 1998, *Qualitative-quantitative research methodology: exploring the interactive continuum*, Southern Illinois University Press, Carbondale, IL.

References

Nicholl, C & Thompson, A 2004, 'The psychological treatment of post-traumatic stress disorder (PTSD) in adult refugees: A review of the current state of psychological therapies', *Journal of Mental Health,* vol. 13, no. 4, pp. 351–362.

O'Connor, S 2014, *Linguistic socialization in the refugee assimilation process: Transmitting cultural capital for self-sufficiency,* Trinity University, America, viewed December 2015, <http://digitalcommons.trinity.edu/infolit_usra/17>.

Olliff, L 2008, 'Playing for the future: the role of sport and recreation in supporting refugee young people to "settle well" in Australia', *Youth Studies Australia,* vol. 27, no. 1, pp. 52.

Oppenheim, A 2000, *Questionnaire design, interviewing and attitude measurement,* 2nd edn., Continuum, London, UK.

Pace, S, 2012 Writing the self into research: Using grounded theory analytic strategies in auto-ethnography, TEXT Special Issue Website Series 13, viewed on 11 January, 2017 <http://www.textjournal.com.au/speciss/issue13/Pace.pdf>.

Palinkas, L, Horwitz, S, Green, C, Wisdom, J, Duan, N & Hoagwood, K 2015, 'Purposeful sampling of qualitative data collection and analysis in mixed methods implementation research', *Administration and Policy in Mental Health and Mental Health Services Research,* vol. 42, no. 5, pp. 533–544.

Parker I 1999, 'Critical reflexive humanism and critical constructionist psychology', in D Nightingale & J Cromby (eds.), *Social constructionist psychology: A critical analysis of theory and practice.* 1st edn., Open University Press, Buckingham UK, pp. 23–36.

Pascual, E 2008, 'Text for context, trial for trialogue: An ethnographic study of a fictive interaction blend', *Annual Review of Cognitive Linguistics,* vol. 6, no. 1, pp. 50–82.

Paul, K & Moser, K 2009, 'Unemployment impairs mental health: Meta-analyses', *Journal of Vocational Behaviour,* vol. 74, no. 3, pp. 264–282.

Payne, R & Graham, J 1987, 'Social class and re employment: Changes in health and perceived financial circumstances', *Journal of Organizational Behaviour,* vol. 8, no. 2, pp. 175–184.

Peterson, R 2000, *Constructing effective questionnaires,* Sage, Thousand Oaks CA.

Pisano, M 1995 'Federal policy and community involvement, Responding to national economic and social trends', *National Civic Review,* vol. 84, no. 1, pp. 30–36.

Polatci, S & Akdo an, A 2014, 'Psychological capital and performance: The mediating role of work, family spillover and psychological well-being', *Business and Economics Research Journal,* vol. 5, no. 1, pp. 1–15.

Punch, K 2013, *Introduction to social research: Quantitative and qualitative approaches,* 3rd edn, Sage, Thousand Oaks CA.

Putnam, R 1995, 'Bowling alone: America's declining social capital', *Journal of Democracy,* vol. 6, no. 1, pp. 65–78.

Putnam, R 1998, 'Foreword to social capital: Its importance of housing and community development', *Housing Policy Debate*, vol. 9, no. 1, pp. 1–215.

Putnam, R 2001, *Bowling alone: The collapse and revival of American community*, Simon & Schuster, New York NY.

Refugee Council of Australia (2011) *Australia's refugee and humanitarian program 2011-12: Community views on current challenges and future directions*, Refugee Council of Australia, <http://www.refugeecouncil.org.au/r/isub/2011-12-IntakeSub-exec.pdf>.

Refugee Council of Australia 2010, *Economic, civic and social contributions of refugees and humanitarian entrants—a literature review*, Refugee Council of Australia, Surry Hills Australia.

Refugee Resettlement Working Group 1994, *Refugee resettlement: Let's get it right in Australia! A blueprint for refugee resettlement services in Australia*, Refugee Resettlement Working Group, Camperdown Australia.

Renzaho, A & Vignjevic, S 2011, 'The impact of a parenting intervention in Australia among migrants and refugees from Liberia, Sierra Leone, Congo, and Burundi: Results from the African migrant parenting program', *Journal of Family Studies*, vol. 17, no. 1, pp. 71–79.

Rubin, A & Babbie, E 2015, *Empowerment series: Essential research methods for social work*, Thomson Higher Education, Belmont, CA.

Ryan, C 2014, *The children of war: Child soldiers as victims and participants in the Sudan Civil War*, IB Tauris, London UK.

Sagor, R 2000, *Guiding school improvement with action research*, Association for Supervision and Curriculum Development, Alexandria, VA.

Sarantakos, S 2013, *Social research*, 4th edn, Palgrave Macmillan, UK.

Saunders, P 2013, 'Reflections on the concept of social exclusion and the Australian social inclusion agenda', *Social Policy & Administration*, vol. 47, no. 6, pp. 692–708.

Schwartz, S, Unger, J, Zamboanga, B & Szapocznik, J 2010, 'Rethinking the concept of acculturation: Implications for theory and research', *American Psychologist*, vol. 65, no. 4, pp. 237.

Seibert, S, Kraimer, M & Liden, R 2001, 'A social capital theory of career success', *Academy of Management Journal*, vol. 44, no. 2, pp. 219–237.

Sherry, E, Schulenkorf, N & Chalip, L 2015, 'Managing sport for social change: The state of play', *Sport Management Review*, vol. 18, no. 1, pp. 1–5.

Shilling, C 1991, 'Educating the body: Physical capital and the production of social inequalities', *Sociology*, vol. 25, no. 4, pp. 653–672.

Shilling, C. 2003, *The body and social theory*, Sage, Thousand Oaks CA.

Shilling, C 1992, 'Schooling and the production of physical capital', *Australian Journal of Education Studies*, vol. 13, no. 1, pp. 1–19.

Siddiquee, N & Faroqi, M 2010, 'Equal employment opportunity in the public service: Theory and practice in Bangladesh', *International Journal of Public Administration*, vol. 33, no. 8–9, pp. 451–462.

Siisiainen, M 2003, 'Two concepts of social capital: Bourdieu vs Putnam', *International Journal of Contemporary Sociology*, vol. 40, no. 2, pp. 183–204.

Singh, P 1979, 'Meaning of work', *Indian Journal of Industrial Relations*, vol. 15, no. 1, pp. 1–12.

Smith, J 1998, 'Humanitarian intervention: An overview of the ethical issues', *Ethics & International Affairs*, vol. 12, no. 1, pp. 63–79.

Sneesby, L, Satchell, R, Good, P & van der Riet, P 2011, 'Death and dying in Australia: Perceptions of a Sudanese community', *Journal of Advanced Nursing*, vol. 67, no. 12, pp. 2696–2702.

Spaaij, R 2011, *Sport and social mobility: Crossing boundaries*, Taylor & Francis, United Kingdom.

Spaaij, R 2012, 'Beyond the playing field: Experiences of sport, social capital, and integration among Somalis in Australia', *Ethnic and Racial Studies*, vol. 35, no. 9, pp. 1519–1538.

Spaaij, R 2013, 'The ambiguities of sport and community engagement', *Ethos*, vol. 21, no. 2, pp. 8–11.

Spaaij, R, Farquharson, K, Magee, J, Jeanes, R, Lusher, D & Gorman, S 2014, 'A fair game for all? How community sports clubs in Australia deal with diversity', *Journal of Sport & Social Issues*, vol. 38, no. 4, pp. 346–365.

Spinks, H 2009, 'Australia's settlement services for migrants and refugees', *Parliamentary Library*, Australia, viewed January 2014, <http://apo.org.au/node /14744>.

Stevens, R 2010, 'Managing human capital: How to use knowledge management to transfer knowledge in today's multi-generational workforce', *International Business Research*, vol. 3, no. 3, pp. 77–83.

Stewart, E 2009, 'The integration and onward migration of refugees in Scotland: a review of the evidence', in *New Issues in Refugee Research*, Working Paper 174, UNHCR, Geneva.

Stone, W 2001, 'Measuring social capital: Towards a theoretically informed measurement framework for researching social capital in family and community life', Australian Institute of Family Studies, Melbourne, Australia, viewed September 2014, < http://cedarscenter.com/resources/Measuring_Social_Capital.pdf >.

Stratigaki, M 2005, 'Gender mainstreaming vs positive action: An ongoing conflict in EU gender equality policy', *European Journal of Women's Studies*, vol. 12, no. 2, pp. 165–186.

Tashakkori, A & Teddlie, C 2003, 'Issues and dilemmas in teaching research methods courses in social and behavioural sciences: US perspective', *International Journal of Social Research Methodology*, vol. 6, no. 1, pp. 61–77.

Taylor, J 2004, 'Refugees and social exclusion: What the literature says', *Migration Action*, vol. 26, no. 2, pp. 16–31.

Teddlie, C & Tashakkori, A 2008, *Foundations of mixed methods research: Integrating quantitative and qualitative techniques in the social and behavioural sciences*, Sage, Thousand Oaks CA.

Throsby, D 1999, 'Cultural capital', *Journal of Cultural Economics*, vol. 23, no. 2, pp. 3–12.

Tipping, S 2011, *Meaningful being: the experiences of young Sudanese-Australians*, Doctoral thesis, University of Melbourne, Australia.

Triggs, G 2015, 'The forgotten children: National inquiry into children in immigration detention 2014', *The Medical Journal of Australia*, vol. 202, no. 11, pp. 553–555.

Turner, M & Fozdar, F 2010, 'Negotiating "community" in educational settings: Adult South Sudanese students in Australia', *Journal of Intercultural Studies*, vol. 31, no. 4, pp. 363–382.

Ungar, M 2010, 'What is resilience across cultures and contexts? Advances to the theory of positive development among individuals and families under stress', *Journal of Family Psychotherapy*, vol. 21, no. 1, pp. 1–16.

Ungar, M 2011, 'Community resilience for youth and families: Facilitative physical and social capital in contexts of adversity', *Children and Youth Services Review*, vol. 33, no. 9, pp. 1742–1748.

UNHCR 2014, 'World at war: Global trends in forced displacement in 2014', viewed 27 June 2015, <http://www.unhcr.org/556725e69.html>.

UNHCR 2015, 'UNHCR Projected global resettlement needs, Resettlement Service, Division of International Protection', *United Nations High Commissioner for Refugees*, Geneva, viewed April 2014, <http://www.unhcr.ch/no_cache/mandat/dauerhafte-loesungen/resettlement.html?cid=12136&-did=10704&sechash=d665804c.>.

Unluer, S 2012, 'Being an insider researcher while conducting case study research', *Qualitative Report*, vol. 17, no. 29, pp. 1–14.

Vanalstine, J, Cox, S & Roden, D 2013, 'The costs and benefits of diversity: Are religious differences most important?' *Journal of Global Business Issues*, vol. 7, no. 2, pp. 9–20.

Veenhoven, R 2000, 'Well-being in the welfare state: Level not higher, distribution not more equitable', *Journal of Comparative Policy Analysis: Research and Practice*, vol. 2, no. 1, pp. 91–125.

Venkatesh, V, Brown, S & Bala, H 2013, 'Bridging the qualitative-quantitative divide: Guidelines for conducting mixed methods research in information systems', *MIS Quarterly*, vol. 37, no. 1, pp. 21–54.

References

Victorian Equal Opportunity & Human Rights Commission 2008, *Rights of passage: The experiences of Australian-Sudanese young people: A report*, Victorian Equal Opportunity & Human Rights Commission, Melbourne, Australia, viewed June 2014, <http://trove.nla.gov.au/work/28101630>.

Ware, V & Meredith, V 2013, 'Supporting healthy communities through sports and recreation programs', Resource sheet no. 26. Closing the Gap Clearinghouse – Australian Institute of Health and Welfare & Melbourne, Australian Institute of Family Studies, Canberra.

Warr, P 1987, *Work, unemployment, and mental health*, Oxford University Press, New York NY.

Watts, M & Mitchell, W 2000, 'The costs of unemployment in Australia', *The Economic and Labour Relations Review*, vol. 11, no. 2, pp.180–197.

Weisberg, H, Bowen, B & Krosnick, J 1996, *An introduction to survey research, polling and data analysis*, Sage, Thousand Oaks CA.

Wemme, K & Rosvall, M 2005, 'Work related and non-work related stress in relation to low leisure time physical activity in a Swedish population', *Journal of Epidemiology and Community Health*, vol. 59, no. 5, pp. 377–379.

Wesely, P 2011, 'Foundations of mixed methods research: Integrating quantitative and qualitative approaches in the social and behavioural sciences by Teddlie, Charles, & Abbas Tashakkori', *Modern Language Journal*, vol. 95, no. 1, pp. 152–153.

Westoby, P 2008, 'Developing a community-development approach through engaging resettling Southern Sudanese refugees within Australia', *Community Development Journal*, vol. 43, no. 4, pp. 483–495.

Whitaker, B, 2002 'Changing priorities in refugee protection: the Rwandan repatriation from Tanzania', *Refugee Survey Quarterly*, vol. 21, no 1–2, pp. 328–344.

Whitehead, T. 2005 Basic classical ethnographic research methods: Secondary data analysis, fieldwork, observation/participant observation, and informal and semi-structured interviewing. Ethnographically Informed Community And Cultural Assessment Research Systems (EICCARS) working paper series <http://www.cusag.umd.edu/documents/WorkingPapers/ClassicalEthnoMethods.pdf>.

Whittaker, C & Holland-Smith, D 2014, 'Exposing the dark side, an exploration of the influence social capital has upon parental sports volunteers', *Sport, Education and Society*, vol. 21, no. 3, pp. 356–373.

Wienclaw, R 2009, 'Surveys in sociology research', *Research Starters Sociology*, vol. 1, pp. 1–5.

Wijaya, S 2014, 'Encounters with local food: The culinary experiences of international visitors in Indonesia', Doctoral thesis, Victoria University, Melbourne, Australia, viewed April 2015, <http://vuir.vu.edu.au/id/eprint/25865 >.

Wilson, R 2008, *The future of work: What does work mean 2025 and beyond?*, UK Department for Children, Schools and Families' *Beyond Current Horizons* Project, University of Warwick, UK.

Yin, R 2013, *Case study research: Design and methods*, 4th edn, Sage, Thousand Oaks CA.

Zainal, Z 2007, 'Case study as a research method', *Jurnal Kemanusiaan*, vol. 9, no. 1, pp. 1–6.

Zetter, R 2015, 'Protection in crisis: Forced migration and protection in a global era', Migration Policy Institute, Washington DC, viewed October 2015, <file:///C:/Users/S3726434/Downloads/TCM-Protection-Zetter.pdf>.

Ziguras, S & Kleidon, J 2005, *Innovative community responses in overcoming barriers to employment*, Brotherhood of St Laurence, Melbourne Australia.

www.ingramcontent.com/pod-product-compliance
Lightning Source LLC
Chambersburg PA
CBHW051940290426
44110CB00015B/2046